William Foster Coffin

1812 - The war and its moral

A Canadian chronicle

William Foster Coffin

1812 - The war and its moral
A Canadian chronicle

ISBN/EAN: 9783742836663

Manufactured in Europe, USA, Canada, Australia, Japa

Cover: Foto ©ninafisch / pixelio.de

Manufactured and distributed by brebook publishing software (www.brebook.com)

William Foster Coffin

1812 - The war and its moral

1812;

THE WAR, AND ITS MORAL:

A

CANADIAN CHRONICLE.

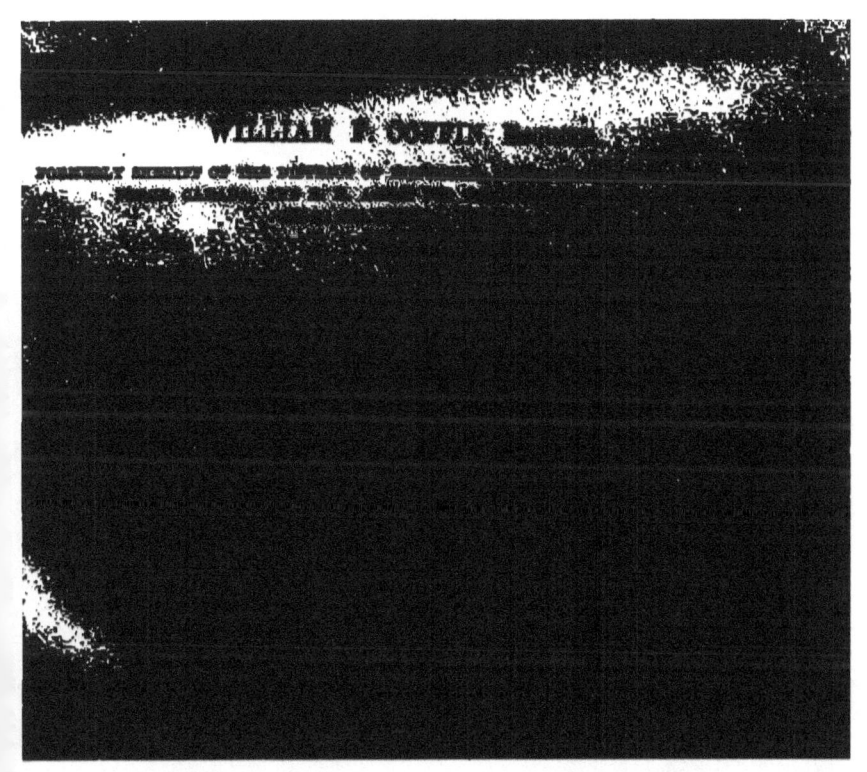

BY WILLIAM F. COFFIN,

To the Right Honourable

Sir Edmund Walker Head, Baronet,

Of Her Majesty's Most Honourable Privy Council,

And late Governor General and Commander-in-Chief of British North America,

This Canadian Chronicle of the War of 1812

Is respectfully dedicated, by his faithful and grateful Servant,

WILLIAM F. COFFIN.

OTTAWA, 2nd January, 1864.

TO THE RIGHT HONORABLE

SIR EDMUND WALKER HEAD, BARONET.

MY DEAR SIR,—I venture to appeal to your respected name as the best introduction for the little work which I do myself the honour to dedicate to you. To you, indeed, it owes its existence. You conferred upon me the appointment I have the honour to hold under the Crown in Canada, and that appointment has given life to an idea, long cherished in embryo.

The management of the Ordnance Lands in this Province has thrown me upon the scenes of the most notable events of the late war. It has brought me in contact with many of the surviving actors. It has revived early recollections of my own.

The achievements of 1812 were the household words of my childish days. For three years, I grew up among the men, and almost among the incidents of the time. In the Spring of 1815, from the Grand Battery at Quebec, I had watched the slow cavalcade which bore Sir George Prevost across the ice of the St. Lawrence, on his return to England.

Fifteen years afterwards brought me back to a country which, for thirty-three years, has been my home. During this long interval, the subject of the war has never ceased to be one of great interest. It has led to many enquiries, and to a gradual accumulation of material, which might have seen light earlier, had I not been daunted by a wholesome precept of my English schooling:

> Si quantum cuperem, possem quoque. Non meus audet,
> Rem tentare pudor, quam vires ferre recusent.

That I do so now, must be ascribed, in great part, to the liberality of my Publisher; in some degree to the pressure of a belief that, under the circumstances of the times, the effort had become a duty; and still more, to the opportunity and incentive you had made.

Permit me therefore, "*si tam parvum carmen, majestas recipit tua,*" to offer to you, in your honourable retirement, this mark of respectful homage. Canada owes to you a deep debt of gratitude. The revival of the military spirit of the country is due to your fostering hand. At your touch the Volunteer force sprang into life. The spirit you infused is inextinguishable. Your parting words will never be forgotten. As a member of that force, "*quorum pars parva fui,*" I offer this humble tribute to your talents, your patriotism, and to your manly, English, independence of character, and have the honour to subscribe myself,

My dear Sir,

With regard and gratitude,

Your faithful servant,

WILLIAM F. COFFIN.

OTTAWA, 2nd January, 1864.

Works consulted and documents furnished—chiefly by personal friends—which have contributed to this Chronicle of War of 1812.

Alison........History of Europe.	Croil.........Dundas, a sketch of Canadian History.
James........Military occurrences of the War.	Mansfield....Life of Gen. Scott.
James........Naval History.	Gifford......History of the War of French Revolution.
Christie......History of Lower Canada.	Sabine.......American Loyalists.
Auchinleck...History of the War.	Veritas......Letters of 1815.
Armstrong...Notices of the War of 1812.	Answer to Veritas..The Canadian Inspector.
Tupper......Life of Brock, and Corres.	Pontiac......Conspiracy of.
Stone........Life of Brant.	Goodrich.....History of the United States— P. Parley.
Neff.........Army and Navy of America.	Greig........History of Montreal.
Schoolcraft...Indian Tribes	Bouchette....Topography.
Garneau.....History of Canada.	Morgan......Celebrated Canadians.
Bibaud......Histoire du Canada.	Montreal Herald, 1811, 1812, 1813, and 1814.

Manuscripts, Memoranda of:

Major General Thomas Evans.	Manuscript Memoir of Sir George Prevost.
James Richardson, D.D.	Journal of General and Governor Simcoe.
Col. Sir Etienne Taché.	Report, Loyal and Patriotic Society, 1817.
Colonel John Clarke, St. Catherines.	Report of Commissioners of Indian Affairs.
Judge Jarvis, Cornwall.	Letter of Philalethes in the United Service Journal, 1848.
Colonel McLean, Scarborough.	
Squire Reynolds, Amherstburg.	Review of Tupper's Life of Brock, in the same.
Serjeant Andrew Spearman.	

The Author tenders his thanks to the Hon. Pierre J. O. Chauveau, Superintendent of Education, L. C., for access to the valuable collection of Books and Documents relating to Canadian History, to be found in the Library of the Jacques Cartier Normal School, Montreal.

ERRATA.

P. 48, line 24, for "Howard," read "Heward."
P. 62, line 7, for "Howard," read "Heward."
P. 29, line 18, for "Admiral Humphreys," read "Admiral Berkeley."

CONTENTS.

CHAPTER I.

PAGE

Preamble... 17

CHAPTER II.

1812—Duration of the War—Feeling in Canada. The War no Canadian quarrel. Value of Canada to England at that crisis. The feeling between the British and American people. British pretensions—Right of Search—Resisted by the Danes—The northern powers—The Americans. British dilemma. Blockade of 1806. Berlin and Milan Decrees. Orders in Council. Constructive Blockade. French and American inconsistency. Troubles of neutrals. Affair of the Leopard and Chesapeake, 1807. American exacerbation. British exclusion from American harbours. American gratitude to France. French sympathy in Canada a mistake. The Eastern States averse to the War. Affair of the President and Little Belt, 1811. Irritation increases. President of United States appeals to Congress. War declared 18th June, 1812. Futile attempt to capture British West India fleet. British disbelief in a war. 21

CHAPTER III.

State of Canada at the outbreak of the war. Military force — Attitude of the people. A vatar of Brock—His character and early career—Letter from Montreal, 1808—Takes command of troops in Upper Canada, 1810—Becomes Lieutenant-Governor, 1811. Hull invades Canada, 12th July. Proclamation—Brock's reply—Meets Parliament. Spirit of the country. United Empire Loyalists. Proctor at Amherstburg, 4th August—Detaches Tecumseh—Defeats Van Horne. On 7th August, Hull retires from Canada. Affair at Magagua. Capture of Michilimacinac, by Capt. Roberts and Toussaint Pothier. Brock with York Volunteers reaches Amherstburg. Interview with Tecumseh. Capture of Detroit, 16th August, 1812.................................. 35

CHAPTER IV.

PAGE

Brock provides for the safety of his conquest and returns to York—Urgent for action—Controlled by an armistice between Sir George Prevost and General Dearborn. Sir George at Quebec. Energy of the Lower Canada Legislature—Provide money—Provide men. The Americans threaten Montreal—Niagara. Detroit. Inroad at Gananoque. Affair at Ogdensburg. Brock returns to the Niagara frontier. Van Renselaer and the Militia—Crazy for a dash. Capture of the Detroit and Caledonia off Fort Erie. Military ardour of the New York Volunteers uncontrollable. Van Renselaer resolves to cross the Niagara frontier. Queenston Heights. Battle 13th October—Death of Brock and Macdonald—Arrival of Sheaffe—Final victory—Surrender by Scott. John Beverley Robinson. Brock's funeral. Scott and the savages.. 50

CHAPTER V.

Armistice between Sheaffe and Van Renselaer. Eastern frontier—Affair at St. Regis. "Capture of a stand of colors"—Retaliation. Hard frost below—Pleasant weather west. American squadron and Commodore Earle. Gallant exploit of the Canadian schooner Simcoe. Chauncey and Captain Brock. Armistice between Smyth and Sheaffe terminated. Descent on Canadian frontier. Americans repulsed. Fort Erie summoned. Bishop won't give up. Smyth retires into winter quarters, and goes south. United States disunited on the war—Canada unanimous. Sufferings and spirit of the people. Loyal and Patriotic Society.......................... 65

CHAPTER VI.

Naval occurrences of the war. Supremacy of England on the ocean. Indifference to foreign progress. American frigates—Unrivalled in construction—Speed—Equipment—Power. Naval duels. The Constitution and Guerrière. The Frolic and Wasp. The United States and Macedonian. The Java and Constitution. Effect of these contests. Exultation of Europe. England nerved and steeled. The Hornet and Peacock. Counter-stroke. Shannon and Chesapeake. Moral effect. The balance redressed. Gallantry on both sides. Effect of these events on the war in Canada... 75

CHAPTER VII.

1813. American preparations on Lakes Ontario and Erie. British Ministry did its best—Canada its duty. Men and money voted. New Brunswick regiment marched from Fredericton on snow shoes. Major General Evans. Sir James Yeo and seamen

CONTENTS. xi

PAGE

arrive from Halifax. British and American forces on the frontier. In the West. Harrison and Proctor. General Winchester defeated and captured at French town. Capt. Forsyth harries Brockville. Reprisals. Sir George Prevost at Prescott. Permits a demonstration. Proscott. Ogdensburg. Colonel George Macdonnell. The Glengarries. Bishop Macdonnell. Dash at Ogdensburg—Dangers of the Ice—The place taken. Capt. Jenkins and Lieut. Ridge. Pierre Holmes. His story. Macdonnell's courage, courtesy, and kindness.................................. 84

CHAPTER VIII.

British armaments at Kingston and York. British force. American strength. Descent planned on Kingston. York and Fort George. Little York—What it was —What it is. Defences in 1813. York attacked 26th April, 1813. Ship of war on the stocks, on British order. First alarm. Pluck of the population. Maclean, clerk of the House of Assembly, killed. Young Allan MacNab. Sir Roger Sheaffe. 97

CHAPTER IX.

Sheaffe. Force at his disposal. His dispositions. MacNeil of the 8th. American approach—Disembark in Humber Bay—Gallant resistance—Slaughter of the Grenadiers. Pike lands—Presses on the town—Enters the old fort—Explosion—Destruction of friend and foe. Pike killed. Sheaffe retires. The place capitulates. American Vandalism. Bishop Strachan. His admirable letter. The farce which follows the tragedy. The "human scalp" turns out to be a perriwig.............. 106

CHAPTER X.

American programme. Modification. Fall of York. Newark threatened. Description of Newark. Fort Niagara. Fort George. Climate and country. La Salle. Sketch of his exploits. Discovers the Mississippi. Fort George burnt. Rebuilt by Denonville. Colonel Dongan, Governor of the Province of New York, objects to the building of a Fort at "Ohniagro." Baron de Longueuil—Record of this family. Fort Niagara taken by the British, 1759. Surrendered to United States, 1796. Upper Canada created a separate Province, 1791. Governor Simcoe. His career. Newark his capital. Visit of Duke of Kent, 1793. Compared with that of Prince of Wales, 1860... 118

CHAPTER XI.

Seat of Government removed from Newark to York. Fort George still Military Head-Quarters. American attack on Fort George and Newark. General Vincent in command. American forces. British strength. American force on landing. British retire. Fort George falls. Vincent occupies Beaver Dam. Description-... 124

CHAPTER XII.

PAGE

Lake Ontario. Kingston. Sackett's Harbour. Expectations and preparations. Dr. Richardson, D.D.—His Career and Record. Departure of Squadron. Sights Sackett's Harbour and withdraws. Capture of American Officer of Dragoons. The Expedition retires—Preparations for landing. Preparations for resistance. General Jacob Brown. Colonel Baccus. Landing effected. Americans defeated—fire the stores and ships on the stocks. The British ordered to retreat. Withdrawal of the Expedition.. 120

CHAPTER XIII.

Return to Vincent at the Beaver Dam—Retires on Burlington Heights—Colonel Harvey—Stoney Creek—British retire from, and the Americans occupy their position—Harvey's plan for night attack—The Americans surprised—Desperate fighting—Americans dispersed—Generals Chandler and Winder taken prisoners—Present aspect of the ground — Old Lutheran Chapel—Burial place of the slain—No memorial stone—Why not ? Americans fall back on Niagara—Abandon camps and supplies.. 140

CHAPTER XIV.

New American Enterprise. Attempt on the Beaver Dam Post. Noble devotion of Mrs. Secord. Her Adventures—Reaches Decan's house in safety. Fitzgibbon. Bœrstler's Advance—Attacked by the Indians—Reaches Thorold. Present aspect of Thorold. Welland Canal. Hamilton Merritt. Col. John Clarke. Old Isaac Kelly—Militia attack on Bœrstler—He surrenders to Fitzgibbon. Mary Secord the real Heroine. Princely generosity of the Prince of Wales. Lieut. Fitzgibbon—His career—A Military Knight of Windsor. History of the Knights. A Reverie.. 146

CHAPTER XV.

General de Rottenburg succeeds General Vincent—Dearborn retires—Boyd in command at Fort George—American Frontier exposed to attack—Colonels Bishopp and Clark—Clark's career—Hazardous and successful foray on Fort Schlosser—Bishopp, emulous of gallant deeds, attacks Black Rock—Black Rock, now and then—Bishopp lands—Defeats the enemy—Captures the place—General Porter rallies the Americans—The British attacked in turn—Bishopp wounded to death—His worthy career in Europe and Canada—Influence over the Volunteers—The Americans enlist the Indians—Lake Ontario—Commodore Chauncey attacks Burlington Heights—Falls—Again sacks York. Sir James Yeo provokes the Commodore out of Niagara—Two American schooners foundered—Two taken—More expected from Yeo very inconsiderately—Yeo did his duty thoughtfully and well—From Ontario to Lake Champlain—Escapade at Gore Creek on the St. Lawrence—Death of Capt. Milne—Supplies how furnished—How transported in winter and summer—Value of the Commissariat—Sir William Robinson—Commissaries in Canada—Isaac Winslow Clarke—His career—Bateaux Brigades................... 158

CHAPTER XVI.

Montreal the centre of supply—Description of Montreal—View from top of the Mountain—Montreal of 1840 or 1864, not the Montreal of 1812—Montreal viewed as the Military Key of Canada—Country around—View of Belœil—Canadian scenery—Canadian people—The *Habitants*, their progress, improvement and characteristics—Strong temptation to invasion—Approach to Montreal and the Richelieu country—Description of Lake Champlain—American force on the New York frontier available for invasion... 173

CHAPTER XVII.

Sir George Prevost and Sir James Craig—Sir James a good man but obdurate—Sir George politic and useful—He identifies himself with the people—They support him and British rule—The Legislature legalize the issue of army bills, and vote additions. militia forces—Exchequer Bills—Sir George prepares for defence—English Volunteers—French Militia—The two people incline to different systems of enrolment—Both readily unite against common enemy—Isle aux Noix—Attempt made to prise this post—Capture of American schooners Growler and Eagle—Reprisals—Officers and men of H. M. brig of war, Wasp, transferred to Lake Champlain—Plattsburg, Swanton, Champlain, destroyed—Burlington challenged—Blockade of the seaboard by the British—Increased American strength on the Lakes............ 181

CHAPTER XVIII.

Stung by reverses the British Admiralty acted with vigour—Ships were equipped of a calibre to meet the Americans—Americans blockaded in their own harbours—Commerce destroyed, revenue ruined—Seamen useless on the ocean, transferred to the Lakes—Naval engagements—Dominica and Decatur—Pelican and Argus—Boxer and Enterprize—Cruise of the President under Commodore Rodgers—Detroit frontier—Unpleasant vicissitudes—Story of the Frontier—Squire Reynolds—His narrative—Early state of the Detroit Frontier—Building of Fort Miami—Who paid for it—Surrender of Michigan Territory and Detroit to Americans under Jay's Treaty 1796—British war vessels on the Upper Lakes allowed to rot—Brock's interview with the Indians—June 1812—First scalp taken by the American McCulloch—Indian exasperation—Resolution to retaliate—Declaration of war received 28th June, 1812—Capture of the Cayuga Packet by Lieut. Rolette......... 192

CHAPTER XIX.

PAGE

Squire Reynold's narrative—Arrival of Brock—Interview with Tecumseh—Affairs on the Frontier 1813—Ball at Malden—From the dance to the field—Colonel St. George—Attack on French Town—Capture of General Winchester—Retreat of Proctor—Wounded abandoned—Rolette hit—Brownstown and the scalps—Fort Meigs—British engineers—Colonel Gratiot—Major Reynolds at the Raisin—Defeat of Green Clay—Retaliation of the Indians—Retreat from Fort Meigs—Council of war—Recriminations—Proctor, Elliott, Tecumseh—Proctor's treatment of the Militia—Second attack on Fort Meigs—A failure—Fort Stevenson attacked—Bravely defended by Major Croghan—Col. Short killed—Stormers repulsed—Proctor retires—Barclay at Malden—Efforts to equip squadron—No men nor material—The two 24's—Calibre and character of guns in the squadrons respectively...... 202

CHAPTER XX.

Captain Barclay and Commodore Perry—Resources of each—Perry's difficulty—Crosses the bar at Presqu'Isle—Description of Barclay's crew and armament—10th September—Battle of Lake Erie—Desperate contest—The Lawrence surrenders—Perry's personal exploit—Changes his ships—Renews the contest—The British squadron captured—Officers all killed or wounded—The resistance of Barclay and his crews—Barclay's heroic character and conduct—Appearance before a Court martial—Honourably acquitted—Barclay's defeat, Proctor's doom—Position of Proctor—Nature of country—Supplies exhausted—Alternative of retreat or surrender—Retreats—Line of march—Difficulties—Followed by Harrison—Kentucky Mounted Riflemen—Tactics in the battle—Character of forest—Not impracticable to horsemen 215

CHAPTER XXI.

Proctor falls back to Baptiste Creek—General Harrison with Perry's assistance follows—5th October—British force halts at Dalson's Farm—Colonel Maclean of Scarborough—His reminiscences—Warburton in command at Dalson's—Proctor retires personally to Moravian Town—Roused before daylight—Intelligence—Troops attacked and retreating—Warburton followed by Shelby and Kentucky riflemen—Description of these troops and mode of attack—Proctor halts his men—Nature of ground and position—Tecumseh—His last words—No abattis made—American attack—Defeat and surrender of the British 228

CHAPTER XXII.

Tecumseh—His character—Origin—Tribe of the Shawanese—From Virginia—Driven into Ohio—Thence into Michigan—The Brothers Elksottawa and Tecumseh—Influence of Tecumseh over Indian tribes, due to his personal qualities—Anecdotes

—Haughty conduct towards the "Long Knives"—His disinterestedness—Indian skill as draftsman—His personal appearance and costume—Stern adherence to England—Last words to Proctor—Attack of the American riflemen—Tecumseh slain by the hand of Col. James Johnston—The four heraldic supporters of Canada—Outrage offered to his remains.. 232

CHAPTER XXIII.

Battle of the Thames—Its effect—In the States—In Canada. Sir George Prevost. Demonstration on Niagara. Vincent concentrates at Burlington Heights. American projects on Montreal. Generals Wilkinson and Hampton. Plan of attack from the West and from Lake Champlain. Hampton advances to Odelltown—Encountered by De Salaberry—Retires—Followed to the Four Corners. Career of De Salaberry—Attempts to surprise the Americans—Discovered—Falls back on the line of Chateauguay. Preparations for defence. Reports on the battle by the American Adjutant-General King... 239

CHAPTER XXIV.

Story of Chateauguay. The "Temoin oculaire." Hampton advances from Four Corners. De Salaberry faces right about, and returns to meet him. First rencontre—Halts—Throws up breastworks and abattis. Disposition of defenders—Ford in the rear. American attack on abattis—Impracticable. Attack on flank and rear, partially successful—Repulsed—Broken by flank fire. Retreating Americans fire on each other. Hampton, daunted, withdraws from front of abattis and retreats. Force engaged. Brilliant conduct of officers and men. Honour to De Salaberry... 252

CHAPTER XXV.

Macdonell of Ogdensburg—The Canadian Fencibles—Descent of the St. Lawrence Running the Rapids—Night March through the Bush—"Always on Hand"—French and English "Shoulder to Shoulder"—Natural Exultation of the French Canadians—Practical Reply to Dishonouring Imputations—Gratitude of the British Government—Queenston Heights—Chateauguay—Chevy Chace and the "Combat des Trentes"—Beaumanoir and Bembro—Croquart................................ 262

APPENDIX.

	PAGE
Letter to Thomas Jefferson, ex-President of the United States of America,	273
Bataille de Chateauguay,	286

1812:

THE WAR AND ITS MORAL.

CHAPTER I.

Preamble.

1812—like the characters on the labarum of Constantine*—is a sign of solemn import to the people of Canada. It carries with it the virtue of an incantation. Like the magic numerals of the Arabian sage, these words, in their utterance, quicken the pulse, and vibrate through the frame, summoning, from the pregnant past, memories of suffering and endurance and of honorable exertion. They are inscribed on the banner and stamped on the hearts of the Canadian people—a watchword, rather than a war-cry. With these words upon his lips, the loyal Canadian, as a vigilant sentinel, looks forth into the gloom, ready with his challenge, hopeful for a friendly response, but prepared for any other.

The people of Canada are proud of the men, and of the deeds, and of the recollections of those days. They feel that the war of 1812 is an episode in the story of a young people, glorious in itself and full of promise. They believe that the infant which, in its very cradle, could strangle invasion, struggle, and endure, bravely and without repining—is capable of a nobler development, if God wills further trial.

---

* Vide Gibbon, Vol. II, pp. 259, 260.

It is impossible for this people to ignore the portents of the time. The blast of war hurtles around them; Its sights are in their eyes, and the sounds in their ears. They feel that they are within the edge of the fatal circle, and await the stroke of the cyclone. It is natural that, at such a time, the popular mind should revert to the experience of the past, and that the war of 1812 should be constantly invoked as an example and as a warning.

Thus, the story of the war has suddenly become a subject of interest which it is difficult to satisfy. Fifty years have come and gone, and of the thousands who survived the contest, how few remain to tell the tale or point the moral! Within the last few months, three honoured men, heroes of 1812, and who emphatically deserve the title,—Sir Allan MacNab, Sir John Beverley Robinson, and Major-General Evans,—have gone to their rest, full of years and well-earned distinction. The voices of those who could animate by eloquent experience, and guide by their counsels, become daily, fewer, fainter, and more indistinct; and we turn with sorrowful respect from the living witnesses of the time, to those who bear record to the gallantry of their deeds and the nobleness of their motives.

The story of the war has been told by eminent writers on both sides of the Atlantic. We have British and American histories; we have biography; and the pages of periodical literature have been, in turn, alike devoted to the events of an epoch when the world was a-glow with arms, and war seemed to be the main vocation of mankind; but the works of the general historian are voluminous and inaccessible to the masses, and the part yielded to Canada is unavoidably small, on an arena occupied by the embattled nations of the earth. The Canadian authorities, faithful and reliable guides so far as they go, are, mostly, out of print and scarce; and they have been succeeded, and their places usurped at our own firesides, by a flood of American publications, sensational as they are termed, written for show, designed for sale, and, to this end, pandering to the worst passions of a morbid nationality. Writers of this class run, frantically, full tilt at Britain, her institutions and her colonies, with death's-head and marrowbones for device; and the bones are broiled, devilled, and seasoned to suit a literary taste prurient and craving as the appetite of the hungry ogre in the nursery tale, who snuffs the wind and mutters—

> Fe, fi, fo, fum,
> I smell the blood of an Englishman:
> Be he alive, or be he dead,
> I'll grind his bones to make my bread.

The present is therefore deemed to be an opportune moment to place the following pages before the Canadian public. A new book on an old subject may offer the attraction of novelty, and, in the present instance, will possess the advantage of an anxious desire for truth. One great object will have been obtained, if it provides an antidote to the American literature of the day; if it counteracts its influence, while it eschews its example. Nothing will be extenuated for the solace of British pride or to palliate British shortcomings; and most assuredly nothing shall be maliciously charged to their adversaries. It will be the endeavor of this narration to invest the story told, as far as possible, with a Canadian character; to present the war in Canada in a Canadian point of view; and, while giving all honor to those to whom honor is justly due, still to impart, as far as can be rightly done, a Canadian individuality to this Canadian Chronicle of the War.

This design has been greatly aided by the kindness of some few of the survivors of the warlike scenes of "fifty years since," who have embellished by the light of their reminiscences a work which has no other claim to originality. In justice to these venerable contributors, their names will be given in proper time and place, in gentle violation of the reluctant modesty inseparable from bravery and worth, and which never has shone more brightly and with less of affectation, than in the present instance.

  And in the nights of winter,
   When the cold north winds blow
  And the long howling of the wolves
   Is heard among the snow ;
  When round the lonely cottage
   Blows loud the tempest's din,
  And the good logs of Algidus
   Roar louder yet within ;

  When the oldest cask is opened,
   And the largest lamp is lit ;
  When the chestnuts glow in the embers,
   And the kid turns on the spit ;
  When the young and old in circle
   Around the firebrands close ;
  When the girls are weaving baskets,
   And the boys are shaping bows ;

  When the gudeman mends his armour,
   And trims his helmet's plume ;
  When the goodwife's shuttle merrily
   Goes flashing through the loom,—
  With weeping and with laughter
   Still is the story told
  How well Horatius kept the bridge
   In the brave days of old.

CHAPTER II.

1812—Duration of the War—Feeling in Canada. The War no Canadian quarrel. Value of Canada to England at that crisis. The feeling between the British and American people. British pretensions—Right of Search—Resisted by the Danes—The northern powers—The Americans. British dilemma. Blockade of 1806. Berlin and Milan Decrees. Orders in Council. Constructive Blockade. French and American inconsistency. Troubles of neutrals. Affair of the Leopard and Chesapeake, 1807. American exacerbation. British exclusion from American harbours. American gratitude to France. French sympathy in Canada a mistake. The Eastern States averse to the War. Affair of the President and Little Belt, 1811. Irritation increases. President of United States appeals to Congress. War declared 18th June, 1812. Futile attempt to capture British West India fleet. British disbelief in a war.

The war of 1812—so called in Canada—extended over three years,—1812, 1813, 1814. War was declared by Act of Congress of the United States on the 18th June, 1812. It was terminated by the provisions of the Treaty of Ghent, 24th December, 1814; which, however, was not ratified at Washington before February 7th, nor proclaimed in Canada until the 21st March, 1815.

Canada in 1812 cared as little, as at present, for a war with her powerful neighbor, but, as at present, cared not to evade it. The ploughshare and the broad-axe are her indigenous weapons, only to be exchanged at the call of honor, and of the public safety. Defence, not defiance, has been and ever will be her motto.

The war of 1812 was no Canadian quarrel. It was forced upon the Canadian people, and fought upon Canadian soil, to gratify the antipathies of two nations, too like to be loving. True it is, the British Canadians of the West did not belie their descent, and shared, without stint, in the weakness and the strength of the British character; nor can it be denied, that the French population of the East woke up to the fight with the gay and gallant spirit of their chivalrous forefathers. But the lot of both was to be betwixt the upper and the nether grindstone, and both faced the inevitable ordeal bravely and well.

Nor is it right to admit, as some have asserted and many have believed, that the assistance of England was purely gratuitous,— that the defence of Canada brought no compensation, that it was in fact an additional burthen at a burthensome crisis; for it is beyond dispute, that the North American Provinces, and Canada especially, were indispensable to England at this period of the Great War in Europe. At the time that she was excluded from the ports of the Baltic, her best supplies of timber came from Canada, and the non-intercourse acts of the United States had thrown her, for this article, almost exclusively on the resources of the North American colonies. One of the strongest arguments for war in the Congress of the United States was that employed in 1811 by Mr. Porter, the Chairman of the Committee on Foreign Affairs, in reference to the conquest of Canada. "These Provinces," said the speaker, "are not only immensely valuable, but almost indispensable to the existence of Great Britain, cut off, as she now is in a great measure, from the North of Europe. The exports from Quebec only, amounted during the last year to near six millions of dollars, in ship-timber, and provisions for support of her fleets and armies." Canada, in fact, made rich return for the expense of defending her, by the supplies afforded to the West India colonies, and to meet the home demand. The war with Napoleon proved the value of these colonies, and a war with Russia might show it again.

Little heed, however, did the men of those days give to questions of this sort. The only question between England and her colony then, was one of mutual assistance. The men of the United States were shrewder calculators, but the feeling which ruled in the British heart was one of bitter irritation. The war, indeed, was, at the bottom, no quarrel between governments. The governments of the day were but the instruments of the time. The real cause of strife was to be found in the temper of the people. It was a personal "turn up" between Jonathan and John Bull.

> Inter
> Hectora Priamidem animosum atque inter Achillem
> Ira fuit capitalis.

The animosity engendered between the British and American nations by the War of the Revolution had not been allayed by the peace of 1783. It had excoriated both parties. The people on both sides were dissatisfied with the results of the contest. Neither had had enough; each had still an old grudge to settle; the British were keen for a fight, the Americans were keener, and grasped at the first inviting opportunity.

From the day when Burke exclaimed against "the passion which many men in very humble life have taken in the American war, and in *our* subjects in America, *our* colonies, *our* dependencies," and denounced "the syren song of ambition which has charmed ears one would have thought were never organized to that sort of music,"* to the close of that contest, the spirit of the British people was the same; That spirit survived the contest. They could forgive the French Fontenoy and Steinkirk, they could exchange stern courtesy with Luxembourg or Marshal Saxe, for they had entertained with still greater courtesy captive French monarchs and marshals; but they had no offset to the humiliations of the American War, nor to the victories of militia generals. They could not give in: their umpires had done so for them, but they were anxious for another round.

---

* Speech previous to the election, Bristol, 1780.

Since the peace of 1783 the British and the Americans had divided between them the carrying trade of the world. They met in every harbour, and in every harbour came to blows. The words "Yankee" and "Britisher," with a sanguinary expletive, were constant terms of mutual reproach, and the popular voices of New York and Liverpool swelled the chorus with accompaniments not always the most soothing;—the feeling between the people was very bad.

The Government of America shared largely in this ill feeling;

> The dog, to gain his private ends,
> Went mad, and bit the man.

The Government of England in all sincerity—hotly pressed and fighting against heavy odds elsewhere—sought no additional quarrel with America. But it was borne down by the burden of its traditions. With the pertinacity of vigorous age, it clung to the assumptions of triumphant and overbearing boyhood. The maritime pretensions of England were, at this time, excessive. Forgetful of all but her naval strength and hereditary renown, she exacted concessions she would have scorned to grant, and to which no spirited nation, more especially one sprung from her own loins, could condescend to submit.

She insisted on the "Right of Search." First, to search neutral vessels for hostile property, whether "contraband of war" or not; and secondly, and still more offensively, on the right to search neutral vessels—even the war-ships of peaceful nations—in quest of deserters. The Americans, on their part, contended that the flag covered the merchandise, that the deck of an American ship was a sanctuary, and that the pretension to search for deserters was a profanation and an outrage.

In the haughty spirit of their Norse forefathers, the Vikings of England had, for centuries, exacted from all nations obedience in the "narrow seas." The power to compel, whether it was to "dip a flag" or, to give up a deserter, continued to be arrogated and exercised. But in time, other men arose who resisted the imposition In 1799 the Danish frigate Haufenau had contested the attempt to search neutral vessels under convoy, and the Danish Minister, Count Bernstorf, had replied to the angry remonstrance of England, that "the captain of the Danish king's frigate, by repelling a violence which he had no right to expect, had done no more than his duty;" and in the summer of 1800 the Freya, another Danish frigate, fought most gallantly in support of the independence of her national flag, and, having lost two men killed and five wounded, struck her colors, and was carried into the Downs.*

To these pretensions, followed by such acts, is to be ascribed the combination of the Northern powers—Russia, Sweden, Denmark, and Prussia—in 1800, to secure, as it was termed, "the liberty of the seas," so that neutral ships should freely navigate the coasts of belligerent powers—that everything but what was expressly contraband should be held to be free—that the declaration of officers commanding ships of war should free the cargoes of their convoys,—and that no search should be allowed." There can be little doubt but that the popular irritation upon such subjects greatly strengthened the hands of Napoleon in his subsequent occupation of the Scandinavian kingdoms. In the year 1800, when the American envoys, Messrs. Elsworth, Henry, and Murray, took leave of the Consular Government of France, they were entertained at a banquet, where the Consul Lebrun proposed the significant toast, "To the union of America with the power of the North, that respect may be procured for the liberty of the seas." †

As the refusal to recognize these "new regulations," as they

---

* Gifford's History of the War of the French Revolution, Vol. I, p. 296.
† Ibidem.

were termed, was the ostensible cause of the war of 1812, it may be permitted here to inquire a little further.

The innate justice of England had been early aroused to a sense of the unreasonableness of these pretensions. The Government of England was prepared to abate this annoyance by treaty stipulations. Indeed, in 1806, negotations to this effect were actually closed by a treaty between England and America, which Mr. Jefferson, for reasons best known to himself, refused to ratify; the practice therefore, objectionable as it was, reverted to the *statu quo ante*. The principles then contended for, are fully recognized now. They have been accepted and acted upon by all civilized nations for half a century. The first nation to violate them has been the Americans themselves, in the late notable exploit of the irrepressible Wilkes.

And it should be kept in mind, that, at this critical period, England was involved in a gigantic contest. Almost single-handed, she had for years resisted the combined powers of Europe, grasped and wielded by the most extraordinary genius of modern times. Every means and device of war had been employed and exhausted in this stupendous struggle. This was no time for concessions which could only strengthen her adversaries. Indeed, as war measures alone, the measures taken would have been justifiable.

In May, 1806, Mr. Fox, then leader of the British Government, had declared the coasts of France and Holland, from Brest to the Elbe, to be in a state of blockade, and enforced the declaration by the exhibition of 160 ships of war, under Lord Keith, in the Channel and on the North Sea.

In November 1806, and in November 1807, Napoleon, by Decrees dated from Berlin and Milan respectively, retaliated. He declared the whole British Islands to be in a state of blockade, authorized the seizure of any vessel, of any nation, bound to Britain, and confiscated British goods, whether contraband of war or not, found sailing under any flag. England again retorted by further Orders in Council, November, 1807, declaring all countries under the power of France to be blockaded, whether *actually blockaded or not;* and that all products of countries so *constructively* blockaded, being taken, in the bottoms or ships of any nation, should be held to be good prize.

Constructive blockade was an innovation in the enginery of war. It was blockading run mad. The right to blockade an enemy's ports in time of actual warfare had been perfectly understood, so long as the blockade was effectual and complete; but the blockade declared by England was of countries, not specific ports, and was declared to exist, whether such countries were actually blockaded or not. England justified her course by contending that, as mistress of the seas, having one thousand ships of war afloat, she practically blockaded the whole world. We will not pause to discuss this process of reasoning; but if fallacious and unjust on the part of England, how should it be designated on the part of Napoleon, who, "without a single ship of the line, and only a few smaller vessels capable of putting to sea, declared the whole British Empire in a state of blockade"?[*]

It is also right to notice, that, by the French treaty of Mortefontaine, to which the Americans were parties in the year 1800, the Maritime code, promulgated by Napoleon himself, had stipulated with ostentatious liberality that "the flag should cover the merchandise." Thus while England, by her Orders in Council, adhered reluctantly and *ex necessitate rei* to obsolete traditions, France, who, with great trumpeting, had abandoned all right, by her Decrees deliberately violated her own treaty stipulations to suit a present purpose. Moreover, it was felt in England, and felt sorely, that while she was fighting the battle of constitutional freedom against

---

[*] Alison., Am. ed., Vol. IV, p. 453.

stark despotism, and was compelled to have recourse to expedients she would otherwise have been willing to waive, free America sympathized and sided with the French Emperor, that

> What in the corporal was but a choleric word,
> Was in the soldier a flat blasphemy.

It must be admitted, at once, that the neutral was sorely tried. Well might he exclaim, under the conflicting circumstances, " a plague on both your houses." He was bandied between the disputants after a fashion equally fatal to trade and temper; and had he turned with equal spirit on both tormentors, little blame would he have had. During this absorbing and protracted contest, wherein every French and every British seaman—by press-gang or conscription—had been claimed for the service of his country, the Americans, safe in their neutrality, had, by degrees, almost monopolized the carrying trade of the world; An enormous commerce had grown up, upon which the British Order in Council and the French Decree fell with ruinous force; and from the nature of things, the gripe of the Briton outreached and outmeasured the stroke of the Gaul. The cruisers of England swarmed on every sea; American vessels, bound to French ports, or to, or from, ports of countries tributary to France, were captured by scores; while the merchantman bound to Britain or her Colonies, was safe except from some occasional French frigate or skulking privateer. While this state of things existed, the bill of damages incurred on French account, was largely against England; but at the same time, had a kindlier or more kindred spirit prevailed in America, it would have been seen, that the interruption of the trade with France was amply compensated by an immense and more profitable trade with Great Britain, and the memory of a generous forbearance would have been productive of fruit to unborn generations.

But, upon the old rankling was piled this new agony; and in

1807, June 22, occurred an incident which greatly exasperated the pre-existing bad feeling. The right of search was rudely tested. The Leopard, a British 74-gun ship, acting under orders from the Admiral of the North American station, overhauled in American waters, the American frigate Chesapeake, and demanded the surrender of certain alleged deserters. The demand was refused, and the refusal was answered by a broadside, to which the Chesapeake replied, but, inferior in strength, struck her colors, having lost three men killed and eighteen wounded, among the latter the commander, Commodore Barron. The deserters were arrested and removed, taken to Halifax and tried, and one, convicted of piracy and mutiny, was hanged.

This act was an outrage—a high-handed act of that school of Tritons in which Commodore Wilkes of the U. S. N. subsequently graduated; but before one word of remonstrance or complaint could reach the British Government, this act of aggression was disavowed. Captain Humphreys, commanding the Leopard, though acting under orders, was recalled. Admiral Humphreys was superseded, and every possible reparation made and offered. It was declared "that the right of search when applied to vessels of war, extended only to a *requisition*, and could not be carried into effect by force."

But the wrath of America was unappeasable—the blow, the irreparable and unpardonable blow had been struck. It was the natural instinct of a young and brave people. On subjects such as these the British were comparatively easy,—their national character was made, but the Americans—a new nation—had a national character to make. They were, therefore, on this occasion, "all feeling and raw life," and brought the brave Commodore Barron to a court-martial for not resisting further, where no good was to be gained or honor won.

The resentment of the American Government was hot and hasty.

Before asking, and without awaiting, reparation, the President issued a Proclamation excluding from the harbors of the United States His Britannic Majesty's ships. As the fleets of France continued to enjoy access to these ports, this act was, at once, hostile to the former and friendly to the latter country. If England had resented the capture of the Trent with similar virulence, the Tuscarora would never have blockaded the Sumpter, for weeks, in Southampton water. But Jefferson, the representative of the democratic principle in American politics, was President of the United States. He and his party betrayed on this occasion, and on many more, strong hatred to England, and marked favoritism towards France. It is undeniable that the American people owed a deep debt of gratitude to France. Lafayette and Rochambeau and De Grasse aided, and more than aided, to achieve the independence of America. America owed to France a grateful return, and exhibited her gratitude by suffering much, and saying little. The democratic party, eager to humble Britain, accepted any humiliation rather than quarrel with France. They submitted to the capture of ships in neutral ports, the sequestration of cargoes, the ransom of merchandise, with a faint remonstrance. French war ships seized American merchantmen at sea, plundered and burnt them,—an example which has been feebly imitated by the notorious Alabama of the present day. They consoled themselves with the belief that the anticipated triumph of the French Emperor in Europe, would ensure their supremacy on this continent. They were prepared to divide the world between them. With this view they accepted wrong from France, and heaped wrong on England. England's difficulty had become America's opportunity. In the words of the historian Alison, "the ostensible object of the war was to establish the principle that the flag covers the merchandise, and that the right of search for seamen who have deserted, is inadmissible; the real object was to wrest from Great

Britain the Canadas, and, in conjunction with Napoleon, extinguish its maritime and Colonial Empire."

Politicians, too, of this early American school, had a notion that French connection and the conquest of Canada were synonymous terms. This was a great mistake, as was found out, some short time after, on the battlefield of Chateauguay; but from the first, it had an unexpected good effect, for the very suggestion of a French policy or the exercise of French influence, tested the British feeling still latent in the hearts of thousands of Americans. In the New England States, a war with England was denounced, which, without any just grounds, destroyed their trade and paralyzed their industry. Citizens of these States expressed an abhorrence of France, and of its rule, and protested against the contemplated introduction of French troops on this continent, which, under the pretext of subduing or seducing the French Canadians, might prove to be subversive of their own liberties.

It is probable, that to this worthy spirit of truthful independence, may be ascribed the fact, that during the whole of the ensuing war, the immense extent of frontier between Lower Canada and the States of Vermont, New Hampshire, and Maine, was unassailed by an enemy. It is well worthy of reflection that, during the whole war of 1812 no hostile irruption was attempted upon the Province, from Lake Champlain to the ocean. The facilities were as great and the temptation as strong, as when the impetuous Arnold forced a passage to Quebec down the valley of the Chaudiére. This feat, executed in 1775, in the depth of a Canadian winter, athwart a howling wilderness, offered an incentive and an example, which could only have been counteracted by the sober good sense and right feeling of the people of the Eastern States in 1812.

Amid these diversities
There is much wisdom to be taught and learnt.

At this period of universal ferment, when decrees, orders in council, proclamations, non-importation and non-intercourse acts, embargos and imbroglios, with their mystical jargon, puzzled, scared and exasperated half mankind, when America rejected British manufactures, and prohibited the exportation of cotton and corn, when the artisans and operatives of England were half crazed with famine,—occurred another untoward event, which exhibited in the brightest light that noble forbearance which is to this day the proud inheritance of a fearless people.

On the 16th May, 1811, the British sloop of war Little Belt, of 18 guns, commanded by Captain Bingham, was pursued off Cape Charles by the American 44-gun frigate President. America was at peace with the whole world. Commodore Rogers had nothing to fear, and had nothing to ask, of a foreign war-ship of any nation, of such inferior force. On American principles, he had no right to overhaul or search. He did overhaul, and hailed; and declared that he was answered by a shot, which led to a determined fight of three quarters of an hour between the ponderous American and his pigmy antagonist. The Little Belt was shot to pieces. Commodore Rogers, on learning the name of his adversary, politely regretted the mistake, and offered help. Bingham demurred to the mistake, and declined assistance. He could help himself, and so he did, and brought his small ship in a sinking state into Halifax, with eleven men killed and twenty-two wounded. This officer averred, with much reason, that his orders prohibited, and common sense forbade the collision he was said to have provoked. The statements on both sides were conflicting; we are left to draw a reasonable inference from the facts. Rogers was tried by court martial, and acquitted amid much national exultation. The American government disavowed hostile instruction, and the British Government acquiesced in the *amende*, and made no remark.

This offering of the cheek to the smiter does not seem to have been appreciated. It very rarely is. The forbearance of England was honest, unselfish, self-denying, but it was entirely misconstrued. Neither reparation, as in the case of the Chesapeake, nor patience, as in that of the Little Belt, could induce a corresponding spirit. The temper of America had festered into rancor. The feeling of the governing masses was not ill-expressed in the lines of Martial:

> Non amo te, Sabidi, nec possum dicere quare,
> Hoc tantum possum dicere, non amo te.

In November, 1811, the President officially appealed to arms. Congress eagerly responded by large votes of men and money. During the winter, warlike armaments were made; in the spring, fresh votes of money and men. At length, and at this juncture, when the Emperor Napoleon, at the head of the largest army the world had seen, was pressing on triumphantly to the boasted subjugation of all the Russias, and Wellington, squabbling with Camarillas and Juntos, was preparing, in silence and apparent discomfiture, for a renewal of the struggle in Spain, the United States declared war against Great Britain; nor did they waver when they learned, a few weeks after, that the obnoxious order in Council, so bitterly resented, had at the time of the declaration of war been actually repealed. War was declared on the 18th of June, 1812, by Act of Congress. Mr. Madison, then President, who had done all in his power to exasperate existing ill-will, and to lash the popular mind to frenzy, eluded the responsibility of the fatal act, and made a catspaw of the legislature.

"Coming events cast their shadows before," particularly to those who can shape events to suit their own purposes. The declaration of war was preceded by an embargo imposed in April, 1812, devised shrewdly, to intercept all sources of transatlantic information with England, and to give to the spoiler her homeward bound West India fleet. It was well known that this rich prize would be on the Atlantic in May or June, unsuspecting and insufficiently protected. By closing their ports, the Americans cut off all communication between the countries, and caused great loss to their own and British commerce, but secured, thereby, all the sailors of the impounded ships, of their own marine, and of other countries also, for future national service on the ocean and the lakes. Instructions must have been given to the American navy long before the declaration of war, for, on the 18th June, the day on which war was declared at Washington, Commodore Rogers—red with the blood of Cock Robin—backed by a stout squadron of three frigates and two sloops, gave chase to the West India fleet, convoyed by the frigate Belvidera, which gallantly rescued every merchantman, and saved herself. Thus failed this cute speculation on the argosies of England, and the cotemporaneous invasion of Canada fared no better.

The people and the authorities of Canada had for long been alive to the imminence of a war. Standing on the brink of the crater they could see the daily progress of the red and angry torrent, destined at any moment to boil over and ravage their own quiet homes. A cry for support and assistance, rather than protection, had long before gone forth, and was met, as it appeared to them, by an inconceivable apathy. The rulers of England believed, or forced themselves to believe, that the United States would never quarrel with their own kith and kin, and their best friend and customer, in unnatural alliance with the despot of Europe. They relied on the right feeling, the shrewd and practical sense, and on the commercial interests—both of North and South—of democrat and federalist. The people of England, rallying from a staggering blow, looked only to their front, regardless of the assailant in the rear. They were, at this moment, fighting for dear life with a gigantic and remorseless foe. "Three days after the American declaration of war, Wellington crossed the Agueda to commence the Salamanca campaign. Six days after, Napoleon passed the Niemen on his way to Moscow, at the head of 380,000 men." *

---

* Alison, Vol. IV, ch. 76.

CHAPTER III.

State of Canada at the outbreak of the war. Military force—Attitude of the people. Avatar of Brock—His character and early career—Letter from Montreal, 1808—Takes command of troops in Upper Canada, 1810—Becomes Lieutenant-Governor, 1811. Hull invades Canada, 12th July. Proclamation—Brock's reply—Meets Parliament. Spirit of the country. United Empire Loyalists. Proctor at Amherstburg, 4th August—Detaches Tecumseh—Defeats Van Horne. On 7th August, Hull retires from Canada. Affair at Magagua. Capture of Michilimacinac, by Capt. Roberts and Toussaint Pothier. Brock with York Volunteers reaches Amherstburg. Interview with Tecumseh. Capture of Detroit, 16th August, 1812.

At the outbreak of the war, Canada was in fact in a defenceless condition. To man the fortresses of Quebec and Kingston, and to cover a frontier of 1,700 miles in length, the whole available force consisted of 4,450 regulars of all arms. In the Upper Province, which presents a water frontier of 1,300 miles, there were but 1,450 soldiers, or about two men and a fraction per mile, without counting garrisons. Sir George Prevost, whose qualifications partook more of a civil than of a military character, governed the country, and commanded in chief. The militia consisted of about 2,000 men in the Lower Province, and perhaps 1,800 in the Upper, not all called out, unarmed and undisciplined, and possessing little of the appearance or of the quality of soldiers, except pluck.

It may well be imagined, and admitted without disparagement to any, that, in the absence of all fitting preparation, the tocsin of war bore upon its echoes dismay to many hearts. The preparations of the enemy had been long made and ostentatiously paraded. Doubtless their extent had been exaggerated, but still they were immeasurably in advance of our own. Indeed the apparent supineness on our part had engendered doubt and suggested disaffection. It is impossible to ignore the alarm, and confusion, and despondency, which settled down, for a time, like a black cloud upon the country, until suddenly, day broke through the gloom, and the stalwart form and sterling character of Brock strode into light.

Like the white horse in a battle-piece by Wouvermans, in every delineation of this war, Isaac Brock stands forth from the canvas, the central figure and commanding feature of the scene. It will not be uninteresting, therefore, to offer, at the outset, a brief sketch of his earlier career. He was born in the Island of Guernsey in 1769, the year which gave birth to Napoleon and Wellington. He was descended from an old and respected family. He obtained his first commission in 1785, served in the West Indies, was promoted rapidly, thanks to the havoc of climate; and, by the force of a vigorous constitution, survived to command the 49th foot as senior Colonel in the expedition to Holland in 1799, where he made his mark under adverse circumstances. In 1801 he was selected with his regiment to serve under Lord Nelson, in his memorable attack on Copenhagen. In 1802, Brock accompanied his regiment to Canada, and was, for the next ten years of his life, identified with the existence of a country which he ultimately governed wisely, defended nobly, and which points to his grave as the monument of his glory. He was a man of natural capacity, self-cultivated, resolute, and endowed remarkably with the qualities of forethought and foresight. His correspondence, imperfectly preserved, makes us regret that so much should have been lost.* These memorials of an honest, modest, and truly brave nature, have furnished the greater part of these details. In person he was tall and athletic, with a commanding bearing and gentle manner. In private life he was irreproach-

---

* Life and Correspondence of Sir Isaac Brock, by Tupper.

able, universally respected by those who did not know him, and loved by those who did. His public life speaks for itself.

In 1806, being senior officer at the time, Col. Brock commanded the troops both in Upper and Lower Canada, and so threatening was the aspect of affairs—six years before the war broke out—" the Americans being employed in drilling and forming their militia, and openly declaring their intention of invading the Province the instant that war is determined on,"* that he took vigorous measures for the defence of the Ancient Capital, and for strengthening Cape Diamond. On the arrival of Sir James Craig, the new Governor General and Commander-in-Chief, he relinquished his temporary command, and returned to his regiment, which was always in splendid order. In 1808 he was appointed to be a Brigadier; and an extract from a letter written to his brother in July of that year is worth reproducing here, as showing the malice aforethought which provoked the war—the pre-determination to " corner" Great Britain—to compel her to resent accumulated wrong—to strike the first blow,—and thus to unite the disunited opinions of the people of the States on the unavoidable necessity of war.

" What will be the result of our present unsettled relations with the neighboring republic," says Brock in 1808, " it is very difficult to say. The government is composed of such unprincipled men, that to calculate on it by the ordinary rules of action would be absurd. We have completely outwitted Jefferson, and all his schemes to provoke us to war. He had no other object in view in issuing his restrictive proclamation; but failing in that, he tried what the embargo would produce, and in this he has been foiled again. Certainly our administration is deserving of every praise for their policy on these occasions. Jefferson and his party, however strong the inclination, dare not declare war, and therefore they endeavor

---

* Correspondence of Sir I. Brock, p. 45.

to attain their objects by every provocation. A few weeks since the garrison of Niagara fired upon seven merchant boats passing the fort, and actually captured them. Considering the circumstances attending this hostile act, it is but too evident it was intended to provoke retaliation. These boats were fired upon and taken within musket shot of our own fort. Their balls, falling on our own shore, were expected to have raised the indignation of the most phlegmatic. Fortunately, the commandant was not in the way, as otherwise it is difficult to say what would have happened. A representation of this affair has been made at Washington, and for an act certainly opposed to existing treaties, we have been referred for justice to the ordinary courts of law." *

This letter was written from Montreal, but Brock was chiefly employed at Quebec up to July, 1810, when he was despatched to take command of the troops in Upper Canada by Sir James Craig. He established his head quarters at Fort George, on the Niagara frontier, but visited all the frontier forts, remaining for some time on the river Detroit, absorbed in observation and preparation for the contest he knew to be before him. In 1811, Sir George Prevost reached Quebec, and in October of that year, Francis Gore, Esq., the Lieut.-Governor of Upper Canada, having returned to England on leave, Brock, now a Major-General, succeeded him, and thus, at a critical moment, the civil as well as the military authority in the Upper Province was combined, most providentially, in the man most competent to confront the emergency. It is instructive to note from his correspondence at this time, how sagaciously he foresaw, how earnestly he forewarned, and to observe how little his counsels were appreciated.

War was declared on the 18th June, 1812, but, by some strange omission on the part of the British minister at Washington, the official notification did not reach Sir George Prevost until the 7th

---

* Correspondence of Sir J. Brock, p. 45.

July. General Brock was not officially notified at all. Happily, private patriotism and enterprise supplied the deficiency. Mr. Richardson of Montreal, afterwards the Hon. John Richardson, had apprised the Governor General of the fact on the 25th June, and the intelligence reached Brock, through a private channel, about the same time. He was then at Fort George. He made the most, at once, of his insufficient means. If not forearmed, he had fortunately been forewarned, by his own forecast. Personally he provided for the protection of the Niagara and Detroit portion of his command. To Major General Shaw he confided the Eastern frontier, of which Kingston was the centre.

The thunder cloud soon burst;—Long before the declaration of war, the American government had despatched from Ohio into the territory of Michigan 2,500 men, under Brigadier-General Hull. On the 12th July, Hull invaded Canada. He crossed the Straits, or Detroit, as it was called by the old French settlers—the earliest of the offshoots from the parent settlement at Quebec—to Sandwitch; where the people, in their habits and language, in their horses, vehicles, and domestic arrangements,—where the long lines of Lombardy poplars, pear trees of unusual age and size, and umbrageous walnut trees,—still remind the traveller of the banks of the Loire. He landed among a simple, inoffensive, agricultural people, indisposed to resistance, and thundered forth a proclamation. This document appealed to the fear of poltroons and the instinct of traitors, denied the right of the red man to defend his own soil, and doomed to death every white man found fighting at his side. It threatened all who resisted with " the horrors and calamities of war," and proffered to the recreant and vanquished " peace, liberty, and security."

To this, on the 22nd July, Brock nobly replied, that the crown of England would defend and avenge all its subjects, whether red or white, and that Canada knew its duty to itself and to its sovereign, and was neither to be bullied nor cajoled into a departure from it.

On the 17th he had opened an extra session of the Legislature of Upper Canada, and it must be owned that, at this crisis, the Legislature was despondent, and the people misgave. But a change in the scene speedily took place; the noble character of Brock rapidly assumed its natural ascendency, the public mind became reassured, public confidence revived, and the lava tide of loyalty, living though latent, surged up and blazed forth as a bale-fire, inextinguishable in the land.

Loyalty to England, fealty to the crown, were the birthright and heir-loom of this people. The first settlers on the soil were the American loyalists, men of educated and elevated minds, who had undergone trials and persecutions, and a fierce fight of afflictions in the cause of the King and of the "auld countree," and who exclaimed in the affecting language of the Psalmist: "When I forget thee, O Jerusalem, may my right hand forget its cunning." They had left home, and friends, and wealth, and station, for a principle sanctified by its disinterestedness, and by the cunning of their hands had enshrined it in the heart of the wilderness. They had borne, for long, the scoffs and jeers of neighbors, who twitted them with a foolish choice, and who, until late trials, have not known the sacred impulse of a great cause. The reflections of the past had been to these men the only —the proud reward of rare sufferings and noble sacrifices. Oh let it not be imputed to them or to their descendants, that they have dwelt upon their loyalty overmuch. Englishmen make no more boast of their loyalty than they do of their honesty, or of their truth, or of any other of those manly virtues, which they justly claim to be national characteristics; but, for generations, few have actually paid the price of their faith, and none can recall the rapture with which the martyrs, for conscience' sake, glory in the scenes of their martyrdom. If the loud hosanna is often on their lips, the spirit is ever present in their hearts. If they lay claim to the " sangre azur," they are ever ready to prove its quality, and to pour it forth in the cause of their Sovereign and of the time-honored flag of England. On this emergency, the United Empire Loyalists were, as ever, true to their antecedents. They thronged to the banner of Brock. The Province rose as a man. Numbers for whom arms could not be provided, returned disappointed to their homes. The rest did their duty nobly, and

> Have left their sons a hope, a fame,
> They too would rather die than shame.

In this interval, while Brock was exhorting his Legislature and forming new levies, his lieutenants in the west had not been idle.

Hull was in a position of great anxiety; he had to draw all his resources from his rear, from distant Ohio, through ways which could not be called roads, and which were infested by savages. The extent of his force increased his difficulties; he had too many mouths to feed, and yet he could not detach in sufficient force to secure his communications. Proctor, who commanded at Amherstburg a force of about 350 men, threatened on his right by Hull, had still nerve enough to detach Tecumseh, the chief of the Shawanee Indians, across the Detroit River, to intercept a convoy commanded by Major Van Horne. The detachment was encountered in the bush, defeated, and scattered, the provisions captured, and the mail, containing the correspondence of the American army, fell into the hands of the savages. This occurred on the 4th of August. On the 7th, Hull, who had crossed to the easy conquest of Canada, and had relied on the country for supplies and upon the people for reinforcements, began to be satisfied of his mistake. He had made one or two abortive attempts on Fort Malden. Colonel Cass, the hero of Ta-ron-tee, had earned this designation by an heroic retreat from before a few Indians at the

Rivière aux Canards, which lies between Sandwich and Fort Malden or Amherstburg. The Rivière aux Canards, in French, or the Taron-tee, in Indian parlance, is a sluggish and sedgy stream, which percolates the wide marshes in the rear country, and unites with the Detroit about five miles above Fort Malden. This creek was crossed, near its mouth, by one of the make-shift bridges of the country. Here, on the 28th July, Col. Cass attacked an Indian scouting party, which, very properly, fell back, losing one warrior, whose body was scalped and otherwise disfigured. The Americans thereupon retired with their trophy—somewhat hastily, for they did not pause to destroy the bridge, which was re-occupied next day by the British, and was protected by two light field-pieces. Next day also re-appeared Colonel Cass, under the fostering wing of Colonel McArthur,—a strong reinforcement—and two guns. The bridge was attacked, two brave men of the 41st, outlying sentries, Privates Dean and Hancock, with that strange and dogged perversity so common among British soldiers, would neither retire nor give in. Hancock was killed—Dean wounded and taken prisoner. After some exchanges of cannon-shot, the Americans again retreated; and an American writer declares "the escape of McArthur and his companions to have been truly miraculous."* The proclamation, which Hull had fathered, but which Cass had written, was found to be theatrical thunder: the Canadians would not revolt; the Indians flocked to the British standard. At this moment the defeat of Van Horne sounded like a knell. Hull was appalled. To cover his "base of supply," he thought it best to change his "base of operations;" so, on the 7th and 8th of August, under the pretext of concentrating his forces, he withdrew himself and his army across the river, and resumed his occupation of Detroit. On the 9th, Proctor, apprised of Hull's retreat, and relieved of all apprehension on his own part, with commendable promptitude determined to follow up his first

---

* Thompson's Sketches of the War, quoted by James, Vol. II, p. 61.

attempt upon Hull's line of supply, and detached Major Muir across the Detroit to intercept a much more considerable force and convoy *en route* to Fort Detroit. This expedition was not as successful as the preceding. Muir, with 100 regulars, 100 militia, and 250 Indians, found himself at Magagua in front of Col. Miller, a good officer, backed by the U. S. 4th Regt. of Infantry, a part of the 1st Infantry, some regular artillerymen, and 400 militia, —about 700 in all. Muir, with great judgment, bethought him of the paucity of the force on the other side of the river, and of the military policy which relinquishes a temporary credit for a future certainty, and so, ordered a retreat to his boats, which was safely effected. Muir and his subaltern Sutherland were both wounded ; the latter died shortly after. Two men were killed and nine disabled. In this action of Maguaga or Brownstown, the Americans, who held the ground on the retirement of the British and Indians, represent their own loss to have been 83 killed and wounded, and the Indian casualties at 100. The National Intelligencer, the American Government organ of the day, boastfully asserted that when the militia returned to Detroit from the battle of Brownstown they bore triumphantly on the points of their bayonets between 30 and 40 fresh scalps, which they had taken on the field. As no mercy was shown to the redskins by the trappers and borderers who constituted the militia, and as scalps were much prized spoils, it may be presumed that the number of these trophies represented fairly the number of the Indians slain.* But this momentary reverse was of no benefit to Hull : Brock was on his track, and did not give him much time to deliberate.

But again, during this interval, while Brock at York was preparing for his swoop in the West, and his lieutenants were harassing and retarding the game, the first British stroke of the war had been delivered 250 miles to the north, at Michilimacinac, in

---

* James, Vol. II, p. 6.

the heart of what was then regarded as the Indian country. This island and fortress is situated at the northern extremity of Lake Huron, in the gorge of the Straits of Macinaw, and blocks the entrance to Lake Michigan. In those days it was regarded as a post of great importance. It is now the Gibraltar of that inland sea. It is strongly fortified, and makes of Lake Michigan a *mare clausum*, where, beyond the reach of treaty stipulations, or of hostile interruptions, armaments may be planned and matured safely, against the rear frontier of Canada.

The vast territory surrounding this lake, now occupied by the States of Michigan, Indiana, Illinois, and Wisconsin, embellished by the cities of Chicago, Milwaukie, Grand Haven, and peopled by 5,000,000 of inhabitants, was, fifty years since, a howling wilderness, the retreat and hunting-ground of savage tribes, whose traditional treatment had taught them to put but little trust in the white man. With the American settlers their relations had been, for long, those of chronic collision and contest. The British had, upon an emergency, accepted the services of an ally whose ferocity they could not restrain, and of whose acts they were ashamed; but if the British, in Indian estimation, had proved to be a cold and ungrateful friend, the Americans had never ceased to be a remorseless and grasping enemy. It is affectation to attempt to deny that at this crisis the Indian alliance was sought by both parties. Accident and action combined to solve the diplomatic doubt by the weight of the British bayonet. It was well known how much the defence of the western frontier depended on the Indians. Great efforts had been made both by the British and Americans to secure the services of these uncertain and suspicious auxiliaries. Here the British labored under great disadvantage. Defence, not defiance, was then, as now, their motto. The policy of the day was to discountenance the idea of war. An Indian alliance could only portend war. It was, at the same time, well known to those familiar with the Indian character, that the first successful blow struck in the west would attract the savage to the successful banner. Macinaw, as it is called for brevity, was an American military post in the heart of the Indian territory. Fort St. Joseph, a British post, established for the protection of the fur trade, was situated 40 miles north of Macinaw, at the debouchure of Lake Superior into the waters of Lake Huron.

Captain Roberts, a brave and energetic officer, was in command at Fort St. Joseph. Brock had reinforced this post in the spring, and Roberts had received instructions which, although embarrassed by the irregular and perplexing interference of Sir George Prevost at a later period, he had prepared himself to carry out. On the 4th July, Brock informed Roberts that war existed, and left him to his own discretion.* Roberts had at hand a congenial spirit. The Agent of the Hudson's Bay Company was Toussaint Pothier, afterwards the Hon. Toussaint Pothier, M.L.C., of Montreal, a French Canadian gentleman, brave, gay, polite, ready for any exploit in court or camp. To him Roberts disclosed the information he had received, and the plan he had formed. "Pardieu, Monsieur," exclaimed the chivalrous Frenchman, gyrating with delight,—and those who remember him can well imagine his glee, —"il faut frotter ces gens la bas, joliement." With such associates in an enterprise, little time was lost. To a force of 33 regulars was supplemented about 160 Canadian voyageurs, half-armed with fowling-pieces and old muskets. Two old iron three-pounders, which had been used for firing salutes and astonishing the natives, were put into requisition; and accompanied by Pothier, who, like Clive in another hemisphere, had flung his pen under his desk and buckled on his hanger, Roberts embarked in a miscellaneous

---

* Tupper's Life of Brock.

flotilla of boats and canoes, attended by a small brig laden with stores. In the grey of the morning of the 17th July, while the legislators at Toronto were snoring in their beds, while the unhappy Hull was cogitating moodily at Sandwich, and the hero of Ta-ron-tee, having fluttered the wild-fowl in Duck Creek, had just retired victoriously, crowned with water-cresses, Roberts landed on Macinaw Island unmolested, got his two guns into a menacing position, disposed of his force ostentatiously, ordered his 33 regulars to the front, and bade Indians and half-breeds yell the war-whoop. At this summons, the American commander, who, to say the truth, was quite unprepared for an attack, felt it to be prudent to surrender his post, with about 75 regulars and a large quantity of military stores and valuable furs. It was the first intimation he had received of a state of war. This well-concerted and well-executed stroke was timely, and, in fact, invaluable. It secured the adhesion of the Indians. It disconcerted Hull, by exposing his rear, and was second only to the crowning exploit of the campaign, the capture of Detroit.

Now came Brock's turn. No man knew better than he, the value of vigour in war, and that rapid offence was often the best description of defence. Having dispatched at once the Legislature and all pressing public business, on the 6th August he left York, now Toronto, for Burlington Bay, and from thence proceeded by land to Long Point, "Point aux Pins" being the rendezvous,* speaking a word of counsel to the Mohawks on the Grand River by the way. At Long Point, he embarked with about 300 militia, all volunteers, and a few regulars, in the ordinary boats of the country, and ran along a dangerous and unsheltered coast for 200 miles, amid heavy rains and tempestuous weather, and exposed constantly to surprise, without losing a man. His constant superintendence, forethought, and precaution, inspired his followers with

---

* General Order, 12th August, Isaac Brock.

unbounded confidence. After four days and nights of incessant exertion, the little squadron reached Amherstburg at midnight on the 13th August; Brock declaring, that "in no instance had he seen troops who could have endured the fatigue of a long journey in boats, during exceeding bad weather, with greater cheerfulness and constancy; and it is but justice to this little band to add that their conduct throughout excited my admiration." *

Here Brock encountered Tecumseh, chief of the Shawanee Indians,—regarding whose character and fate more will be said hereafter. It is wonderful with what an instinctive perception of character these two men instantly took to each other. Brock descried at once the sagacity and intrepidity of the Shawanee chief. Tecumseh, in one of his glowing orations, apostrophizes Brock as the warrior who, "standing erect in the bow of his canoe, led the way to battle." It reminds one of Cæsar's standard-bearer launching himself upon the shores of Britain. The incident occurred in crossing the Detroit River two days after; Brock exposing himself, not from ostentation (for his courage was most unpretentious), but to win the confidence and rouse the enthusiasm of his Indian allies. Brock concerted with Tecumseh the plan of his operations against Fort Detroit. The chief listened eagerly, with glistening eyes but undemonstrative attitude. He expressed his approbation with Indian brevity, and his readiness to act by a gesture. Brock asked him, "Could the Shawanees be induced to refrain from spirits?" Tecumseh answered that "Before leaving their wigwams on the Wabash, they had vowed not to touch rum till they had humbled the "Big Knives," meaning the Americans. Brock remarked, "Adhere to this resolution and you must conquer."

Brock acted with promptitude and vigor. The correspondence of the American army had come into his hands by the defeat of

---

* General Order, Amherstburg, 14th August, Isaac Brock.

Van Horne, on the 4th August. The despatches of General Hull disclosed his own misgivings and the demoralized state of the army under his command. Brock saw the opportunity, and grasped at it, at once. With a force of the most miscellaneous character, not half the numerical strength of the enemy, he determined to cross the river Detroit, and beard him in his den. On the 15th August, he summoned Hull to surrender. The latter took two hours to consider the invitation, and declined it. That night Tecumseh crossed the river with about 600 warriors, and occupied the roads and woods below Detroit, intercepting the American communications. The spot selected for landing was Springwell, four miles below the fort, on the only American line of retreat. The river at this point is about three-fourths of a mile wide, deep and strong. Before daybreak on the 16th, the force under Brock, consisting of 330 regulars and 400 militia, with four light pieces of artillery, crossed the river, and advanced upon the fort. He was flanked upon the left by the Indians in the woods, and on the right by a small vessel of war, the Queen Charlotte. Brock led on rapidly. He had taken the measure of his foe, and knew that daring was the best title to success. " Of the force at his disposal," says Armstrong, the American Secretary of War, " four hundred were Canadian Militia, disguised in red coats."* The sequel proved the imitation not to have been a bad one. The York Volunteers, under Hatt, Howard, Bostwick, and Robinson, the men who had escorted Brock to Amherstburg, thrown out as skirmishers, were well forward in the front. Astonished by the vigor of the advance, and perhaps disconcerted by the unearthly outcries of the Indians, the Americans abandoned an outpost, well placed, strongly picketted, and defended by two 24-pounders, and retreated into the main fort. Preparations were made for an assault, when suddenly, was seen to emerge from the works, an

---

* Armstrong, Vol. I, p. 35.

officer bearing a flag of truce. Brigadier-General Hull had resolved to capitulate, and proposed a cessation of hostilities. Articles were formalized then and there, under which the whole Michigan Territory, Fort Detroit, a ship of war, 33 pieces of cannon, stores to correspond, and military chest, 2500 troops, and one stand of colors were surrendered to the British, who, thereupon, betook themselves to dinner. The first act of Brock on entering the fort was to release from captivity Dean, the gallant private of the 41st, who behaved so nobly at the Ta-ron-tee. He sent for the man at once, and shook hands with him cordially, in front of the whole force.*

The surrender of Detroit electrified all Canada. It was the first enterprise in which the Militia had been engaged, and the courage and success of their Volunteers animated and encouraged all. No more was there of doubting or of wavering; disaffection slunk out of sight. Brock became the idol of Upper Canada; and no man ever, by his dauntless example, both moral and physical, and by effecting much with small means, had more honestly won the homage of a people.

---

* Mem.: Col. A. McLean.

CHAPTER IV.

Brock provides for the safety of his conquest and returns to York—Urgent for action—Controlled by an armistice between Sir George Prevost and General Dearborn. Sir George at Quebec. Energy of the Lower Canada Legislature—Provide money—Provide men. The Americans threaten Montreal—Niagara. Detroit. Inroad at Gananoque. Affair at Ogdensburg. Brock returns to the Niagara frontier. Van Ranselaer and the Militia—Crazy for a dash. Capture of the Detroit and Caledonia off Fort Erie. Military ardour of the New York Volunteers uncontrollable. Van Ranselaer resolves to cross the Niagara frontier. Queenstown Heights. Battle 13th October—Death of Brock and Macdonald—Arrival of Sheaffe—Final victory—Surrender by Scott. John Beverley Robinson. Brock's funeral. Scott and the savages.

On,—on again, with the gallant Brock and his fortunes, for on the fortunes of that noble man hung the fate of Upper Canada, still threatened by overwhelming numbers on the Niagara frontier and on that of the St. Lawrence. It was well known at the time, that the demonstrations on Lower Canada were a feint to hamper Sir George Prevost and retard supplies, and that the strength of the enemy had been thrown on the Upper Province. On the Niagara frontier they had accumulated in great force. The indisposition of the Eastern States for the war, and the tendency of the democratic malady to French hallucinations, had preserved to the Lower Canadians the privilege of being the last to be devoured.

After providing for the security of his conquest, and re-assuring the sparse population of Michigan by a Proclamation, confirming to them their property and the enjoyment of their laws and religion, Brock sailed on the 22nd August in the schooner Chippewa for the Niagara frontier.

We may well imagine the patriotic thoughts and high aspirations which at this time thronged the active and vigorous mind of this thorough soldier. His correspondence with his brother tells the tale in his own cheery and modest way.* He knew that he was surrounded. An unconscious lion in the toils, he had torn the meshes to atoms in one direction, and beheld with fearless eye the fire and the steel in his rear, and on his flank. He would neutralize numbers by activity and *vim*. In one week he would have swept the whole American frontier from Buffalo to Fort Niagara; he would have dispersed the reluctant and imperfect levies there formed, and have destroyed the then insufficient armaments. Such a blow, struck at that time, would have pacified that frontier, averted two years of desolation and misery, and have secured for nobler deeds his own invaluable life. Nor was this all. This blow was to have been followed up by a stroke at Sackett's Harbour, the standing menace to Central Canada, just then wakening into armed life, and pregnant with so much of annoyance and humiliation in after years. By the middle of September the enemy would have been anticipated at every point, and Upper Canada would have been safe. Rough lessons such as these might have inculcated reason, and the war itself would have collapsed.

Such, or like unto these, were the patriotic plans of Brock, when, on the waters of Lake Erie, conveyed by the British armed schooner The Lady Prevost, he encountered the demon of obstruction in the shape of an armistice. The British Orders in Council, the ostensible cause of the war, had been revoked by an Order in Council of the 23rd June, seven days after war had been declared by Congress; and so impressed was the British government with a firm belief in American moderation, and in the peaceful efficacy of the remedy exhibited, that on receipt of the intelligence they merely directed that " American ships and goods should be brought in and detained until further orders," † and " forbore from issuing

---

* Life and Correspondence of Brock, p. 102.

† *Vide* Orders in Council, October 13, 1812, and 23 June, 1812.

letters of marque and reprisal, under expectation that the United States would, upon notification of the Order in Council of the 23rd June, forthwith recall the said declaration of war." This hopeful credulity clogged their own movements and those of their subordinates, and nearly proved fatal to Canada. Prevost, pacific by nature, and bound by the pacific instructions of the Imperial government, on learning the repeal of the Orders in Council, presumed Mr. Madison to be as pacific as himself, and proposed to General Dearborn, chief on the northern frontier, an armistice, which, in terms and operation, was as useful to the enemy as it was unfavourable to us, and which all but neutralized the moral effect of the victories which had been achieved in the west. It gave the enemy time to breathe, to think, to transport stores and reinforcements unmolested, and, when it had served their turn, was repudiated by the President. It admitted of the removal of nine fine vessels from Ogdensburg—removed from under the guns of Fort Wellington at Prescott—to Sackett's Harbour, and gave Commodore Chauncey that ascendency on Lake Ontario which enabled him subsequently to destroy Little York.* Brock urgently renewed his instances. He was then at Kingston. "Attack Sackett's Harbour from hence. With our present naval superiority, it must fall. The troops at Niagara will be recalled for its protection. While they march, we sail; and before they can return, the whole Niagara frontier will be ours." In reply, Brock received peremptory orders from Sir George Prevost to do nothing; to remain on the defensive and not provoke the enemy. It is just to believe that in doing this, the Governor General but obeyed the peremptory and painful orders of his superiors. Within his own sphere he had been prompt and energetic. He had convened the Legislature of Lower

---

* Narrative of Simon Van Ranselaer, Lieut.-Col., A.D.C. to Gen. Van Ranselaer, Niagara.

Canada on the first rumour of war, and had obtained from them cordial support.* They indorsed his "Army Bills" to the extent of $1,000,000, and they voted $60,000 for five years, to meet the interest and expenses. By a preceding Act of May of the same year they had authorized the embodiment of 2000 militiamen, and in the event of war, the calling out of the whole militia force of the Province, and measures had been energetically taken to give effect to this legislation.

"A cordon was formed along the frontier of Lower Canada from the Yamaska to St. Regis, where the line of separation between the United States and Canada touches the St. Lawrence, consisting of Canadian Voltigeurs and part of the embodied Militia. A light brigade of *elite*, regulars and militia, was formed at Blairfindie, under the command of Lieut. Col. Young of the 8th Regt., consisting of the flank companies of the 8th, 100th, and 103rd Regts., with the Canadian Fencibles, the flank companies of the 1st Batt. of Embodied Militia, and a small brigade of the Royal Artillery with six field-pieces.†

"On the Montreal frontier the road to the United States from the camp at L'Acadie through Burtonville and Odeltown was rendered impracticable by *abattis*. The Voltigeurs, with extraordinary perseverance, effected this fatiguing duty in short time, under the superintendence of their commanding officer, Major de Salaberry.‡

"On the other hand, the Americans augmented their preparations rapidly, and Gen. Dearborn threatened Montreal with invasion by St. Johns and Odeltown. Their force at Niagara and on the Niagara frontier, under Brig.-Gen. Van Ranselaer, was already formidable, and afforded good ground of apprehension to Gen. Brock of a speedy irruption from that quarter; while Gen. Har-

---

* 16th July, 1812. ' † Christie, Vol. II, p. 40. ‡ Ibid.

rison was actively employed in collecting an army at the river Raisin, near Detroit, from Ohio and Kentucky. The naval establishment at Sackett's Harbour in the meantime increased with celerity, and the ascendency of their fleet on Lake Ontario was, by the indefatigable exertions of Commodore Chauncey, now almost established." *

Two insignificant affairs occurred on the Upper St. Lawrence, this early autumn, but little creditable to either party. Capt. Forsyth with 150 riflemen crossed from the American side (on the 9th September) to Gananoque, where he fluttered the turkeys, captured a few old muskets, wounded the wife of a militia officer who kept a store there, burnt the building and its contents, and returned home with a good deal of predatory exultation.

En revanche, and provoked by frequent interruptions of his convoys from Montreal, Col. Lethbridge, in command at Prescott, attempted a descent on Ogdensburg, opposite, in open day. He pushed off, on the 4th October, in the forenoon, with a force of 750 regulars and militiamen, in 25 batteaux, escorted by two gun-boats. They were received by a heavy fire of artillery, boats were struck and sunk, some disabled, all fell into confusion. The flotilla dropped down the stream out of fire, and returned whence they came, with three men killed and four wounded. It was a rash and unauthorized enterprise, ill-concerted, and led with more of courage than conduct.

Brock, chafing but obedient, had returned to Niagara. He writes thence to his brother, 18th September 1812: "A river about 500 yards wide divides the troops. My instructions oblige me to adopt defensive measures, and I have evinced greater forbearance than was ever practised on any former occasion. It is thought that without the aid of the sword the American people

---

* Christie, Vol. II, p. 40.

may be brought to a due sense of their own interest. I firmly believe that I could at this moment sweep everything before me between Fort Niagara and Buffalo. . . . The militia, being principally composed of enraged democrats, are more ardent and anxious to engage, but they have neither subordination nor discipline. They die very fast. It is certainly singular that we should be two months in a state of warfare, and that along this widely extended frontier not a single death, either natural or by the sword, should have occurred among the troops under my command, and we have not been altogether idle, nor has a single desertion taken place." *

The "enraged democrats" at length brought things to a crisis. The American leaders had assembled on the Niagara frontier,— 36 miles in length from Buffalo to Fort Niagara—a force of about 6,000 men. A large number consisted of militia, of whom Col. Baines, having encountered them on his official visit to Gen. Dearborn, says to Brock: "I found a very general prejudice prevailing with Jonathan of his own resources and means of invading these Provinces, and of our weakness and inability to resist, both exaggerated in a most absurd and extravagant degree." *

These paladins, with little discipline, and no subordination, exhibited great impatience at what they were pleased to term, the dilatoriness of their officers, in not " clearing out the British frontier right off," and their impetuosity was greatly sharpened by a successful exploit on the part of Lieut. Elliott of the American Navy, who was then engaged at Black Rock in fitting for service an armed schooner. This officer, backed by 100 good seamen, in the early morning of the 9th October, boarded and carried, off Fort Erie, the brig of war Detroit, and the private brig Caledonia, laden with stores and spoils from Amherstburg. This feat, which was

---

* Brock Correspondence, p. 108.

well and gallantly done, could never have been attempted, had not Brock, at an earlier period, been restricted to defensive measures. Black Rock and its batteries would have disappeared, and the armed vessel Elliott had in hand, would have been in ours, or in flames. As it was, the Detroit grounded and was destroyed, but the eclat of the exploit turned the heads of the gallant militia, and they insisted, incontinently, either to be led to victory or to go home.

General Van Ranselaer, who commanded the whole force, was manifestly under the impression that a good deal of glory was to be got at small risk, and was unwilling to allow the glittering prize to slip through his fingers. He had been informed by a deceitful spy, that Brock had left for the Detroit frontier. He resolved therefore, on the adventure. On the morning of the 11th October, an attempt was made, but failed. Boats were wanting—oars were deficient—it rained hard, and the general prospect was disagreeable. The attack on Queenston heights was, in consequence, deferred to the 13th.

There is not on this continent a more imposing situation or a lovelier scene, than is presented from the noble plateau immortalized as Queenston Heights. Rising in rich undulation from the alluvial shore, which, at a distance of seven miles, subsides into Lake Ontario, they form the height of land through which, for twenty miles back, the river and cataract of Niagara cleave their resistless way. They trend away westerly until they reach Hamilton, and constitute the great embankment which dams back the superincumbent waters of Lake Erie. The approach to the heights from the village of Queenston is strikingly beautiful. It reminds an Englishman of the grassy glades and hanging woods of his native land. An ascent of 250 feet, tortuous and broken, is now crowned by a grand column of buff sandstone, artistically designed, and not unworthy of the memory which Canada reveres. Brock's monument is a credit to the taste and gratitude of the country. From the summit the eye commands a varied landscape of woodland and farm land, of umbrageous forest and rich cultivation—of village and of villa— church spire and cosy homestead—the blue Ontario in the distance, flecked with sails; such as may well gladden the hearts of those under whose eye the land has grown, and make them glory in the flag, emblematic of the system, which fosters and protects it. The noble river, boiling, rushing, eddying,—which, 500 yards wide, rushes through the gorge at the right hand side of the spectator, now spanned by a gossamer bridge, 800 feet of wire tracery,—separates, as with a barrier of steel, the "clearings" of experiment from the domain of experience—the United States from British territory. On that rich October morning, glowing with the gorgeous tints of the autumnal foliage, and softened by the mellow haze of the first flush of the Indian summer, how attractive must have been that lovely scene to the eye of the American invader,

Baptized in molten gold and swathed in dun.

In the early morning, before day broke, the desperate few, the "forlorn hope," had manned the first boats, and under the command of Colonel Van Ranselaer, gained the Canadian shore. The force there stationed consisted of two companies of the 49th and about 200 of the York militia. One 18-pounder gun was in position, on a spur of the heights, and a carronade raked the river from a point about a mile below. The American force, covered by the fire of two eighteen pounders, and two field pieces from their own side, effected a landing with little loss. One officer was slain in the boats by a ball from the gun at the point. More troops and some militia-men crossed, until about 1,300 men were in line, and in front of them the British outposts. The resistance made was desperate; the assailants were as resolute. The voices of the American officers could be heard above the rattle of the musketry with the cry of "On men! on! for the honour of America." The reply, again, was a dogged cheer, and the rattle of musketry. In a short time, Col. Van Ranselaer was desperately wounded in four places. Good men and officers had fallen around him. The captains commanding the 49th companies had both fallen wounded. The fire of the 18-pounder was of no avail in that part of the field. It would have been more fatal to friend than to foe. At this moment Brock rode up. Awakened at daybreak by the firing, and fully anticipating attack, he called for his good horse Alfred, and, followed by his staff, galloped up from Fort George. He passed without drawing rein, through the village, reached the 18-pounder battery, dismounted, and was covering the field through his telescope, when a fire was opened on the rear of the field work from a height above, which had been hardily gained during this brief interval by Captain Wool and a detachment of American regulars, up an almost inaccessible fisherman's path. The volley was promptly followed by a rush; Brock and his suite had no time to remount; they quickly retired with the twelve men who manned the battery. There was neither space, nor time, nor thought, for generalship—all was sheer fighting. Williams of the 49th, with a detachment of 100 strong, charged up the hill against Wool's men, who were repelled, but reinforced, charged again; notwithstanding which " in the struggle which ensued the whole were driven to the edge of the bank."[*] Here, with the storming foe before them, a precipice of 180 feet behind, and the roaring Niagara beneath, some craven spirit quailed—an attempt was made to raise the white flag— Wool tore it down and trampled it under foot. The re-inspired regulars opened a scathing fire of musketry; Brock who, in front, roused beyond himself, had forgotten the general in the soldier, conspicuous by his height, dress, gesture and undaunted bearing, was pointing to

---

[*] Wool's letter to Van Ranselaer, Buffalo, October 23, 1812.

the hill, and had just shouted "Push on the brave York Volunteers," when he was struck by a ball in the right breast, which passed through his left side. He fell. His last words were, that his death should be concealed from his men, and that his remembrance should be borne to his sister. Thus fell, and thus died a brave soldier, an able leader, and a good man, who honoured by his life and ennobled by his death the soil on which he bled, and whose name remains, ever beloved and respected, a household word and a household memory in Canada.

Shortly after, McDonell, his Aide-de-Camp, a Lieut.-Colonel of Militia, and Attorney-General for Upper Canada, obeying the last behest of his chief, leading on the "brave York Volunteers" and breasting the hill on horseback, was struck from his saddle. He died next day, and, regardless of self, his last thoughts were with his departed commander and friend.

The charge of the Volunteers had compelled the enemy to spike the 18 pounder and retire; but at this moment, the best officers and bravest men down on both sides, and the rest exhausted, a lull took place in the fighting. The Americans retained the hill, with the precipice at their backs; the British retired under cover of the houses on the outskirts of the village. Both parties looked for reinforcements.

As has been before remarked, the Americans occupied at this time a position full of peril. Though Wool had received an accession of force, their number was unequal to the adventure, and they were cooped up on the brow of the hill, with their foe in front, whose strength they knew must increase, and the beetling precipice and the boiling river in their rear. Nothing could save them but a retreat, or large reinforcements. The first expedient was impracticable. The reinforcements were within sight, within call, yet denied their aid. The "enraged democrats" had abated all their savagery. The men, a few days before, so desperate to do or die, quailed at the sight of danger, and urged qualms of conscience and constitutional scruples as a plea for their poltroonery. Canada forsooth was not New York State, and they could not lawfully risk their precious lives, except in defence of their native soil. The brave men on the opposite hill-side were, therefore, left to their fate.

On the other hand, General Sheaffe, who commanded at Fort George, had, under instructions from Sir Isaac Brock, got his men together on the first alarm. With about 300 regulars of the 41st and 49th regiments, two companies of Lincoln militia, and a handful of Indians, he had followed rapidly to the scene of the conflict. He took the road from Newark to St. Davids, which enabled him to debouch on the heights about two miles to the west of Queenston. He heard, on his way, of the fall of Brock, and pushed on the more eagerly, to avenge his death and retrieve the day. With all his speed, marching through roads such as they then were, he could not reach the Plateau long before noon. Here he was reinforced by Norton, and Brant the younger, Indian chiefs, and a body of their followers, and by about 200 volunteer militia men from Chippewa, making the whole force equal to 800 men. It will be seen, at once, that the invaders were surrounded, their backs to the river and to their own recreant countrymen, Queenston with its defenders breathing vengeance on their right, and Sheaffe on their front and left flank. Gradually and systematically, the fatal semicircle of fire and steel narrowed and thickened. Wool, who had bravely done his best, was down with wounds. Scott, who has since filled so large a place in the history of his country, succeeded him, and not unworthily. The Americans fought on manfully, but hopelessly. The fatal semicircle narrowed more and more—a volley here—scattered shots there—amid the wild yell of the Indian, the shout of the soldier, the shriek of the wounded, the hoarse word of command,—amid smoke and dust, and tumult, and groans and execration, the last vengeful rush was made, and every living American swept from the summit of that blood-stained hill.

Of the survivors, part scrambled down by the path they had ascended, part clinging to rocks and shrubs endeavoured to escape, but the lithe Indian proved the better cragsman, and the descent was fearfully accelerated. Many were dashed to pieces : many drowned—two men were seen to strip deliberately, and take to the whirling river, remarking significantly, that they might as well be drowned as hanged. Here, on the rocky selvage, at the foot of overhanging cliffs, unarmed and defenceless, the remainder assembled and, at once, resolved to surrender.* Scott, accompanied by Captains Totten and Gibson, with Totten's cravat attached to his sword point, not without great danger from the infuriate savages, emerged from the rocks, near where the Suspension Bridge now stands, and meeting a British picket, were conducted to General Sheaffe. Short was the parley between men in their condition, and a commander in whose hands were life and safety. Major-General Wadsworth and about 1,100 American officers and soldiers surrendered, unconditionally, prisoners of war. The American loss by bullet, steel, and flood, had been near 400 men.

Among the present residents, whom the fortunes of peace have cast on our frontier, is one John McCarthy, who served in the American regulars at the battle of Queenston heights. He now lives between old Newark (Niagara) and Queenston. He relates that, in preparation for the last assault of the British, the American officers caused their men to load and lie down, with the order not to rise or fire a shot until they " got the word." Twenty men were detailed at intervals in the rear, with pieces loaded, and directions openly given, to shoot down any man disobey-

---

* Mansfield's Life of Scott, p. 48 ; Stone's Life of Brant, Vol. II, p. 512.

ing the first order. He states that the British were within forty yards before the word came, that the volley was instantaneous and fatal, but never stopped the rush, which cleared the hill like chaff before a gust of wind.

The British force engaged during the day consisted of the remnants of the two companies of the 49th attacked in the morning who had been bravely sustained by Cameron's, Howard's, and Chisholm's companies of the York militia. Sheaffe brought to their support 380 of the 41st. Crook's and McEwen's flank companies of the 1st Lincoln; Nellies and W. Crook's companies of the 4th Lincoln, Hale's, Durand's, and Applegate's companies of the 5th Lincoln, Major Merritt's yeomanry corps, and a party of Swayzee's militia artillery. Colonel Clark of the militia came up from Chippewa with Capt. Derinzys' and Bullock's company of the 41st, Capt. R. Hamilton and Stone's flank companies of the 2nd Lincoln and Volunteer Sedentary militia, Young Norton, Brant the younger, and about 50 Mohawks. A company of colored men under Captain Runchey was on the ground, and did good service. The whole force at the close of the day did not exceed one thousand rank and file. Of this number about 80 were killed and wounded, Indians included.

The British had been greatly exasperated by the fatal event of the morning. The men of Lincoln and the "brave York Volunteers" with "Brock" on their lips and revenge in their hearts, had joined in the last desperate charge, and among the foremost, foremost ever found, was John Beverly Robinson, a U. E. Loyalist, a lawyer from Toronto, and not the worse soldier for all that. His light, compact, agile figure, handsome face, and eager eye, were long proudly remembered by those who had witnessed his conduct in the field, and who loved to dwell on those traits of chivalrous loyalty, energetic talent and sterling worth which, in after years, and in a happier sphere, elevated him to the position of Chief Justice of the Province, and to the rank of an English Baronet. The late lamented death of Sir John Beverly Robinson, Bart., and C. B., demands, as an homage to the grief of Canada, this passing tribute to his memory. Bright names hallow story as well as song.

Thus terminated this remarkable contest. It has been the practice of all writers, with pardonable partiality, so far to identify Brock with Queenston heights, as to make his name inseparable from the victory; but, honor to whom honor is justly due, and Brock was the last man to deny it to an old friend who had fought by his side in the 49th, in many a stricken field. The battle was won by Sheaffe—a U. E. Loyalist, born in Boston, who had served the king from the days of Bunker Hill. Brock lost his life early in the morning—the fight flagged in consequence—was re-fought, and won by Sheaffe at 3 in the afternoon. Sheaffe was rewarded for his success by a Baronetcy. Brock died unconscious of the honors he had earned. On the day of his death, at the foot of Queenston heights, the guns of the Tower of London proclaimed his victory at Detroit. He had been made a Knight of the most honourable order of the Bath. His banner and his spurs were laid upon his tomb. Like a wreath of " immortelles," they cover a solitary name, " alone in its glory." Brock died unmarried. His remains were interred with those of his Provincial Aide-de-Camp, Col. McDonell, at Fort George, in a cavalier bastion which had been constructed under his superintendence. On the erection of the column to his memory at Queenston heights, they were removed, and rest there. The soldier who commanded at the American fort, Niagara, on the occasion of the funeral, hoisted his flag half mast, and fired minute guns during the ceremony, shot for shot with our own.*

---

*It may be pardoned to the pen which traces these lines, if it is inspired by something of an hereditary interest in the events narrated. The chief mourner at the funeral of Brock was General Sheaffe. Two of the pall bearers were Lieut.-Colonel Coffin, Provincial Aide de Camp, and James Coffin, Esquire, Deputy Assistant Commissary General, both uncles to the writer. As General

A picturesque incident of this semi-savage warfare is related. Col. Scott, by his stature and intrepidity during the day, had attracted the particular attention of the Indian Chieftains. Fortune favoured him so far, that his escape was ascribed to some peculiar "medicine," or to witchcraft. On the evening of the day of the surrender, Scott was dining with General Sheaffe, when a messenger came from persons without, who wished to speak with the "tall American." Scott rose, with a jocular observation, and proceeded into the narrow entrance, where he found himself confronted by two Indians, Jacob Norton and Brant the younger. The latter in English, rapidly questioned him "as to his wounds," "balls through his clothes," "they had fired at him all day without effect." The former somewhat rudely took the Colonel by the arm, as if to turn him round for inspection. Scott indignantly flung the intruder from him, exclaiming "Hands off, you scoundrel: you shot like a squaw." The Indian blood was roused instantaneously, knives and tomahawks were drawn. Scott grasped his sword, but the odds were against him in a narrow passage, when, in at the door way stepped Colonel Coffin, Provincial Aide-de-Camp to General Sheaffe, who seeing things at a glance, drew a pistol and put it to Norton's head, calling for assistance, which in one moment was on the spot from the room behind. The Indian Chiefs, recovering from their sudden gust of passion, and abashed by their own violence, slowly dropped their arms, and retired. The officer to whom Scott possibly owed his life was then Aide-de-Camp to the General, and on the 14th January following, was appointed Deputy Adjutant General of the militia of Upper Canada, which post he filled with universal respect, for twenty-four years.*

Sheaffe had married their sister, and was their first cousin, his name is added, with, it is believed, a not ignoble pride, to the familiar record of men who—all U. E. Loyalists—had served their king and country truly in times of trial.

* Mansfield's Life of Scott, p. 47; Stone's Life of Brant, Vol. II, p. 214.

CHAPTER V.

Armistice between Sheaffe and Van Renselaer. Eastern frontier—Affair at St. Regis. "Capture of a stand of colors"—Retaliation. Hard frost below—Pleasant weather west. American squadron and Commodore Earle. Gallant exploit of the Canadian schooner Simcoe. Chauncey and Captain Brock. Armistice between Smyth and Sheaffe terminated. Descent on Canadian frontier. Americans repulsed. Fort Erie summoned. Bishop wont give up. Smyth retires into winter quarters, and goes south. United States disunited on the war—Canada unanimous. Sufferings and spirit of the people. Loyal and Patriotic Society.

It is unfortunate that Sheaffe, if his own master, should have marred the fair proportions of his success by an armistice which has given rise to much animadversion. He apparently might, and if he could, he *ought* to have crossed the river forthwith, and to have swept the coast of the renegade crew who had disgraced our common manhood, and the Niagara frontier, on both sides, would have been spared much of future evil. Brock, as he got into his saddle on the morning of his death, had ordered Major Evans of the 8th Regt., who remained in command at Fort George, to open fire on Fort Niagara, directly opposite, and so effectually was the order obeyed, that, in a short time, the place was dismantled and abandoned, and might easily have been taken possession of the following day. But it should be kept in mind, that Sheaffe had to protect a frontier of 36 miles with about 1500 men—that he had on the other side 6000 opposed to him; that in assailing the enemy's frontier he exposed his own to superior numbers at remote points, and that a failure on his part would have been a sacrifice of the successes gained, would have opened the road to Burlington Heights and York, would have thrown the enemy in Proctor's rear, and have endangered the safety of the Province. Independent of the rashness of an advance, there were *in favour* of an armistice many substantial grounds.

As before said he was weak, in face of an enemy superior in numbers, and embarrassed by a crowd of prisoners, whom he had to guard as well as feed. He expected reinforcements, the safe and speedy arrival of which would change the aspect of affairs. It is obvious too, that he acted under unseen pressure, and that, in this respect, he was not his own master. Temporizing was the government " order of the day ;" Sir George Prevost had imposed it upon Brock, he in his turn had impressed it upon Proctor in the west, and Sheaffe, with soldierly subordination, did as he understood.* Sir George Prevost disapproved of this armistice when reported to him; but the British ministry, as Sir George said, had " hampered the contest with strange infatuation," and it cannot be wondered at, that absorbed in a vast life-and-death struggle in Europe, they prayed to be ridded, by any concession, of the worriment of a *petite guerre* in America. On the spot, and in our own view of our own interests, we see things in a larger and truer point of view; and it should be kept in mind that the propriety of the armistice was never questioned in England.

The Americans were nothing daunted by this reverse. To the popular eye, the disaster at Queenston heights read as a success. The authorities, as well as the writers of the day, spoke of the death of Brock, as they now do of the fall of Stonewall Jackson, as equivalent to a victory. It has even been contended that the temporary tenure of the crest of the hill, up to the arrival of the reinforcements under Sheaffe, was in itself a victory. The British held the Redan in front of Sebastopol for two hours, before they retired, and yet it may be doubted if any American writer would admit this honourable feat of desperate valour to be a success.

But successes of another and unexpected character—successes on the ocean, to be enlarged upon hereafter, had, at this

---

* Life and Correspondence of Brock, Tupper, p. 116.

critical moment, elated the mind of the government and people, and imparted an immense impulse to the national energies. The reluctant good sense of the country was drowned in the general intoxication. The government urged on with vigour its preparations for further invasion. Late as the season was, they had calculated to take Canada at a disadvantage, when hermetically sealed by winter from extraneous help; and, to impart to the tragedy, which had been enacted amid the melodramatic scenery of Niagara, its due proportion of farce, they appointed one General Smyth to the command. This gentleman was the Bombastes Furioso of the day. In proclamations he stands unrivalled. Never was there "a most noble army" more "bethumped by words,"—but his exploits appear to have been limited by phrases.

Leaving General Smyth to apostrophize his "Hearts of War," in front of General Sheaffe, we will proceed to the New York frontier of Lower Canada, where General Dearborn had assembled 10,000 men, and from Plattsburg menaced Montreal. But the French Canadian militia, like the dragon's teeth sown by Cadmus, sprang to arms; the land bristled with bayonets. Major de Salaberry, in the infancy of his fame, had the command of the outposts, and, under his inspiration, these undisciplined levies speedily showed that they were too much in earnest to be trifled with. After some parade of demonstration, on the 20th November, an attack was made on a picket at Lacolle, by a force from Champlain Town. The picket consisted of frontier militia and a few Indians under Col. McKay, of the North West Company, who had borne the news of the war to Mackinac, had returned to Montreal, to throw himself into the field at the head of his Indians, and who, in 1814, performed services still more important in the capture of Prairie du Chien on the Mississippi.* This gentleman so handled his small force, that the

---

* Col. William McKay was father of Robert McKay, Esq., an eminent advocate of Montreal.

enemy, in the dark, fired upon their own people, killing several, and then, much disconcerted, fell back on Champlain Town, from whence they came; and thereupon Dearborn, in deference to the mandates of climate, retired into winter quarters.

On our way back from the Plattsburg-Montreal section of the international frontier, we will touch at the Indian village of St. Regis where the line 45° strikes the St. Lawrence. It is the westernmost, and extreme point of the frontier between Lower Canada and the State of New York. The Upper Province on the north shore of the St. Lawrence and Lakes had been formed into three military divisions—left, centre, and right—the left extending upwards from the old French fort of Coteau du Lac, up the line of the St. Lawrence, included Kingston. The centre embraced York and the Peninsula of Niagara; the right comprehended the Detroit frontier and the Upper coasts of Lake Erie. St. Regis in Lower Canada, on the south shore of the St. Lawrence, opposite to Cornwall, was surprised on the morning of the 23rd October by a force of 400 men detailed from Plattsburg. The outpost or picket, at this point, consisted of twenty men and an officer of Canadian Voyageurs. Lieut. Rototte, Sergeant McGillivray, and six men were killed, the remainder taken prisoners. In a cupboard of the wigwam of the Indian interpreter, was found a Union Jack, on gala days the worthy object of Indian adoration. This windfall was announced to the world as the "capture of a stand of colors," "the first colors taken during the war." Dozens of them might have been obtained, at far less cost, in any American shipyard.

This affront was resented forthwith. On the 23rd November, small parties of the 49th Foot and Glengarry Light Infantry, supported by about 70 men of the Cornwall and Glengarry militia, about 140 in all, under Lieut.-Colonel McMillan, crossed the St. Lawrence and pounced on the American fort at Salmon river, opposite to St. Regis. The enemy took to the block-house, but finding themselves surrounded, surrendered prisoners of war. One captain, two subalterns and forty-one men were taken, with four batteaux and fifty-seven stand of arms. No " stand of colors" was captured with the Americans, as it is not usual to confide standards to the guardianship of detached parties of forty or fifty men in any service.

But while winter, growing gradually up the river, had already imposed an icy barrier to all military operations in Eastern Canada and on the line of the river St. Lawrence, the climate of the Western Province, the more moderate as it declines westward, admitted, to a much later period of the year, of naval combinations and of the movements of troops. At a time when the St. Lawrence, from Quebec downwards, is barred by thick ribbed ice, and the vast territory intermediate between the Atlantic and this noble river is an impassable wilderness of snow; where the breath freezes in the very nostrils of men; the immense tract of country west of, and among the Lakes, enjoys a climate very like that of England;—somewhat less of humidity, perhaps, and a little more of sun. At Detroit, the river freezes occasionally, as does the Rhine, and as does the Thames, and leads to much the same exhibition of jollity, booths and bonfires, races and roast oxen; but the vast expanse of the lake surface moistens and softens the atmosphere—the waters are, for military purposes, at no period of the season reliably impracticable, and the West is, during winter, and in ordinary seasons, as pleasant a country to fight over as any part of Flanders.

Thus, on the 9th of November, 1812, the American fleet from Sackett's Harbour, consisting of the Oneida brig of 16 guns, and six heavy schooners, chased the Royal George, commanded by Commodore Earle, into Kingston. At an earlier period the Commodore had withdrawn from an attempt on the Oneida in Sackett's Harbour, and much had been said to his disparagement in consequence. We have been reminded significantly, that the Canadian

Commodore did not belong to the Royal Navy. The imputation should have been spared until it had been fully ascertained how much of his apparent backsliding was ascribable to British mismanagement. What was the strength of his crew? What the state of his equipments? What his orders? His conduct simply indicated the character of all the orders of that time. We do not hesitate to say that the Canadian seaman, on his own waters—man to man—is as good as the briniest salt that ever trod deck; and as a rule, for pluck or conduct, the raw Canadian material is equal to any found in Yankeedom, or Christendom either, and in proof we quote the daring escape of the Canadian schooner Simcoe, James Richardson, commander, by running the gauntlet of the American flotilla. The story is thus told:

On the 20th November, the Americans had cannonaded the town of Kingston, and got the worst of it, at long bowls. They had hauled off, beating out of the channel into the open lake, under heavy press of sail, when they discovered the Simcoe, a fine 200-ton schooner, bound from Niagara to Kingston. She had been employed in the transportation of troops and stores, and was returning in ballast. The American force, armed with long heavy guns, intercepted her completely. Richardson, not relishing the idea of capture, and the transfer of so fine a vessel to the American marine, attempted at first to run her ashore on Amherst Island, but the wind baffled this design. In the meantime one of the enemy's schooners got under his lee, and opened fire, but, attempting to tack, "missed stays." Richardson's nautical blood was up in a moment. He cheered his men. "Look, lads, at these lubbers! Stand by me, and we will run past the whole of them, and get safe into port." The answer was a ready cheer. The helm was instantly "put up," and spreading all sail, with a stiff breeze blowing, the daring Simcoe bore down direct on the harbour, passing a little to the northward of the enemy, who, ship by ship, delivered their fire of round and grape, and vainly endeavoured to cross her bows. She shot by them all, with riddled sides and sails, but not a man hurt, running the gauntlet for four or five miles. Before reaching port she was struck under water by a 32-pound shot, filled, and sank, but was easily raised afterwards, and repaired. As she sank the crew fired their only piece of ordnance, a solitary musket, with a cheer of defiance, which was taken up and echoed by the thousands of citizens, troops, and militia who thronged the shore.*

A few hours after, Commodore Chauncey, in command of the American squadron, captured a schooner having on board Capt. Brock, a brother of the deceased General, with plate and effects of his late relative. Chauncey paroled the captain, and, with graceful generosity, restored to him all the captured property he had in charge.

The armistice between Gen. Smyth and Sir Roger Sheaffe terminated on the 20th November. With Gen. Smyth gasconading was a gift. He had primed his men with proclamations, but fired the train with a long lanyard. He had prepared 2500 men for an invasion of Canada. He presided at the embarkation, saw the men off safely, and retired to "organize further."

"The tornado burst on the Canadian shore," to use the words of the American annalist,† at the upper end of Grand Isle, between Fort Erie and Chippewa. It was met by the gallant Col. Bishopp, who commanded about 600 men,—360 regulars, and 240 militia, under Major Hatt and Capt. Bostwick. The first demonstration took place on the 27th November. Small outposts of the British were temporarily overpowered, guns were spiked; Lieutenants King, Lamont and Bartley, of the Royal Artillery, perversely fighting, with that stupid indisposition to give in, natural to British youngsters,

---

* Memoranda of the Rev. Dr. Richardson, D.D.
† Nile's Weekly Messenger, quoted by Auchinleck, 119.

were badly wounded; but when morning broke, Bishopp and Ormsby were down upon the invader. The guns were recaptured and unspiked; a second division of American invaders repulsed with much loss; and an aide-de-camp of the American general, with about forty men and some other officers, were taken prisoners. Smyth, who had already proclaimed himself victorious, was puzzled. Considering the disparity of numbers the British ought to have surrendered long before—he was sure they meant to do so—the case of Hull was precisely parallel. He would give them an opportunity,—and so despatched a flag of truce to Fort Erie, politely requesting a surrender—a suggestion which was declined, in the best possible temper, by the imperturbable Bishopp.

Smyth ordered his men again into the boats, and then, to disembark and dine, and then, to repeat the same manœuvre, until at length, on the 1st December, he decided to abandon all idea of crossing and conquest, and to go into winter quarters, which was done, it must be said, to the intense disgust of his army. Winter quarters led to military conventions, and to resolutions very disconcerting to the General, who finding himself to be threatened with tar and feathers, departed forthwith South, was removed in a summary way from the U. S. service, and subsided finally into a member of Congress: and thus ended the campaign of the year 1812, not inauspiciously for Canada.

It proved two things—first that the people of the United States were disunited on the subject of the war, while the people of Canada were united to a man. The Legislature of Maryland openly denounced the war. The governments of Massachusetts, Connecticut, and Rhode Island, had refused the quota of militia demanded of these States respectively. Such men as Quincey declared in the House of Representatives at Washington, that "since the invasion of the Buccaneers, there was nothing in history more disgraceful than this war."

SPIRIT IN CANADA—LOYAL AND PATRIOTIC SOCIETY. 73

The voice of Canada was unanimous—in the Upper and in the Lower Province—French and English—Protestant and Catholic—men of all parties and all policies—the voices of all were still for war. They had not sought it,—they had shunned it,—but it had been forced upon them, and they were ready to fight it out. Recollect, that this was not the sentiment of a vagabond population, but of the farmers, whose fields were left uncultivated, and families destitute, while they risked their lives for their national independence. Nor were these sacrifices, all: let us consider the privations endured. Men were suddenly summoned from their firesides, homely but plentiful, to encounter a campaign, imperfectly armed, insufficiently clad, uncertainly fed. And yet no complaints were heard —they suffered and fought on.

But the knowledge of their distress pervaded the community and touched every heart. First, the people of York originated a subscription, and the young ladies devoted themselves to the work of preparing flannels for the men. In December 1812, rose the " Loyal and Patriotic Society of Upper Canada ;" Thomas Scott, Chief Justice, President, and John Strachan, William Campbell, John Small, William Chewitt, J. B. Robinson, William Allan, Grant Powell, and Abel Wood, as Directors. The object of this Society was to provide comforts for the men, support for destitute families, succour for the wounded, compensation to the plundered, and assistance to all who required and deserved it. The appeal of this Society met with an instant and generous response. In London, under the auspices of the Duke of Kent, was subscribed at once £5,000 ; in Jamaica, £1,419 ; in Nova Scotia, £2,500 ; in Montreal, £3,130 ; in Quebec, £1,500 ; in York, £1,868 ; in Kingston and Eastern Districts, £800. In other places both within and without the Province other large sums, amounting altogether to £14 or £15,000. These moneys were employed very judiciously, to the relief of great distress, leaving at the close of the war a considerable balance in the hands of the Treasurer, but, at the time, this generous appreciation of their efforts had a grand effect. It sank deep into the hearts of the people of Canada. Inspired by the sympathy and enthusiastic support of their fellow-subjects in all parts of the world, the loyal men of Canada rallied to the flag of their native land—*in utrâque fortunâ parati*—with the sentiment in their hearts which they have handed down to their children, expressed in Praed's Charade—

> Fight as your fathers fought,
> Fall as your fathers fell :
> Thy task is taught—thy shroud is wrought—
> So—forward, and farewell.

CHAPTER VI.

Naval occurrences of the war. Supremacy of England on the ocean. Indifference to foreign progress. American frigates—Unrivalled in construction—Speed—Equipment—Power. Naval duels. The Constitution and Guerrière. The Frolic and Wasp. The United States and Macedonian. The Java and Constitution. Effect of these contests. Exultation of Europe. England nerved and steeled. The Hornet and Peacock. Counter-stroke. Shannon and Chesapeake. Moral effect. The balance redressed. Gallantry on both sides. Effect of these events on the war in Canada.

Not to interrupt, as far as could be avoided, the thread of the preceding narrative, no mention has been made of those remarkable naval duels which imparted so much of a bold and startling interest to the American contest, so called, of 1812. The first of these occurrences, which took place towards the end of that year, electrified and dazzled America, and blinded the popular vision to the reverses which had been encountered in Canada, while a series of well fought engagements, resulting, in rapid succession, to the disadvantage of Great Britain, signalized the opening of the year 1813. Up to this period of time, England had held dominion of the seas. The oceans of the globe owned her sway. The Spaniard and the Frenchman, the Dutchman and the Dane, had confessed her prowess. From Cadiz to Copenhagen, from Gibraltar to the Nile, she ruled the main. It was with astonishment, not unmixed with glee, that those who had suffered discomfiture, now witnessed her disaster. The haughty lioness had been bearded in her den, by her own sea-cubs, who proved themselves, in deadly conflict, to be not unworthy of their origin.

In 1812 Great Britain had one thousand pennants afloat. At

the outbreak of the war, the American navy consisted of four frigates and eight sloops, but they were all ships of new and skilful construction, combining great power with great speed, and both, in the number of guns and weight of metal, exceeding their nominal strength. The embargo supplied these choice cruisers with admirble crews, while the officers, in seamanship and bravery, were second to none. It had been remarked by observant travellers in preceding years, that the Americans were building vessels of their respective classes, very superior to our own, but the British Admiralty of the day were deaf to suggestion or advice. They laughed to scorn all such Yankee inventions.

> The reverend greybeards raved an' stormed
> That younker laddies
> Should think they better were informed
> Than their auld daddies.

Thus, when war came, a solitary frigate, splendidly armed, equipped, manned and officered, proved more than a match for ships of war, nominally equal, but in fact, greatly inferior; while her speed enabled her to set at defiance all vessels or combinations of superior force. The frigates too, of England, scattered on every sea, were not only, individually, unequal in strength, but, from their numbers, imperfect in appointment and under-manned. All this ought to have been foreseen and provided for. In the absence of provision came the catastrophe. We have already seen how, in the first naval attempt of the war, the Belvidera had maintained the skilful supremacy of England, but this was followed by blows of different augury. In August, 1812,* the Constitution encountered the Guerrière. The American, in tonnage, weight of metal, and number of men, was half as heavy again as the Englishman. The former was fresh out of port. The latter returning from a long cruise to refit, with fore-

---

* August 19, 1812

mast and bowsprit sprung. Captain Dacres, in true bull-dog fashion, fought for two hours, yard-arm to yard-arm. He was crushed, dismasted, wholly wrecked—seventy-nine men killed and wounded, and thirty shots received below the water-line. He struck, without disgrace, to an antagonist uninjured comparatively in hull and rigging, and whose casualties amounted to fourteen.* The Guerrière was sinking when she struck. She was fired by the enemy and blown up.

Next, in October, 1812, ensued the fight between the Frolic and the American Wasp, sloop of war, of the same nominal force, but the broadside, equipage and tonnage greatly in favour of the American. The Frolic, damaged in a gale, was refitting rigging. She was soon reduced to the condition of a log on the water, and was carried by boarding, the only living occupants of her decks being three officers and the man at the wheel. The British loss in a conflict of an hour was thirty killed and between forty and fifty wounded. Both ships were taken in the afternoon of the same day by the Poictiers, 74 guns, and sent into Bermuda.†

---

* The Guerrière had been captured from the French, and for the beauty of her model was taken into our service. She was therefore an old ship, and her scantling only admitted of the use of long 18-pounder guns, while the Constitution carried 24 pounders on her main, and 32 pounders on her upper deck. The comparative fighting power of the two ships may be thus given:—

Constitution.	Guerrière.
58 guns.	48 guns.
Throwing 1536 lbs. shot.	Throwing 1034 lbs. shot.
Crew, 460.	Crew, 240.
Tonnage, 1538.	Tonnage, 1092.

† Frolic.	Wasp.
18 guns.	18 guns.
Broadside, 262 lbs.	Broadside, 268 lbs.
Crew, 92.	Crew, 135.
75 hors de combat.	5 killed, 5 wounded.
Tonnage, 384.	Tonnage, 434.

On the 25th October came a still sturdier blow. The United States encountered the Macedonian, 56 guns to 44, and the disparity still more increased by weight of broadside, tonnage, and crew. The fight was fierce,—at long range,—in close fight,—in attempts to board,—in a tremendous sea. The Macedonian was so crippled as to become unmanageable, and being exposed to raking broadsides, she could not answer. After a contest of two hours and upwards, with mizzenmast gone by the board, main and foretopmast shot away, thirty-six men killed and sixty-eight wounded, she slowly and sadly lowered her flag. The disparity of force is best shown by the comparative losses. The British frigate lost 104 killed and wounded ; the American twelve.*

Nor was this the last disaster of the year. On the 20th Dec., the Java frigate, under command of the young and gallant Lambert, left Spithead for the East Indian Station. Lambert had been at Quebec in 1808, in the Iphigenie frigate, where he had attracted much attention, as the *beau ideal* of a British sailor. Brock speaks of him with warmth in his familiar letters. He sailed from Spithead with a motley crew—gaol-birds, as they were called—being many of them poachers and smugglers, desperadoes, devoid of discipline, but, as the event showed, full of fight; many of them, however, had never fired a cartridge. Lambert, who had some American experience, remonstrated. He was answered with a sneer: he was told that a voyage to Bombay and back would make a crew: and went to his death, doomed but determined. On the 29th Dec. he fell in with the Constitution—The inequality was much the same as in the preceding contest with the Macedonian. The Constitution at first stood away, long range being her *forte*, but Lambert was a

---

* United States.
Broadside, weight of metal, 864 lbs.
Crew, 474.
Tonnage, 1533.

Macedonian.
Broadside, 528 lbs.
Crew, 254.
Tonnage, 1081.

seaman, and one of the bravest of the brave. He knew that his only chance was at close quarters, and by dint of good seamanship, at length ranged alongside of an antagonist, on his part nothing loath. The fight lasted two hours and a-half; Lambert attempting to board, fell mortally wounded. With no greater crash to the brave hearts around, down came, at the same time, the foremast of the Java, clogging the deck with wreck. Lieut. Chads took the command, and desperately fought on ; the rigging and running gear ignited from the discharge of the guns. At last not a piece could be brought to bear, and the gallant ship, helpless and hopeless, surrendered to the foe,—but so utterly riddled and ruined, that the American Captain Bainbridge, having saved the remains of her crew, left her to the flames, and the charred and shattered *torso* of the Java, " into the deep went down." * Lambert fell, a hero as he had lived, and expired six days after. His " gaol-bird " crew, true Britons at heart, and inspired by his devoted gallantry,

— died, all pluck and bottom,
To save a sire who blushed he had begot 'em.

The size of these American frigates may be estimated, on stating the fact that the largest 74 gun ship in the British navy at that time—the Dragon—was two feet shorter, though two feet wider, than the President, the Constitution, or the United States, rated as 44 gun frigates; and that while frigates of the class of the Guerrière, the Macedonian, and the Java, carried each twenty-eight long 18 pounders and sixteen 32 pounder carronades, the American 44's, so rated, carried thirty-two long 24 pounders and twenty-two

---

* Java, 44 guns,   Constitution, ut suprà.
Men,   292   Men,   460
Killed, 22   Killed, 10
Wounded, 92—114   Wounded, 48— 58
      178   402

32 pounder carronades. At long range they were superior in weight and precision of fire, and immeasurably superior at close quarters.*

The effect of these successive disasters can hardly be exaggerated. England stood, for the moment, stunned. The continent of Europe shouted with joy. "Down with the sea-dogs, *à bas les loups marins*," was the polyglot cry; but the old sea-dog shook himself sulkily, showed his teeth, muttered an ominous growl, and betook himself at once to remedy the evil. Never does England bear herself more bravely, never does she look more worthy of her fortunes, than in the face of misfortune. The Admiralty, slow to move, when moved, swept on, with the force of the tide which rebuked the Courtiers of Canute. Efforts were made to strengthen the squadron on the American coast, and single vessels were equipped, and manned, fit to encounter the leviathans of America; a further calamity spurred them on. On the 14th February, 1813, the American Hornet stung to death the British Peacock.* Both were sloops nominally of the same force, but the Hornet had two guns more than her opponent, and the weight of her broadside was double. In men and size she was much superior. The contest continued for an hour and a half. The Peacock was so torn to pieces, that she sank with thirteen of her own men, and four Hornets, striving, nobly but vainly, to save their foemen from a watery grave.†

As in the frigates, so was the disproportion in the American sloops of war. "For instance the sloop Hornet carried eighteen 32 carron-

---

* Veritas, p. 145.

† Peacock.	Hornet.
Broadside guns, 9.	Broadside guns, 10.
Weight of broadside, 192 lbs.	Weight of broadside, 297.
Men, 110.	Men, 162.
Tons, 386.	Tons, 460.

ades, four long 9 and two long 6 pounders with 162 picked men; the British sloop Peacock had sixteen carronades of 24 lbs. and two long 9's, with 110 men." *

At last came the counter-stroke. Among the many gallant officers, anxious to meet the Americans on equal terms, was Captain Broke, in command of the Shannon. He had under his command a crack ship mounting 52 guns, and a crew carefully trained to gunnery and small arms. They knew their commander, and their commander knew them; and this mutual confidence made its mark in the hour of need. Broke, off the American coast, had learned that the frigate Chesapeake of 52 guns was then in Boston fitting for sea, whereupon he dismissed his consort, the Tenedos, a frigate of 36 guns, with instructions to keep out of the way while he had a fair " turn up" with the foe, and then, with Castilian punctilio, sent a cartel to Capt. Lawrence requesting in the most respectful terms " the honour of a meeting to try the fortunes of their respective flags."† Lawrence, as brave a sailor as ever trod quarter deck, had anticipated the invitation, and was prompt in his acknowledgments. In brief space, 11th June, 1813, Broke saw the American under weigh, and standing down upon him, surrounded by yachts and boats, while the cheers of his enthusiastic countrymen rang through the welkin. An entertainment had been prepared on shore for the return of those who were thus arrayed and sent to conquest, but the feast was served with funeral baked meats.

The contest which ensued it is difficult to give in detail. It was short, sharp, and decisive, most bravely fought on both sides, but the magnificent gunnery of the British gave them an advantage from the outset, which was crowned by boarding. From the deck and from yard-arm, simultaneously, the American was carried, in a

---

* Veritas, p. 146; Letter 9.
† Letter from Broke to Lawrence, James, Vol. I, p. 199.

desperate hand-to-hand struggle, led by Broke, who was severely wounded in the fray. Lawrence had fallen cheering on his men, and died shortly after the action, honoured and lamented. His body was buried at Halifax with every mark of military respect. In fifteen minutes from the firing of the first gun, the Chesapeake was a prize to the Shannon; and in that brief space 145 brave men on the American side, and 83 on the English had passed to their account. The moral effect of this victory was tremendous—a succession of disasters was repaired at a blow. The deadly spell was broken, and England again held in her grasp the talisman of success. It was recovered by her own resolution to repair defeat, and by a tardy, but just, appreciation of the merits of others.*

In all these actions the strength of vessels, weight of metal and number of men were decidedly in favour of the Americans—the meed of valor was equally divided. In courtesy and manly bearing the American generously vied with the Briton. Lawrence and Lambert alike consecrated with their blood the flags of their respective countries. The echoes of the indiscriminating sea sing a requiem, everlastingly, for the souls of the brave men who followed their example.

> Yet more the billows and the depths have more,
> Light hearts and brave are gathered to thy breast:
> They hear not now the booming water roar;
> The battle thunder will not break their rest.
> Keep thy red gold and gems, thou stormy grave!
> Give back the true and brave!

---

* ARMAMENTS.

	Shannon.		Chesapeake.
Broadside guns,	25		25
Weight of metal,	535		590
Number of crew,	306		376
Tonnage,	1066 tons.		1135 tons.

The early successes of this naval campaign exercised great moral influence on the general conduct of the war. They more than compensated in the American mind for the national shortcomings on shore. The seaboard cities were then the centres of population and of opinion. The tastes, the pursuits, the sympathies of the people were with their sailors. The present exultation gave no thought to the future, or to disagreeable admonitions on the distant frontier of Canada. The Government also were not unaware that the present advantages on the Lakes might, with their opportunities, be greatly improved, and the prestige of victory be transferred from the ocean to these inland seas.

CHAPTER VII.

1813. American preparations on Lakes Ontario and Erie. British Ministry did its best—Canada its duty. Men and money voted. New Brunswick regiment marched from Fredericton on snow shoes. Major General Evans. Sir James Yeo and seamen arrive from Halifax. British and American forces on the frontier. In the West. Harrison and Proctor. General Winchester defeated and captured at Frenchtown. Capt. Forsyth harries Brockville. Reprisals. Sir George Prevost at Prescott. Permits a demonstration. Prescott. Ogdensburg. Colonel George Macdonnell. The Glengarries. Bishop Macdonell. Dash at Ogdensburg—Dangers of the ice—The place taken. Capt. Jenkins and Lieut. Ridge. Pierre Holmes. His story. Macdonnell's courage, courtesy, and kindness.

It has been said before, that one effect of the war had been to concentrate the national resources, both of men and material, and to dispose them most conveniently for operations on either arena, of land or lake; immense preparations were made at once. Sackett's Harbour on Lake Ontario, and Presqu'isle on Lake Erie, were supplied with comparative facility from New York and Philadelphia, and a naval force, created with great rapidity, very superior to any with which Great Britain, engaged in every sea, and so distant from her colonies, could encounter the emergency.

The preparations, therefore, for the campaign of 1813, were carried on with increased vigour by the American Government. The British Ministry, it may be believed, did their best, but at great disadvantage. Thronged and beset by difficulties, it is not unnatural that they should still have temporized, still have indulged in a lingering hope that more pacific counsels might yet prevail, or that the chapter of accidents would open at a leaf propitious to the fortunes of Britain.

Nor was Canada wanting to itself. The Legislature of Lower Canada had assembled on the 29th Dec., 1812. The Army Bill Act was renewed and extended. £500,000 were authorized to be put into circulation. £15,000 were granted to equip the embodied militia. £1,000 to provide hospitals, and £25,000 towards the support of the war. A duty of 2½ per cent. on all merchandize imported into the Province was also granted for the support of the war. The expenses of the militia for the current year had been £55,000, or $220,000.* The whole expenditure of the Government was £98,777.

In addition to the force already raised, the militia was augmented by a draft in Lower Canada. A battalion was embodied in Quebec, (the 6th) for Garrison duty. A Canadian Fencible Regiment, a regiment of Glengarries, and a regiment of Voltigeurs were recruited diligently, and with success.† The New Brunswick regular regiment, (the 104th,) in the month of March explored, for the first time, the wintry wilderness lying between Fredericton on the River St. John and the St. Lawrence. These hardy men per-

---

* Christie, Vol. X, p. 72.

† The Montreal Canadian Courant—an extinct Literary Volcano—of the 4th May, 1812, copies from the Quebec Gazette of a preceding date:

"THE VOLTIGEURS.

"This corps now forming under the command of Major De Salaberry is completing with a despatch worthy of the ancient warlike spirit of the country. Capt. Perrault's company was filled up in 48 hours, and was yesterday passed by His Excellency the Governor; and the companies of Captains Duchesnay, Panet and L'Ecuyer, have now nearly their compliment. The young men move in solid columns towards the enlisting officers, with an expression of countenance not to be mistaken. The Canadians are awakening from the repose of an age secured to them by good government and virtuous habits. *Their anger is fresh* —the object of their preparation simple and distinct. They are to defend their King, known to them only by acts of kindness, and a native country long since made sacred by the exploits of their forefathers."

formed this feat, actually, upon snow-shoes, confronting hardships and surmounting obstacles, to which the late march of the Guards through the same scenes, admirable in itself, as it ever must be, was but a holiday freak. The staff and the Commissariat of those days had not undergone the teaching of a Crimean campaign—the more honourable to those who, by dint of individual exertion, contrived to supply those deficiencies, and among them no man shone more conspicuously than the late Major General Thomas Evans, C.B., long identified with the social circles of Montreal and Quebec, and who was then a Captain in the 8th Infantry.

In their wake followed Captains Barclay, Pring, and Finnis of the Royal Navy, with five lieutenants and a few seamen, overland, from Halifax. From Quebec they proceeded rapidly to Kingston, took the fleet there in hand, and laid themselves out, sturdily, to the work of fitting and equipment. In May they were joined by Sir James L. Yeo, from England, backed by about 450 British sailors.

It may be well to recapitulate here the strength of the respective forces on the frontier, both of Upper and Lower Canada, at the commencement of the campaign of 1813. Armstrong, the American Secretary at war, stated that the force commanded by General Dearborn, within District No. 9, that is to say, on the Plattsburg-Montreal frontier, was over 13,000 men of all arms. The force at the disposal of Sir George Prevost at this point did not exceed 3,000 regulars and militia.

At Sackett's Harbour 200 regulars and 2,000 militia; at Lake Champlain, available for operations on Central Canada or the left Division, 3,000 regulars and 2,000 militia. To oppose this force there were scattered at Kingston, Prescott, and other posts on the line, about 1,500 men.

On the Niagara frontier, the enemy had assembled 8,800 regulars and 2,000 militia. To these men were opposed 1,700 men in Fort George, and 600 men on the rest of the frontier, 36 miles in length,—2,300 in all.

On the Western frontier, General Harrison held in hand some 2,000 men, while opposed to him in command of the Right division of Upper Canada, Proctor wielded about 1,000 troops, and 1,200 Indians and militia.

The first operations of the year were adverse to the Americans. The conditions of climate on the Western frontier admit of military movements at a time when Central Canada is difficult, and Lower Canada impracticable. Early in January, 1813, General Harrison, who, at the head of the Ohio levies, hung upon the border of Michigan, made demonstrations on Detroit, weakly garrisoned, and held by Colonel Proctor, who had been left in command by Brock. The season, though favourable to an advance from the American side, from the South, precluded all idea of British reinforcements from the North. On the 11th, Proctor learned that an American division under General Winchester, had reached Frenchtown on the River Raisin, with the intention of attacking Brownstown, still more in advance towards Detroit. Proctor boldly grappled with the danger. He saw that the American force had advanced beyond the shelter of support, and he flung his whole strength on Winchester before Harrison could reach him. At break of day, on the 22nd, Proctor attacked the enemy's division, about 1,000 strong, being the flower of the Northwestern army, and encountered, from dread of the Indians, a desperate resistance. The buildings at Frenchtown were held, but a part of the American force broke to their rear, and endeavoured to escape by the road on which they came. In the pursuit, the American General was captured by Round-head, a Wyandot chief, and brought to Proctor. The Americans, who had retreated under cover, still fought with desperation.* Indian severities and their own inhuman reprisals crowded

---

* Christie, Vol. XI, p. 69. A more detailed narrative of these occurrences will be found hereafter, Chapters XVIII and XIX.

before their eyes, like spectres of doom, assuming bodily shape, in swarms of dusky warriors, heralded by demoniac yells. Winchester, apprehensive that the buildings held by his men would be fired to the hopeless destruction of every defender, agreed to surrender himself and his whole force. Five hundred and twenty-two men and officers, with arms, stores and ammunition, became the prize of the British; about 400 were killed and wounded. Proctor commanded 500 regular soldiers and militia, with about 600 Indians, and lost 180 *hors de combat*. He and his troops received a vote of thanks from the Canadian House of Assembly then in session, and he was promoted to the rank of Brigadier General. For a time, the Michigan territory was safe, and Detroit secure.

We will now turn from the right division of Upper Canada, to the division of the left, or the frontier of the Upper St. Lawrence. On the 6th February, Capt. Forsyth, the invader of rustic tranquillity at Gananoque, made a nocturnal raid on the pigs and poultry of Elizabethtown, now Brockville, where he wounded a militia sentry, sacked the cattle pens, and did not spare the private houses, nor the gaol, and carried off fifty-two of the inhabitants into captivity,—among them two Majors, three Captains, and two Lieutenants, elderly gentlemen, who, as a compliment, retained their commissions in the militia. This exploit led to a brilliant reprisal, and deserves notice moreover, as a proof, how far this part of the frontier is assailable in winter—the ice, indeed, affording facility for small predatory excursions.

The Lower Canadian Legislature rose in February, and on the 17th Sir George Prevost left Quebec for Upper Canada. On his route he found at Prescott Lieut.-Colonel Pearson, an active and enterprising officer, who urged upon him an attack on Ogdensburg in retaliation for the recent descent on Brockville. Prevost doubted and demurred; but while the proposal was under discussion, it was discovered that two deserters had escaped from the British side with the intelligence of the presence of the Governor in Prescott, and of his contemplated movement westward, no light incentive to the enemy to intercept his progress. It was therefore deemed expedient to distract attention from His Excellency by a diversion, and Pearson was permitted to plan a demonstration on the ice of the St. Lawrence,—like the torreador of a Spanish bull-fight,—partly to disconcert, and *hocus* the bull, and partly to test the mettle and strength of the animal.

Prescott was then a small village, protected by a palisaded fort, and block-house; since enlarged, surrounded with heavy earth works, and now known as Fort Wellington. It is situated above the Rapids, or continuous, rough, and broken navigation of the St. Lawrence, which for 40 miles interrupts communications with Montreal, and was a place of rendezvous, for voyageurs and batteaux, and a depot for military stores. It stands on an exposed part of the frontier, within cannon shot of Ogdensburg opposite. Below, the Canadian shore of the St. Lawrence is, to a great extent, covered by impassable rapids, and above, with a short interval, the coast is in like degree masked by the rocks of the Thousand Islands. But in that interval, from Prescott to Brockville—a distance of twelve miles—a lovely champaign country opens to the view, undulating upwards in rich verdure, as if born of the green waters of the noble river, and bearing on its fertile uplands, cornfields and orchards, mills and farm houses, villas and villages, nestling among primeval trees, all very beautiful to look upon, but difficult to defend, either in summer or winter.

Opposite to Prescott stands, now, the flourishing city of Ogdensburg, containing 7000 inhabitants, in those days a populous village, very democratic in its proclivities, and anti-British in religion. It was then, also, a fortified military post, garrisoned and armed, but still more effectually protected by the breadth of the St. Lawrence, at this point, a mile and a quarter wide. One rash attempt upon the place made in open day, in the soft and golden autumn, had, as already related, been repulsed. In the later autumn and early winter, the floating masses of descending ice prohibit the use of boats, but by the end of December the river generally " takes," presenting when solid, a continuous surface, but interspersed here and there with open intervals of rushing water, and with uncertain intervals of unsubstantial ice, pitfalls, and worse to the incautious footstep, and very trying to the nerves, if nerves were known at that early period of the Canadian formation. It had been, of course, impracticable to test or try the strength of the ice under the fire of Ogdensburg.

The proposed demonstration was in itself an adventure full of peril, but the man who led was no trifler. Pearson had been ordered away, and his second in command, Lt.-Col. G. Macdonnell, conducted the enterprise. Colonel Macdonnell being for the nonce a militia officer, like the Free Lance of former days, was given to fighting on his own inspirations, and it was hinted that Pearson did not altogether disapprove of the latitudinarianism of his subordinate. This gallant officer came of a good stock. Descended from the old, and a native of the new Glengarry, he led to the fight such a following as Vich Ian Vohr himself, might have been proud to muster. He commanded the Glengarry Fencibles, raised wholly in Central Canada, and on the occasion of the raid on Brockville, had been dispatched to remonstrate with the American commander on the un-military character of his excursion. He had been received with a discourtesy not usual to the educated officer of the American army, had been taunted somewhat in the style of " Mine Ancient Pistol," and had been challenged to a fight on the ice ; a fancy he was not disinclined to gratify, and he had at his bidding the very men to help him.

These men were the Glengarries. In the rear of Prescott, due North and East, fronting on the St. Lawrence, and a few miles distant from the stream, lies what is known as the Glengarry country, of Canada, composed of the present united counties of Stormont, Dundas, and Glengarry. At the time of the war these tracts of country were known as the Eastern District of Upper Canada. After the peace of 1783, the Eastern District had been appropriated by the British Government, as a place of refuge for the U. E. Loyalists, and it so happened that among these early and war-worn settlers, a majority consisted of Scotch Highlanders, the descendants of men who, after Culloden, had been transported to the plantations, and whose instincts of loyalty were such, that regardless of names, genealogies, or dynasties, they looked to the principle, and whether it was for James, or whether it was for George, struck heartily and home in the abiding sentiment of Claverhouse:

"Ere the king's crown comes down, there are crowns to be broke."

The dauntless devotion of these men attracted a still further accession of chivalrous loyalty. To the Jacobites of 1745—to the U. E. Loyalists of 1775, was added a gallant band of Scottish soldiers who had fought the battle of the Crown against Republican France from 1792 to 1803. Men who had battled under Hutchinson and Abercrombie, who had pushed the French grenadiers at Aboukir, and had borne the brunt of the Turkish cavaliers at Rosetta. The brief and illusive peace of Amiens (1802) led to the disbandment of many fine British regiments, and among them a Catholic regiment of Highlanders, raised some years before, mainly through the instrumentality of Alexander Macdonnell of Glen Urquhart, a Catholic clergyman of great energy of character and benevolence of disposition.* He had been appointed chaplain of the corps, and in the hour of their destitution proved to be a fast and faithful friend. By unremitted exertion, he obtained from the British Ministry of the day the permission and the means, to transport the men of the late

---

* Morgan, Celebrated Canadians, p. 262.

Glengarry regiment to Canada. He led them into the wilderness, and engrafted on the waste, their faith to God and their fidelity to the throne. Good Catholics, faithful and loyal men, they have never departed from that first, noble teaching. The earnest priest and tried friend, through life, never deserted them. Partaking of the character of the mediæval churchman, half bishop, half baron, he fought and prayed, with equal zeal, by the side of men he had come to regard as his hereditary followers. With the universal acclaim of all good men of all denominations, he rose to the Episcopate and died Bishop of Kingston, mourned in death as he had been revered in life.

The Bishop had been most active in rousing and recruiting the Glengarries during the preceding winter. The fiery cross had passed through the land, and every clansman had obeyed the summons. The Glengarry Fencibles garrisoned the frontier, and their gallant leader, (George the Red) a near relation of Bishop Macdonnell, now rallied his followers behind the earth works of Prescott for his proposed demonstration on Ogdensburg.

> And wild and high the "Cameron's gathering" rose,—
> The war note of Lochiel,—which Albyn's hills
> Have heard, and heard too have her Saxon foes :—
> How in the noon of night that pibroch thrills
> Savage and shrill! But with the breath which fills
> Their mountain pipe, so fill the mountaineers
> With the firm native daring which instils
> The stirring memory of a thousand years,
> And Evans', Donald's fame, rings in each clansman's ears.

Little time was wasted on preliminaries. It had been the practice of the British for some time previous, to exercise daily on the ice. Half the river fairly belonged to them, and not having, hitherto, carried their mimic warfare beyond these limits, they had continued to drill and manœuvre, unmolested. On the morning of the 22nd February, Macdonnell descended on the ice at the head of 480 men,—two-thirds and more Canadian militia, supported by two field pieces. He played and purred for some time with velvety touch, prepared for a spring. The American officer in command, Forsyth, was at his breakfast. He was informed, in haste, that the British fun, that morning, looked very like earnest; but assuming the privilege of the "old soldier," he simply "pooh-poohed" his informant. The British were only at drill, "they were not the men to trouble him in that impudent way," and so, betook him afresh to his corn cakes and hominy. He occupied an old French work on the western side of the Oswegatchie, a small affluent of the St. Lawrence, at its mouth, situated behind where the lighthouse now stands. He had eleven guns in position, 500 men at his back, and a glacis before him a mile wide, exposed and smooth as a tablecloth. Macdonnell manœuvred briefly, and then dividing his force into two columns, advanced rapidly to the attack;—speed and resolution alone could save them. The Americans, more wary than their chief, sprang to their guns; musketry and cannon opened on the advancing columns. The left, under Macdonnell himself, rushed rapidly on, under a heavy fire, and through the deep snow ascended the river bank, and swept from the left into the village of Ogdensburg, overwhelming all opposition. Here from the eastern bank of the Oswegatchie, he commanded to a great extent the flank and rear of old French Fort Présentation, and the batteries which raked the river; but his own guns were behind hand, they had stuck in the deep snow bank and rough ice, broken and piled, at the river bank. By furious efforts they were forced to the front, and not a moment too soon. While this was doing, Jenkins, who commanded the right wing, a gallant New Brunswicker, and a Captain in the Glengarries, had, most emphatically, taken the bull by the horns. Seven pieces of artillery, backed by 200 good troops, smashed the head of his advance; gallantly he rallied his broken column, not a living man shrank; springing forward with a cheer, his left arm was shattered by a shot; nothing daunted, forward and still cheering on, his upraised right arm was disabled by a cluster of grape. Thus crippled, his voice still failed not, nor his gestures, until he fell from loss of blood,* but he was nobly followed. His gallant Glengarries, with broken formation, through the deep snow, in front of the deadly battery, were re-forming for a charge with the bayonet, when, fortunately, Macdonnell's guns on the left got within range. Captain Eustace, with the men of the King's, crossed the Oswegatchie and captured the eastern battery, and together, both attacks swarmed into the body of the place, to find it vacated, except by dead and dying, the enemy having withdrawn to the woods in their west rear, where there was no means of intercepting their retreat. The Americans lost about 75 men and officers, eleven pieces of cannon, a large amount of military stores and four armed vessels burnt in the harbour. The British lost eight killed and fifty-two wounded, the larger proportion, as may well be supposed, in front of the old French work assailed by Captain Jenkins.

This feat was performed chiefly by the men of the country, by the militia and Fencibles, both Canadian and Glengarry. These men did not plead qualms of conscience or constitutional scruples, as an excuse for not daring the ice, which undulated and cracked and gaped beneath their feet. One hundred and twenty of the King's regiment, under Captain Eustace and " Lieutenant Ridge of that corps, who very gallantly led on

---

* Captain Jenkins was a man of striking appearance and bearing,—the admiration of his men. He was, as stated in the text, a native of New Brunswick, the son of an American loyalist and brave old soldier. His left arm was amputated at the shoulder; his right arm was saved, but almost in a useless state. He survived in this condition some years. Mrs. Sampson of Kingston,—the estimable wife of a man as much respected as she was beloved, the late Dr. Sampson,— was a sister of this distinguished officer. His only daughter, the wife of Sutherland Stayner, Esquire, lives near Richmond, C. E.

the advance,"* and forty of the Royal Newfoundland regiment, under Captain Lefebvre, led the left column, and, as ever, were foremost in the fray, but the remainder of the force, and particularly the men under Jenkins, were farmers' sons fighting in defence of their homes, and right nobly did they redeem, that day, the pledge made to mother and sister and wife by the old fireside. Col. Frazer of the militia was bravely supported by his officers and men. Lieut. Empey of that force lost a leg. Lieut. McAulay and Ensign Macdonnell of the Glengarries, Ensigns Kerr of the militia, and Mackay of the Light Infantry, who had each charge of a field-piece, and Lieut. Gangueben of the Royal Engineers, are all honourably mentioned by Colonel Macdonnell in his graphic and soldierly despatch.

There still lives in Ogdensburg an old Canadian militiaman, by name Pierre Holmes. His father had been a British soldier, his mother a French Canadian of Sorel. French is his natural language. He is very old and very poor. He works about, doing "chores," cutting wood, and drawing water for the grandsons of those against whom he fought on this memorable occasion, and who appear to regard the lively old man with especial favour. He relates how that he was a "*petit tambour*" of the Canadian Fencibles in those days; how the British paraded for a while, threw out skirmishers, and advanced on the ice "*drapeaux déployés et tambours battants;*" how boldly Macdonnell led, how, by swearing and sweating, he got his guns out of the deep snow; how, he cared for his prisoners; how, he released one indignant captive, who had been rudely treated by an over lively volunteer, and

---

* *Vide* Macdonnell's despatch, February 23rd, 1813. This dashing officer subsequently married the eldest daughter of the Hon. Samuel Gerrard of Montreal. Their eldest daughter is married to Edward L. Freer, Esquire, Canada Postal Department, and the second to George, son of the Hon. George Moffatt, of Montreal.

sent his unworthy assailant to the black-hole; how, he prohibited and forstalled all pillage. It appears, that in crossing the river, a little of the olden rieving temper had revived among the Highlandmen, and the word "spulzie" had passed, and many faces glistened with glee at the hopeful prospect; but to their intense disgust Macdonnell anticipated them. He put a sentry upon every door in Ogdensburg; "and so," exclaimed the auditor of old Peter Holmes' narration, "you got no plunder after all?" "Plunder!" shrieked the old man, in the angry accents of indignant recollection, " Plunder! *Non, monsieur, non pas même une torquette de tabac?*"*

Macdonnell took his revenge by force of contrast; he was courteous to his enemies, protected prisoners, spared the poultry, respected elderly gentlemen notwithstanding their rank in the militia, and paid every American teamster employed in transporting the captured stores to Prescott four dollars *per diem* in hard silver, as the price of his services.

---

* Pierre Holmes, as has been before said, is very old and very poor. By some misadventure or inadvertence, or want of knowledge, or of energy rightly applied, he never got the 200 acres of land awarded to him as "Tambour Major" at the end of the war. Is it now too late; can nothing even yet be done for the brave old man?

CHAPTER VIII.

British armaments at Kingston and York. British force. American strength. Descent planned on Kingston. York and Fort George. Little York—What it was—What it is. Defences in 1813. York attacked 26th April, 1813. Ship of war on the stocks, on British order. First alarm. Pluck of the population. Maclean, clerk of the House of Assembly, killed. Young Allan MacNab. Sir Roger Sheaffe.

In the mean time, Sir George Prevost, on the 23rd February, had reached Kingston in safety, and there, animated by his presence, the exertions made to restore the equality of the British with that of the American naval armament on lake Ontario. One ship of war had been laid down at York, now Toronto, in the preceding year; and another, the Wolfe, of 24 guns, was in an advanced stage at Kingston, but men and stores were both wanting. The American shipwrights at Sackett's Harbour, through the energy of their government, fore-reached, hand over hand, those in the British ship-yards. Sir James Yeo and his seamen did not arrive until May, so that Commodore Chauncey, amply supplied and equipped from the sea-board arsenals, rode undisputed master of Ontario from October, 1812, to the middle of May, 1813. How he used his opportunity will be shortly shown. The whole coast of this beautiful lake was open and exposed to attack. A descent on Kingston had been planned and was expected. The Americans had six fine schooners and a ship, mounting together 72 guns, all admirably appointed and manned by choice seamen, disposable for an invasion at any point.

The real military objects of attack were Fort George, Niagara, and Kingston. Little York, the point selected, was notably defenceless and indefensible. Little York then contained about 1000 inhabitants and was the seat of the government and legislature of Upper Canada. This fact gave it an adventitious importance. It possessed then, and does still, a very good harbour for vessels of moderate draught, perhaps the real secret of its future fortune. The young capital of a new born country, it was not, even then, unworthy of high aspirations. It had, already, become the residence of the chief officers of the legislature and government, of the dignitaries of the law, and the hierarchy of the church; men living in modest affluence and noted for genial hospitality. Amongst them had settled many of the most distinguished of the U. E. Loyalist refugee families, whose proudest characteristic, engrafted on the native patriotism of the country, has produced a plant of indigenous growth unsurpassed in all the climates of the Empire. York was then the centre of the intelligence, the learning and of the nascent progress of the land, and it has well fulfilled its promising destiny.

Little York is now the beautiful city of Toronto, containing 50,000 inhabitants,—a mart of commerce, a school of learning, the abode of energy and enterprise, talent and taste. It is adorned by some of the finest edifices, public and private, in Canada. The buildings of the University would add embellishment to Oxford. The law courts rival in elegance those of Dublin. The Bank of Toronto would adorn Pall Mall.

In April, 1813, the town was a scattered collection of low-roofed villas, embowered in apple orchards. An old French Fort or earthwork, constructed to resist the Indians, stood on the shore of the lake about a mile from the inhabited part of the Bay. Two embrasured field works, dignified by the name of batteries, covered the entry to the harbour. These works were armed with three old French 24 pound guns, captured in 1760; the trunnions had been knocked off at the time, but, for the nonce, they had been exhumed from the sand and clamped down upon pine logs, extemporized as carriages. The town was entirely open in the rear and on the flanks, an easy prey to an enemy waging war in the spirit of a buccaneer. An unfinished ship of war on the stocks, was, in a military point of view, the only legitimate object of attack; and her destruction might have been, at any time, effected by a couple of boat's crews.

This ship had been laid down as before said, in the preceding year, when the British had the command of the lake, and expected to keep it, and would have done so, had the Imperial government shown befitting energy at the outset, or had the later inspirations of Sir Isaac Brock been listened to. But the pall of an enforced procrastination hung over the Provincial authorities. A lofty disbelief in the wickedness of man, and in the imminence of a war, had paralyzed and neutralized the precautions judiciously commenced, and the Americans had been permitted to gain the ascendancy. The ship could not be taken to pieces, nor, in the winter, be disembedded from the ice. All that could be done under the circumstances was to push on the work,—as a happy-go-lucky experiment—to complete and save her, if it might so chance; and, if not,—to destroy her.

Commodore Chauncey, and General Dearborn, the American General in Chief, after due deliberation, preferred a cheap predatory certainty at York to a glorious uncertainty at Kingston; and on the 25th April,—at a period of the season when the Lower St. Lawrence was barred by rugged piles of rotting ice—when roads and rivers were impassable, and all assistance, support, or supply, impossible,—the American squadron left Sackett's Harbour, sixteen sail of vessels, conveying a land force of 2,500 men.

Videttes had been, long before, posted, in constant watch, on Scarborough Heights, with orders to fire alarm guns, and, on sight of a hostile fleet, to ride into town. It was late on the evening of the 26th April, when the first report hushed every voice, and stilled for a moment the startled hearts of a whole population. Night fell as the news arrived, and with it came hurry, confusion and dismay. We read of such things, and in the interest of the story, lose sight of the agony of the hour, when the tide of terror topples over the dyke which has sustained it so long, and drowns out human endurance, sense, and reason. Whatever may have been the expectation and preparation,—whatever the hopes and fears; it is a tremendous thing to realize,—that the spoiler is at the door, that the happy home may be given to the flames, that the tender wife and radiant children of to-day may be outcasts and wanderers to-morrow. The excited mind aggravates and exaggerates these apprehensions. It may be picturesque to tell of, but it is an appalling thing to see—

> The thronging citizens with terror dumb,
> Who whisper with white lips, " The foe, they come, they come!"

At the same time, it is wholesome to remind the present generation of the experience of the past.

But the men of Toronto paused not long to whisper, nor could white lips be said to be, in any way, prevalent. The bounding blood stood still, for an instant only—men, who saw the whole extent of the danger, who knew the impotence of defence, also knew their duty, and every pulse of the popular heart throbbed with the rage of resistance. Old and young, rich and poor, high and low, rushed to arms. The maimed, the wounded, the invalid, the reckless school-boy, the grave judge of the land,—all shouldered their muskets, and fell into the ranks. McLean, clerk of the House of Assembly, seized his rifle, and was killed at early dawn among the men of the 8th. Young Allan MacNab, a lad of 14 years, whose name has been, ever since, identified with Canadian story, stood side by side with a veteran father, shattered with wounds, sire and son, equally eager for the fray. But the British force was utterly inadequate for resistance. Altogether, it did not exceed 600 men. Two companies of the 8th or "King's Own" were accidentally in the town on their way from Kingston to reinforce the garrison of Niagara, and unhappily swelled the slaughter with but little service to the cause.

This force was under the command of Major General Roger Hailles Sheaffe, an old and brave officer, who, after the death of Brock, had retrieved the fight on Queenston Heights, and had been honoured for his success by a Baronetcy. Sheaffe was a Massachusetts boy, born in Boston, educated from an early age for the army, into which he entered young, under the powerful influence of the house of Northumberland. In the 49th foot, he served, side by side with Brock in the West Indies, in Holland and at Copenhagen, and with his revered comrade came to Canada. Here he encountered, after many years of separation, his cousin Margaret, daughter of John Coffin, a U. E. Loyalist refugee,* who

---

* The Loyalist refugees from the United States in those days, found the pathway of flight a hard road to travel. Roads between the inhabited parts of the States and Canada, there were none. The only communication for a family laden with its household goods was by water: A large number of the refugee Loyalist families from the Eastern and Middle States of the seaboard of America found their way into Canada by the river Hudson, Lake Champlain, and the river Richelieu, to Sorel. From this point they took a fresh departure up the St. Lawrence to Kingston, or Little York or Newark, and intermediate places of settlement. The family of the late Sir John Beverly Robinson came into Canada by this route.

John Coffin, named in the text, brought his family round from Boston to Quebec in a schooner which, being the conjoint property of himself and a partner, who adhered to the Republican party, was shortly after captured by a British cruiser, and declared good prize. John Coffin, with nine children reached Quebec in 1775. In 1778 he was proscribed by name in the "Boston

had followed the colours under which Sheaffe fought, from Boston to Quebec. An old attachment was revived between the cousins, strengthened by the romantic incidents of many chequered years, and in 1808 they were married. He had left his wife and young children at Quebec, and his military headquarters were at Fort George. Having succeeded on the death of Brock to the civil as well as the military command in Upper Canada, York was of course the seat of his Provincial government, but at the time of the descent he was almost, by mere chance, on the spot.

Confiscation Act,"* and his property confiscated as a penalty for his adherence to the Royal cause. His return to Massachusetts would have been visited by death without benefit of clergy.

He was in Quebec, under arms, during the siege 1775-76. On the memorable morning of the 1st Jan., 1776, John Coffin defended the same battery at the *Près de Ville*, in the Lower Town of Quebec, with the well-known Captain Barnsfare, when assailed by the American forces. In front of this battery fell General Montgomery, and the chief officers of his staff, and with them the last hopes of the American cause in Canada. The following documents which remain in the possession of the family, prove by the best evidence, that whatever may be the merit justly ascribed to Captain Barnsfare for the defence

---

* "Boston Confiscation Act," Sept., 1778, ch. 48.—" In Massachusetts a person suspected of enmity to the Whig cause, could be arrested under a Magistrate's warrant, and banished, unless he would swear fealty to the friends of liberty; and the select men of towns could prefer charges of political treachery in town meetings; and the individual thus accused, if convicted by a jury, could be sent into the enemy's jurisdiction. Massachusetts also designated by name and, generally, by occupation and residence, three hundred and eight of her people, of whom seventeen had been inhabitants of Maine, who had fled from their houses, and denounced against any one of them who should return, apprehension, imprisonment, and transportation to a place possessed by the British, and for a second voluntary return, without leave, death without benefit of clergy. By another law, the property of twenty-nine persons, who were denominated " notorious conspirators," was confiscated—of these fifteen had been appointed " Mandamus councillors," two had been Governors, one Lieut.-Governor, one Treasurer, one Attorney General, one Chief Justice, and four Commissioners of Customs.—[Lorenzo Sabine, Historical Essay prefixed to Biographical Sketches of the American Loyalists, p. 78.

of this post, an equal measure of praise was, at least, due to the American Loyalist, John Coffin.

The first of these letters was written by Sir Guy Carleton, afterwards Lord Dorchester, who was Governor and Commander-in-Chief of the Province of Quebec, and who was in Quebec during the whole siege.

JENNINGSBURY, Dec. 25, 1779.

SIR,—I have received your letter, and am sorry to learn your brother's misfortunes render it now necessary for him to apply for any assistance beyond his own industry, having observed in all his conduct from his arrival in the Province of Quebec until I left it, a constant attachment and zeal for the king's service, as well as the manner of a prudent, worthy man, I could not but interest myself for him; yet his conduct and judicious behaviour on the morning of the 31st Dec., 1775, gave him a still stronger claim on me; for to him *with the assistance of Barnsfare*, I attribute the repulse of the rebels on the side of Quebec when Mr. Montgomery attacked in person, while the success on the other was very different, and brought the town into no small danger. Now, whether we consider the strength of the post, the number allotted to its defence, or the former services of the officer who commanded, we might have expected as much at least from him—a remarkable proof this, that former services and greater numbers may be outdone by superior vigilance and good sense of gentlemen, though not used to arms. After all this, sir, I cannot but lament, that it is nowise in my power to forward Mr. Coffin's wishes; I might, 'tis true, bear witness to his merits, but this probably would hurt not serve, such is the state of things. I have, therefore, only to assure you of my esteem for him, and that I am

Sir,

Your most obedient and most humble Servant,

(Signed,)   GUY CARLETON.

To Mr. NATHANIEL COFFIN,
    Pall Mall, London.

The second is a letter written by Colonel Allan McLean, H. M. 87th Regt., commanding the garrison during the seige of Quebec, 1775–76.

QUEBEC, 28th July, 1776.

SIR,—As I am in a few days going to England with dispatches from the Commander-in-Chief, I should be glad to know if I could be of any service to you: power to do you any material service I have none; but your conduct during the siege of Quebec last winter and spring makes it a duty on my part to give you my testimony and approbation of every part of your conduct. Truth must always have some weight with his Majesty and his Ministers, who, I am certain, wish to reward deserving men like you. To your resolution and watchfulness on the night of Dec. 31st, 1775, in keeping the guard at the *Près de Ville* under arms waiting for the attack which you expected ; the great coolness with which you allowed the rebels to approach ; the spirit which your example kept up among the men ; and the very critical instant in which *you directed* Captain Barnsfare's fire against Montgomery and his troops ;—to those circumstances, alone, I do ascribe the repulsing of the rebels from that important post, where, with their leader, they lost all heart.

The resolutions you entered into, and the arrangements you made to maintain that post, when told you were to be attacked from another quarter, was worthy of a good subject, and would have done honour to an experienced officer. I thought it incumbent on me to leave with you this honourable testimony of your service, as matters that were well known to myself in particular ; and I should be happy at any time to have it in my power to be useful to you, and do assure you that I am with truth and regard,

Sir,

Your most obedient humble Servant,

(Signed,) ALLAN MACLEAN.

To Mr. John Coffin, Quebec.

The third is a communication signed Henry Caldwell, Lieut.-Colonel commanding the British Militia at the siege of Quebec. This gentleman was father to Sir John, and grandfather to the late Sir Henry—Baronets of that name. He certifies by a document given under his hand at Quebec, May, 1787, that " John Coffin, Esquire, served in the British militia, under my command, during the siege of this town by the rebels, from Nov. seventy-five to May seventy-six, during all which time he conducted himself and behaved with the greatest spirit, zeal, and activity in the king's service, which by his example was very much promoted, particularly on the attack of the 31st Dec., when he very much distinguished himself."

He left a large family—four daughters : the eldest married Colonel McMurdo; the second, the Hon. John Craigie, brother to Lord Craigie, Edinburgh ; a son of this lady is now a British Admiral ; the third became Lady Sheaffe ; the fourth died in Quebec.

And seven sons. One was killed, a Lieutenant in the Navy; another, Francis Holmes, rose to the rank of Admiral in the same noble service; two died high in rank in the Commissariat—one a Major in the Army; a sixth was member Legislative Council, and Colonel Mil., Lower Canada; and a seventh Adj.-General Militia, Upper Canada.

His descendants reflect with pride, that the above-named exiles earned their rank by long and faithful services; but it is a subject of still greater pride to acknowledge that they all owed their opportunity to the devoted loyalty which has ever characterized their family, and to the generous appreciation of it by their Sovereign and country.

These descendants in Canada and in England are many. Among those in Canada may be named Mrs. Hamilton of Quebec, mother of Robert Hamilton, Esquire, and of the Hon. John Hamilton of Hawkesbury, U. W., Mrs. Dean, wife of James Dean, Esquire, Quebec, and William Holmes Coffin, Prothonotary of the Superior Court in Montreal.

CHAPTER IX.

Sheaffe. Force at his disposal. His dispositions. MacNeil of the 8th. American approach—Disembark in Humber Bay—Gallant resistance—Slaughter of the Grenadiers. Pike lands—Presses on the town—Enters the old fort—Explosion—Destruction of friend and foe. Pike killed. Sheaffe retires. The place capitulates. American Vandalism. Bishop Strachan. His admirable letter. The farce which follows the tragedy. The "human scalp" turns out to be a perriwig.

As many imputations, some thoughtless, many reckless—all equally unjust and ungenerous—have been cast upon the reputation of Sir Roger Sheaffe in relation to the defence of York, it may be allowed to a kindred hand, in this place, to vindicate his memory.

York in itself was incapable of defence. All the troops in Western Canada would have been insufficient to protect it. The regular garrison, if it can be so termed, consisted of a company of Glengarries and 50 men of the Royal Newfoundland regiment, apart from the militia. This force had been augmented accidentally, as has been before said, by two companies of the King's Regiment under Captain McNeil. Sheaffe's first duty as a soldier, and as a general, looking to the defence of his military command, was, to abandon a place never intended to have been defended, and to preserve his force for the protection of the country. The capture of this detachment, at this time, would have been an irretrievable loss, and, in its effects, fatal to the Province.

His first duty, therefore, was, to destroy all public property which would otherwise benefit the enemy, and to fall back either on Kingston or Niagara. The direction of this movement depended on the developments of the enemy. If they had landed on the side of the Don, he would have retired on Burlington heights. They assailed him on the west, and he withdrew towards Kingston. General Armstrong, the American Secretary at war, wrote to General Dearborn, privately, from Washington, 13th May, 1813 : " We cannot doubt but that in all cases in which a British commander is constrained to act defensively, his policy will be that adopted by Sheaffe, to prefer the preservation of his troops to that of his post, and thus carrying off the kernel leave us only the shell."* If York had been left defenceless and unprotected ; if a ship of war in the hands of the shipwright had been recklessly exposed to destruction, the fault was not with Sheaffe, nor with his direct superior Sir George Prevost, as charged by Veritas, but with the authorities in England who trifled with the emergency until too late, and then, spent treasures in life and money to repair an irreparable error.

On the first alarm, Sheaffe had got his men in hand, and awaited what the morning should bring forth. At early dawn, the American squadron was seen bearing down on Gibraltar Point, and the western flank of the town. The plan of attack was at once disclosed. The mouth of the harbour was the threatened point. While the ships of war engaged the three mutilated guns, an overwhelming force would be thrown ashore, and all retreat to the west would be cut off. Sheaffe, thereupon,.detached the best part of his force to keep the enemy at bay, to check the advance, to afford time for the destruction of public property, and to cover his slow retreat to Kingston. Captain McNeil, at the head of the two companies of the 8th, was ordered on this service, about 200 militia rallied on the flanks of the regulars, and Colonel Givens, with a small body of Indians, always notable in the war, already

---

* Armstrong, Vol. I, p. 87.

occupied the woods on the west side of the town, skirmishing to ascertain the precise place of landing.

An eyewitness has described the scene. The American fleet, in beautiful order, bore down before a fresh breeze which carried them beyond the intended point of disembarkation. They had fallen to the southwest as far as the eastern extremity of Humber Bay, ere the ships of war rounded to, and brought their heavy broadsides to bear on the shore. Sail was rapidly taken in, the boats assembled under cover of the vessels,—men promptly embarked, and the stalwart rowers,—the best seamen in the American service,—bent ready to the oar.

By this time McNeil, assured of the point of descent, had brought his men down the shore road, and had drawn them up in line, on the top of the bank which bounds the western side of Humber Bay, a startling red line, right in front of the American batteries, and at half cannon shot from the muzzle of the guns. It was a dauntless, but desperate expedient, " *c'était bien magnifique, mais ce n'était pas la guerre.*" The first American broadside swept the men down like grass before the scythe. Under cover of their broadsides, amid the din and smoke, the American boat's crews dashed to the shore.

The disembarkation was well handled. So soon as the keels touched ground, the riflemen under Forsyth, sore with recollections of Ogdensburg, were overboard, in the water, up the bank, down among the bushes, invisible, except where the rapid puffs of white smoke bespoke their fatal presence. The boats backed off instantaneously, and returned for reinforcements. McNeil himself and the greater part of his brave grenadiers had been killed by the first cannonade; the remnant, scattered and shattered, fell back from before the lashing fire, and the American rifles, always desparately resisted, held their own. A bitter, skirmishing fight ensued among the trees. But the eager reinforcements hurried to the shore. General Pike of the American army, an officer of repute, landed in the rear of the riflemen, at the head of a division at least 1000 strong, and the torn relics of the British detachment,—the *reliquiæ Danaum*,—slowly fell back upon the town.

Meanwhile, Sheaffe had collected his stores, dispatched his convoys, and ordered his retreat upon Kingston. The light company of the King's regiment, an additional reinforcement for Niagara, was rapidly approaching from that direction, and afforded opportune support. The ship and the dockyard, and a large quantity of marine stores were destroyed,—much removed ; the residue, for the most part indestructible in material, fell finally into the hands of the enemy.

General Pike, on his part, had pushed forward, feeling his way through the bush, and fighting with an enemy who defended every tree. His advance was slow but steady. At about 2 P. M., he emerged from the forest in the rear of the old French Fort and insignificant harbour defences. The fleet having effected the disembarkation weighed anchor and stood up into the harbour itself. The simplicity of this operation proves all practical defence to have been impossible, and that any more protracted resistance would have doomed the town. The American troops pushed on and soon enveloped the Fort. It contained at this time within its *enceinte* the government or "King's House," some public offices, the usual complement of barracks and store houses, and a powder magazine, built into the bank on the lake shore. This must have been a recent structure, as Brock, in 1811, complained that " the only powder magazine was a small wooden shed only sixty yards from the King's House." For safety's sake this dangerous appendage had been removed to a strong stone building constructed in the water front of the Fort.

The Americans swarmed into the works, fiery with fighting, and flushed with success, when, suddenly—with the crash and concussion of an earthquake,—the powder magazine exploded at their feet, spreading havoc through their ranks. Of the assailants 250 were instantaneously killed or wounded ; of the defenders many perished.

> Up to the sky, like rockets, go
> All that mingle there below :
> Many a tall and goodly man,
> Scorched and shrivelled to a span,
> When he fell to earth again,
> Like a cinder, strewed the plain.
> When in cradled rest they lay,
> And each nursing mother smiled
> On the sweet sleep of her child,
> Little thought she such a day
> Would rend those tender limbs away.

Pike had pushed on to the front and was in the act of questioning a militia soldier, one Joseph Shepherd, whose family still reside in the township of York, when—with a flash and eddying smoke—the infernal blast swept through the air. A heavy mass of stone struck the General down. In like manner, Shepherd was crushed at his side, and was borne off in the arms of his relative and fellow soldier, Joseph Dennis, now of Buttonwood, Weston. The gallant general and more humble soldier, both died of the injuries received, within a few hours, victims alike in the cause of their respective countries.

The contest itself was stayed by this catastrophe ; it had endured for eight hours. The surviving troops had withdrawn, well covered and unmolested by the enemy ; all that could be done had been done, and York capitulated through the local officers of militia. What remained of the public stores was surrendered, two hundred and sixty-four militia men laid down their arms. Sheaffe left behind him of the regulars 62 killed, 72 wounded ; one wounded officer with one sergeant major and four men of the artillery, prisoners of war ; and fell back deliberately and without obstruction upon Kingston. Such are the facts, the inferences are left to the judgment of every intelligent man, soldier or not.

> * * * Si quid novisti rectius istis
> Candidus imperti, si non, his utere mecum.

It is painful to relate that the American army shamefully abused its success, and perpetrated acts of vandalism, which at a later period, and in a distant scene, entailed just retribution.

The details cannot be given more effectively, than in the vigorous language of the Rev. Dr. Strachan, D.D., now the venerable Bishop of Toronto, who in a letter addressed to Thomas Jefferson, Esquire, of Monticello, ex-president of the United States of America, and dated York, 30th January, 1815, expressed himself as follows:—" In April, 1813, the public buildings at York, the capital of Upper Canada, were burnt by the troops of the United States, contrary to the articles of capitulation. They consisted of two elegant halls, with convenient offices, for the accommodation of the Legislature and of the Courts of Justice. The library, and all the papers and records belonging to these institutions were consumed; at the same time the church was robbed, and the town library totally pillaged. Commodore Chauncey, who has generally behaved honourably, was so ashamed of this last transaction, that he endeavoured to collect the books belonging to the public library, and actually sent back two boxes filled with them, but hardly any were complete. Much private property was plundered and several houses left in a state of ruin. Can you tell me, Sir, why the public buildings and the library at Washington should be held more sacred than those at York?"*

We have here the testimony of an eyewitness, whose evidence is beyond challenge. There is not in Canada a man whose career has been more thoroughly dovetailed into the moral structure of

---

* *Vide* Appendix No. 1. Letter from Dr. Strachan to Thomas Jefferson, Esquire, *in extenso*.

society, in welfare and in sorrow, than that of John, the revered Bishop of Toronto. From a beginning of noble humility, by dint of talent and honest energy, he now adorns the episcopate. Sixty-four years since, in the grand field of educational labour, he struggled with, and mastered a rugged soil, which has rendered noble increase. It was his great privilege, to have modelled the minds and characters of the men, who have since made the country, and who have left upon its broad surface, the "tower mark" of sterling. Whatever differences of opinion may have been, at times, entertained as to his course, that course has ever been straightforward, truthful, and uncompromising; and at the age of eighty-five he enjoys, in the lusty winter of his years, the well earned respect and esteem of all classes of men in Canada. His testimony on the subject of the severities, persistently exercised by the American armies, is unimpeachable. His remarkable letter will be found at length in the Appendix.

Again, after the tragic scenes which have been narrated, came the farce. The Americans occupied some days in removing the naval and military stores. The commanders found solace in the composition of despatches and in the compilation of catalogues. The "spolia opima" were all duly recorded, but the sensational trophy of the day, embalmed in a special report from the innocent seaman in command on lake Ontario, was "a human scalp" alleged to have been found "suspended from the chair of the speaker of the House of Assembly." The official circles at York were a little scandalized and more amused at this announcement; by some it was regarded simply as a *mauvaise plaisanterie*, others it puzzled, but at last it eked out, that the shocking trophy so loudly paraded, was in reality a *periwig*,—an official *peruke*, dropped in the confusion, and transported in triumph to Washington, to find a place by the side of the "stand of colours" captured in the wigwam of the Indian interpreter at St. Régis.

The Americans evacuated York on the 2nd May, 1813.

CHAPTER X.

American programme. Modification. Fall of York. Newark threatened. Description of Newark. Fort Niagara. Fort George. Climate and country. La Salle. Sketch of his exploits. Discovers the Mississippi. Fort George burnt. Rebuilt by Denonville. Colonel Dongan, Governor of the Province of New York, objects to the building of a Fort at "Ohniagro." Baron de Longueuil—Record of this family. Fort Niagara taken by the British, 1759. Surrendered to United States, 1796. Upper Canada created a separate Province, 1791. Governor Simcoe. His career. Newark his capital. Visit of Duke of Kent, 1793. Compared with that of Prince of Wales, 1860.

The programme of the American commanders had at first embraced the reduction of Kingston, York, and Fort George or Newark. The attack on Kingston had been abandoned; York had succumbed; and Newark, distant only a few hours' sail, unsupported and indefensible, lay at their mercy.

Contrary winds, however, thwarted all endeavours, and they did not arrive off the coast of Niagara before the 8th of May. They disembarked at the mouth of a streamlet known as Four-mile Creek, on the American shore of Lake Ontario, and, as its name implies, situate about four miles to the east of Fort Niagara. Here, for nearly three weeks, the expedition lingered, while Chauncey was employed in removing his wounded to Sackett's Harbour, and in transporting from thence reinforcements and heavy ordnance, preparatory to the attack on the British position at Fort George.

We may occupy the interval by describing the main features of this part of Canada.

The mouth of the river Niagara afforded one of the finest harbours on Lake Ontario. Safe of access, secure in its anchorage, and protected from every wind, it was at the same time exposed to this drawback in a state of warfare — it was open to the fire of both shores, and was, therefore, useless to either party. The river is at this point about 800 yards wide. On the eastern shore, where it joins the lake, stands Fort Niagara. Fort George and its dependency, the town of Newark, stood on the western bank of the river, somewhat withdrawn from the lake shore. Fort Niagara commanded the entrance to the river; Fort George dominated the harbor, and made it untenable by an enemy.

But the town of Newark, on the British side of the river, lay under the guns of Fort Niagara, opposite; and though Fort George, in the event of an attack, might retaliate and punish aggression, it could, in no way, protect the town. The course of human events had reversed all human relations; and Fort Niagara, which, from its foundation, had been to the town a fostering friend and defender, had, by the provisions of treaties and the fate of war, been converted into a shape of fear and a standing menace.

The traditions of the spot are as interesting as the site is beautiful. The scene is at once historic and picturesque. Within sound of the roar of Niagara; within sight of Queenston Heights; surrounded by a country of unrivalled fertility; a tessellated parterre of fruit, flowers, and foliage; where the grape, and the peach, and the apple and pear flourish side by side; in a climate soft and genial; under skies as blue as those of Italy, and bathed in an atmosphere more pure and translucent. Here, on the banks of a river exulting and abounding, whose winding-way, like that of the High Street at Oxford, is its main feature of beauty, and just where its waters blend with the *aqua marine* of Ontario, rise now the ramparts of Niagara and the venerable ruins of Fort George, the Sestos and Abydos of that Golden Horn.

The scene is worthy, at once, of the pencil of Claude and of the pen of Froissart, for it teems with memories of the deeds of adventurous men. Here, in 1678, the heroic La Salle, built his first fort; a few miles further on, above the cataract, on Navy Island, opposite to the mouth of Chippeway Creek, he built his first ship. Men yet living recollect to have seen, in early youth, on this, then, well-wooded island, the charred remains of burnt ships and other relics of his extemporaneous dockyard. From hence, in 1679, he launched his first bark of European structure, on the unknown water, of the upper lakes. He named her the Griffon, armed her with seven guns, and with his friend Tonti, and the celebrated Recollet, Père Hennepin, dared the watery wilderness of Erie, threaded the mazes of the Detroit, gave a name to lake St. Clair, penetrated into lake Huron, visited Michilimacinac, explored Michigan, and closed his great career by discovering the Mississippi and founding Louisiana.

The trading post at the mouth of the Niagara, erected by Robert Cavalier de La Salle, was burnt a few years afterwards; and, in 1687, was re-established by the Marquis de Denonville, Governor General of Canada, in a more permanent form, on the site of the present Fort Niagara. Denonville describes the locality as "the most beautiful—the most pleasing—the most advantageous site that is on the whole of this lake."

But the establishment of a French fortress upon the English side of the river Niagara, aroused at once the jealousy and the indignation of the Provincials; and Colonel Dongan, the English Governor of the province of New York, remonstrated strongly against the building of a French fort at "Ohniagro;" and in 1687 he solicited from the board of trade of the province of New York, an order to build a "campagne fort at Ohniagro."

The works, established by Denonville, were abandoned in 1688, and so remained until 1725, when the Baron de Longueuil* com-

---

* This Baron de Longueuil must have been the second of the name. He had

menced a stone cavalier, and completed it in the next year. Chaussegros, the French engineer employed, represents that the work was erected on the spot where an ancient fort had been built by order of Denonville.

With the fall of French dominion on this continent, came the fall of Fort Niagara. It had been by degrees enlarged and strengthened, and in 1759 was held for the French King, by M. Pouchot, who had under his command some 500 men. It was

---

served from his youth in the French armies, and died Governor of Montreal. The third Baron de Longueuil, Charles Jacques Le Moyne, was born at the Chateau de Longueuil, 26th Jan., 1724. He commanded the French troops at the battle of Monongahela, 9th July, 1755. He was made Chevalier de St. Louis, and Governor of Montreal. The Marquis de Vaudreuil relates in a despatch dated 8th September, 1755, that this distinguished officer, serving under Baron Dieskau, had disappeared in a skirmish on the shores of Lake George, and was believed to have fallen a victim to Indian treachery, if not to Indian cruelty. He was then 31 years of age. He left an only daughter to whom the Barony descended, and who as Baroness de Longueuil married Captain Grant of the 94th Regt. at Quebec, 7th May, 1781. This noble and exemplary lady, who was the embodiment of all the graceful and generous and chivalrous qualities so much prized by the French Canadians, died in 1842 at the advanced age of 85 years, an object of universal respect, as she was to the last, the object of universal love. Her son, the Hon. Charles Grant, M.L.C., succeeded to the Barony and title. He had married Caroline, the eldest daughter of the late General John Coffin of Alwington Manor, New Brunswick, and niece to the late Admiral Sir Isaac Coffin, Bart. This lady still lives with her brother, Admiral John Townsend Coffin, in Bath, Somerset, England. The late Baron, who died in 1848, was succeeded by his son, the present Baron de Longueuil, who resides on the Continent of Europe. The House of Longueuil is connected by marriage with the Baby, De Beaujeu, Le Moyne, de Montenach, de Lanaudière, de Gaspé, de la Gorgendiére, d'Eschambault, and several other of the old families in Canada.

And of these old families it is one of the oldest and of the most honourable. Le Moyne is the patronymic of the maison de Longueuil. They are of Norman

besieged by Brigadier General Prideaux, at the head of 8200 men and 600 Indians. The place was regularly invested, parallels opened, and batteries established. On the 20th July, General Prideaux was killed by the bursting of a cohorn ; and the command devolved on Sir William Johnston, of Mohawk celebrity. On the 24th July, an attempt was made to relieve Pouchot, by a French and Indian force from lake Erie. The besiegers obtained intelligence of the advance, and encountered it by an ambuscade

---

extraction, descended originally from a Count of Salagne en Biscaye, who took part in 1428 with Charles VII. and Joan d'Arc, la Pucelle d'Orleans, against the English. This Count de Salagne married Margaret de la Tremouille, daughter of the Count des Guines who was also Grand Chambellan de France, one of the oldest families of the kingdom. [Taken from a " Chapter on Canadian Nobility" in Maple Leaves, an interesting contribution to Canadian Literature, by J. M. Lemoine, Quebec.]

The Barony de Longueuil in Canada was a creation of the Grand Monarque. Louis XIV, by royal Letters Patent, bearing date at Versailles, 27th January, 1700, erected the Seignory of Longueuil into a Barony, and rarely indeed have distinctions been conferred for more distinguished services. In those days it was the practice to detail on the face of a patent of honour the honourable exploits of which it was the recompense. The same practice now enhances the value of the Victoria Cross. This document, which is recorded in the Register of proceedings of the Superior Council of Quebec, recapitulates, first, " The services rendered to us by Charles Le Moyne, Esquire, Seignior of Longueuil, who left France in 1640 to reside in Canada, where his valour and fidelity were so often conspicuous in the war against the Iroquois, that our Governor and Lieutenant Governors in that country employed him, constantly, in every military expedition, and in every negotiation and treaty of peace, of all which duties he acquitted himself to their entire satisfaction ; also the services of his eldest son, Charles Le Moyne de Longueuil, who had borne arms from his youth in the Regiment de St. Laurent, and as a Captain of a naval detachment in Canada since 1687, who had an arm shot off by the Iroquois in a combat at Lachine, wherein seven of his brothers were also engaged—furthermore of the services of Jacques Le Moyne de Ste. Hélène, another son, Captain

on the side of Lewiston, under the command of Captain James de Lancey. The French were surprised, deserted by their Indian allies, and defeated. Pouchot was informed of the extent of the disaster by Sir William Johnston, and was offered most honourable terms, which he accepted, after a defence which entitled him to all that was offered. Thus on the 25th July, 1759, Fort Niagara fell into the hands of the English.

The fort remained in British possession up to the year 1788,

---

in the Marine, who was killed in defending Quebec against Phipps in 1690—also of Pierre Le Moyne d'Iberville, another son, Captain of a sloop of war, who captured Fort Corland in Hudson's Bay, and still commands a frigate. Also, of another, Joseph Le Moyne de Bienville who was killed by the Iroquois in an attack on Repentigny ; also of Louis Le Moyne de Chateauguay, who fell in the taking of Fort Bourbon in Hudson's Bay ; also the services of Paul Le Moyne de Marricourt, an Ensign in the navy and Captain of a Company in the naval detachment of marines in service on shore. That for these and other considerations, equally creditable, but too lengthy to enumerate here, the most Christian king elevates the Seigniory of Longueuil to the rank, name, title, and dignity of a Barony, in favour of the said Charles Le Moyne, his children, heirs and descendants. Rarely indeed, on the wider fields of Christendom, have there been arrayed worthier titles to knightly distinction.

Long as is the list of those meritorious men contained in this Royal document, it does not enumerate them all nor their services. Charles Le Moyne, " who left France in 1640" the leader in the above Letters Patent named, was the father of eleven sons. It will be observed that each is distinguished by the name of the *fief* or other property with which he had been invested. Six are named in the *acte* of 1700. Besides these, two brothers, Joseph Le Moyne de Sevigny and Gabriel Le Moyne d' Assigny, both died in the King's service. Antoine Le Moyne died young. Antoine Le Moyne de Chateauguay succeeded Louis Le Moyne de Chateauguay who was killed in 1694. Jean Baptiste Le Moyne de Bienville succeeded to the Le Moyne de Bienville who was killed defending a burning house against the Iroquois.

In a memorial from Jean Baptiste Le Moyne de Bienville to the king, dated New Orleans, Jan. 25, 1723, after setting forth his services, he describes him-when it was surrendered to the Americans, though not practically abandoned until 1796, under Jay's treaty. During the period of French possession, a village, in connection with the fort, had grown up on the western side of the river, being French territory, and, therefore, more safe. The fort was looked upon as an outpost more likely to occupy the attention of regular assailants, and deter plunderers; and the village, secure in its insignificance, reposed under its wing.

---

self as a Chevalier de St. Louis, and Commander General of the Province of Louisiana. He states in it, that of eleven brothers only four were then surviving. Baron de Longueuil—himself Bienville—Sevigny, and Chateauguay, and that they had all received the cross of knights of St. Louis. These details were collected in Paris by —— Falconer, Esquire, son of the late Dr. Falconer, of the Circus, Bath, and brother in law to William Roebuck, Esquire, M. P. for Sheffield, England.

But the most distinguished of this band of brothers—the one whose name will live while the Father of Rivers continues to flow to the sea, was the discoverer of the Mississippi. La Salle, as is stated in the text, ascended the lakes and descended the Mississippi, and was therefore justly entitled to claim the first discovery of the prodigious territory watered by that majestic river and its affluents; but the first person of European origin who entered the Mississippi from the sea—was the born Canadian, Pierre Le Moyne d'Iberville. He was an officer of the French marine. He had seen much hard and fierce service in Canada and Hudson's Bay. He was made Captain of a frigate in 1692. He visited France in 1695. He left it with three vessels. Entered and ascended the Mississippi nearly one hundred leagues, established a garrison and returned to France in 1699. He was decorated with the Croix de St. Louis. He subsequently made two successful voyages to the same coast; left settlements, and in 1720 was promoted to the rank of *"Capitaine de vaisseau."* In 1706, he was again despatched to the Mississippi charged with an important command. He died on his way, at the Havanah, 9th July, 1706. He was born at Montreal. What Burckhardt and Speke and Grant have done for the Nile—La Salle did for the Mississippi, but the mouth and the mysterious delta of the river, and the site of the present great city of New Orleans, were discovered by a Canadian, Pierre Le Moyne d'Iberville.

But when, in 1796, the French fort became an American outwork, the whole aspect of the frontier changed. The fortress, which had afforded protection, became a coign of vantage and exposure. The artillery, which had provided defence, menaced destruction. In the interim, in 1791, was passed the act 31, Geo. III, which divided Canada into two provinces, and conferred a constitution which was confided to the judicious administration of Governor Simcoe. This officer found the military head-quarters of his government at Fort Niagara, and established his miniature capital in the transfluvial town, to which he gave the name of Newark. Governor Simcoe was a remarkable man, and a becoming companion of the *dramatis personæ* of this historical scene. Unlike La Salle, he was not the creature of his aspirations. He did not, in quest of an Eldorado, or of the fountain of perpetual youth, discover a vast territory, but in the steady practical spirit, in the spirit of the Puritan Pilgrims, he founded in Upper Canada a great English colony. He was an Englishman by birth, had been educated at Eton and Oxford, and animated by a passion for a military life, at the age of 19 obtained an Ensigncy in the 35th Regiment. His first essay in arms was in America. He was distinguished at once for military knowledge, activity, and sense. His earnestness and proficiency had their reward. In 1777, Sir William Howe appointed Simcoe to the command of the Queen's Rangers, a partisan corps which performed conspicuous service during the war of the Revolution, and was finally disbanded after the surrender of Cornwallis at Yorktown, 19th Oct. 1782. He has left a Journal of the operations of this corps, well worthy of the perusal of the military student. In the intervals of camp life, in the leisure of winter quarters, Simcoe had become a student himself, and had trained his mind to the discharge of great duties on a wider field of usefulness. Colonel Simcoe returned to England. He had acquired reputation. He was elected to Parliament in 1790. He took an active part in the debates on the Bill which divided the Province of Quebec and gave a Constitution to Upper Canada. He was appointed the first Lieut.-Governor under that Constitution. He devoted himself to the judicious settlement of the colony. The present site of London was selected originally by him as the site of the capital of Upper Canada. But, at that early period, it was inaccessible— York received, and retains the honour. Simcoe devoted himself to surveying the country, improving and peopling it. He invited the Loyalists from the United States, and he attracted settlers, military and others, by a prompt allotment of lands and a just rule. He planted the British Constitution in a virgin soil, put it upon trial, in a fair field without favour, and appealed to results; and a trial of seventy years has justified his faith in the success of the experiment. He left behind him, through the land, the marks of his footsteps—*vestigia nulla retrorsum*. In 1794 he was ordered to St. Domingo. Thence to England, where in 1801 he was employed in the western counties in organizing resistance against expected invasion. He was then a Lieut.-General. In 1806 he was sent to Portugal—was taken ill on the voyage, and returned to England to die in the meridian of life, aged 54. Had he lived he might have shared in the immortality of Wellington. His energy and talent and experience were full of promise. He died unconscious of the fact, that before he reached his native shore, he had been appointed to succeed Lord Lake in the chief military command in India.

His residence was in a log building, of some pretensions among log dwellings, situate on the Canadian side of the river, in the town of Newark, and known as Navy Hall. His council sat in a wooden shed, and the council-chamber was, in those primitive and peaceful days, used by Catholics and Protestants alternately, as a place worship—the lion laid down with the lamb in patriarchial quietude.

The first parliament of Canada assembled in 1792, 17th Sept., in a marquee-tent—one remove in the scale of ascending civilization from the aboriginal council-lodge. In 1793 Governor Simcoe entertained, at Newark, His Royal Highness the Duke of Kent, the father of our beloved Queen. It is recorded, that if the lodging was indifferent, the fare was good. It is related in contemporary memoranda that the guests were feasted " with game, and all the dainties the season and the wilderness could produce, such as white-fish, trout, wild-fowl, roast beef, ale, old port, and Madeira, of better quality," adds the narrator, in the true spirit of the *laudator temporis acti*, " than can be got in the present year of grace, 1862."*

His Royal Highness had been conveyed to Niagara in the King's schooner, Mohawk, commanded by Commodore Bouchette, the grandfather of the present Commissioner of Customs. On landing, " as soon as horses with saddles and bridles could be mustered," the royal party wended their way by the river road, recently opened by the troops: the *portage* road, frequented by traffic, had previously been restricted to the eastern, or American, bank of the river Niagara. The road to the cataract was an Indian path through the woods; and an Indian ladder, which consists of a succession of pine trees, with the branches lopped short as a foot-hold, led down for 160 feet, to the foot of the Fall. Down this hazardous descent, in despite of all expostulation, His Royal Highness resolved to venture, and, with the nerve and physical strength of his race, accomplished it successfully—returned with a capital appetite, and in a log hut on the quivering brink of the abyss, " ate what the house afforded, and enjoyed himself exceedingly."†

It is interesting to contrast this royal reception in the back bush, with the reception of His Royal Highness the Prince of Wales, in

---

* Memoranda of Colonel John Clark, of St. Catherines.
† Mem. Col. John Clark.

the same locality, seventy years afterwards. The endurance of the grandson was not exposed to trials such as these; and those trials which civilization imposes upon princes, were encountered with a genial grace which reminded the present generation of the traditionary kindliness of the grandsire. And yet it may be doubted if the Prince of Wales enjoyed the crowd, and the crush, and the congratulations, and the cheers, which rose above the roar of the cataract, with half the zest, with which the Duke of Kent, with the flush of exhilarating exercise on his cheek, and the perfume of the pine branches on his hands and garments, partook of the rude cheer of the forest, in the door-way of a shanty, in full front of the Falls of Niagara — the sole monarch of all he surveyed — within sight and sound of the grandest spectacle that ever greeted royal eye.

CHAPTER XI.

Seat of Government removed from Newark to York. Fort George still Military Head-Quarters. American attack on Fort George and Newark. General Vincent in command. American forces. British strength. American force on landing. British retire. Fort George falls. Vincent occupies Beaver Dam. Description.

In 1796 all the forts on the frontier of the United States,—La Presentation, or Ogdensburg, called also Oswegatchie; Oswego; Niagara; Fort Miami, were finally transferred in accordance with Jay's treaty, to the American authorities. At Niagara the change produced much inconvenience. In the short space during which Newark had possessed the advantages and the honours of the capital, it had increased commercially. It had grown under the fostering influence of centralization; but it would have been improvident and unsafe to have left the government and the archives of the legislature exposed to unpleasant alternatives, and Governor Simcoe, with prompt prudence, removed the seat of government to Toronto, which in honour of a royal Duke, he had named York.

Newark, however, still retained much of its former importance. It continued to be the head quarter of the troops; and the bastions and curtains of Fort George gradually rose up in grim rivalry to the more regular and substantial fort on the other side of the river. Fort Niagara still retains the strong development and regular aspect imparted to it by scientific French engineers, before the conquest of Canada. It is now a large, well-constructed work, faced with stone, ditched and palisaded, fit at any time for military occupation and service. The defences of Fort George have, long since, dissolved into huge, unmeaning, inoffensive mounds of earth — monuments of an expenditure of life and treasure, without result and almost without object.

The uselessness of the fort, in a military point of view, and the lamentable expense and loss entailed by its occupation, were memorably shown on the occasion of the hostile descent now to be related. The whole British force quartered in Fort George and cantoned in Newark, on the 27th May, 1813, amounted to 1340 men, with eight field guns, under the command of General Vincent. Four twenty-four-pounders, captured from Hull, had been brought from Detroit, and were mounted on the bastions of Fort George; a fifth was planted *en barbette*, in a redoubt, lying between Newark and the lake shore. Fort George afforded some defence against an enemy descending the river Niagara, in the rear, but the town obstructed fire upon an assailant approaching from the lake shore. It is evident that if an enemy, superior in number, had thrown a force across the river above the town and Fort George, instructed to form a junction with troops to disembark at One-mile Creek, Newark and its defenders would have been cut off, and enclosed within a narrow triangle — the river on one side, the lake shore on the other, and the enemy's line the base. It would thus have been invested by 6,000 * good troops in front, and exposed to the fire from Fort Niagara in the rear. That this manœuvre had been contemplated is to be inferred from the fact that a flotilla of boats had been assembled at the Five-mile Meadows, about two miles below Lewiston. It was also a pet project with the American Secretary of State for war.†

---

* Ingersoll.

† If, instead of concentrating his whole forces, naval and military, on the water side of the enemy's defences, he had divided the attack, and, crossing the Niagara below Lewiston, had advanced on Fort George by the Queenstown road, the investment of that place would have been complete, and a retreat of the garrison impracticable.—*Armstrong*.

The forces of the Americans were ample, and in every way adequate to the attempt. Generals Dearborn and Lewis, Boyd, Windsor, and Chandler were at the head of at least 6000 men. The American squadron, under Commodore Chauncey, consisted of eleven vessels of war, with a fighting broadside of 52 guns—many of them long thirty-two and eighteen-pounders. His crews mustered 900 choice seamen. This immense superiority was well-known to the British general; and it is only to be lamented that a sentiment of military punctilio, exacerbated, possibly, by the reproaches recently flung upon Sheaffe, should have induced him to dare a useless contest against overwhelming odds, and to have sacrificed 445 good soldiers, whose services at Stoney Creek would have been invaluable. Vincent, however, had resolved not to give way without a fight, and disposed his men accordingly. He placed an advanced detachment of the Glengarry and Newfoundland regiments, numbering about 250 rank and file, with 40 Indians, under Norton, in a ravine and copse at the outlet of One-mile Creek, a small rivulet situated about one mile west of Newark; in their rear, within supporting distance, was the left column, under Colonel Myer, 470 strong, protected by three light field pieces; while his right column, 600 bayonets, under Colonel Harvey, was drawn up between Newark and Fort George, except about 50 men of the 49th foot and 80 of the militia, who occupied the fort itself.

At day-light on the 27th May, the American flotilla — ships of war and swarms of boats —were discovered bearing down before a light breeze, from the eastward upon Missisagua Point. At the same time the batteries of Fort Niagara opened upon Fort George and Newark; but a heavy fog settling down suddenly, the cannonade ceased for a while, with little harm done, except to the town. During the lull, three heavy schooners swept in, so as, to enfilade the British twenty-four and nine-pounder guns *en barbette*. About 8 a.m. the fog lifted and discovered the American flotilla bearing down in three lines, towards One-mile Creek. As the boats approached the shore, the British advance sprang to the bank, and tore them with so severe a fire, that the men cowered down for safety. Then the Oneida, and the Madison, and the Lady of the Lake, opened with their heavy cannon, and like Graham's artillery, at St. Sebastian, playing over the heads of the stormers, threw their shot over their own boats into the exposed ranks of the British, and with admirable precision. The fate of the brave McNeil, at York, was re-enacted, and the storm-struck line staggered back on its supports.

So soon as the boats touched ground, the Americans plunged into the water, and rushed to the shore. Their officers rallied and formed them with bravery and coolness; but the brief time occupied in formation, enabled the left column, under Myer, incorporating the remnant of the advance, to reach the top of the bank; and the Americans were repeatedly driven back and thrust down at the point of the bayonet; but the brigades of Winder and Chandler had reinforced the first. The twenty-four-pounder gun at Missisagua had been silenced; the nine-pounder, served by militia, bravely fought on, until almost every gunner had been killed or wounded; and the deadly fire from the ships enfiladed Myer's column. The Colonel himself was down, desperately hurt. Every mounted officer, but one, was hit, and the exception lost his horse. Of a column of 470 strong, 204 regular and 85 militia were *hors de combat*. Fortune kindly spared the man who was most wanted. Harvey took Myer's place, and falling back on his own right column, which he had left for the moment in charge of Plenderleath, drew up his whole force in order of battle in the plain. This was to the west of the town and fort, on the line of retreat.

So soon, however, as the enemy had landed on the top of the bank and formed, a cloud of light troops and riflemen had been thrown upon the road to Burlington Heights, to intercept this movement. The American army had divided into two columns, and, strongly supported by artillery, followed in the same direction. To delay further, simply to indulge the dogged rage of resistance, were to tempt destruction. Vincent, yielding in his extremity, ordered his outlying posts at Fort Erie and Chippewa to join him, and directing Fort George to be blown up, gathered up the shattered remnants of his forces, and fell back upon the strong position of the "Beaver Dam," unmolested, leaving behind him, on the stricken field, 445 of his best and bravest men.

About noon, on that day, the Americans took quiet possession of Fort George. The 50 men of the 49th, who had been left to destroy the magazines, being entirely cut off, fell into the hands of the enemy. The American loss amounted to about 150. On reaching the Beaver Dam, Vincent was joined by Colonel Bishopp, from Fort Erie, and Major Ormsby, from Chippewa; and thus reinforced, mustered 1,600 rank and file. Had he destroyed Fort George and retired to this position at early dawn, he would, in the words of Mr. Secretary Armstrong, "have adopted the policy of Sheaffe, have preferred the preservation of his troops to that of his post, and carrying off the kernel would have left the enemy the shell."

Vincent had retired to the Beaver Dam, covering his retreat on Burlington Heights. A beaver dam, or beaver meadow, is a common feature of the wilderness. The sagacious labourer has long since receded before the footsteps of the settler, and the range of the trapper ; but his handy-work remains in evidence of his industry and skill. It is the practice of the beaver, when nature does not offer a pond or lake fit for the safe structure of his dwelling, to form an artificial overflow. He selects a gorge between hills, or uplands on each side of a running stream, and with his teeth, and paws, and some slight aid from his tail, he cuts down trees, and floats them to the site selected; with his paws he moves stones, and earth, and branches; he intertwines, and overlays, and plasters—and thus he creates a dam, with a rare certainty of instinctive calculation as to the depth and area of water to be obtained, and of the strength and substance required for its retention. Many of these beaver dams have been found twelve feet in thickness at the base, as many feet in height, and extending across valleys of considerable width. It is the work of conjoint labour, organized and applied with the economy of human intelligence. The construction of the dam has, most probably, flooded a large tract of land in the rear, and has destroyed vegetation; but on the disappearance of the engineer, the dam has fallen into decay; a new vegetation of rank grass has sprung up on the subsidence of water, and in the rear of the deserted beaver dam has grown up a beaver meadow. This is an attraction to the early settler — it affords to his cow, pasture in summer, and hay in winter; and his first shanty is placed in its vicinity.

The military position of the Beaver Dam was about twelve miles from Niagara, on the road to the Heights; and one Decau had built a stone house hard by, which became at once a depot for military stores, and a *point d'appui*. The dam itself, an embankment, might then have been looked to, as a breastwork in case of attack, but little trace remains of it now. It was then chiefly valued as commanding the cross-road to Ten-mile Creek, now St. Catherines, where Major de Haren lay, with 220 men.

CHAPTER XII.

Lake Ontario. Kingston. Sackett's Harbour. Expectations and preparations. Dr. Richardson, D.D.—His Career and Record. Departure of Squadron. Sights Sackett's Harbour and withdraws. Capture of American Officer of Dragoons. The Expedition retires—Preparations for landing. Preparations for resistance. General Jacob Brown. Colonel Baccus. Landing effected. Americans defeated—fire the stores and ships on the stocks. The British ordered to retreat. Withdrawal of the Expedition.

Leaving General Vincent to rally around him his outlying detachments, and to organize his retreat upon Burlington Heights, we will now turn to events of equal moment, which took place at the same time, at the eastern or lower extremity of Lake Ontario. Here, where the waters of the lake contracting, assume the dimensions of a river, the St. Lawrence, embracing in its thousand arms the far-famed "Thousand Isles," commences, under that name, its glorious and rapid course to the sea. On the north shore of the lake, at the mouth of the River Cataraqui, stands the town and fine harbour of Kingston, whilome selected, and with much judgment, as the seat of government for United Canada. It would be out of place here, to dwell upon the passions and the prejudices, or the policies, which have made this costly and coveted prize, ever since the disturbance of the arrangement mentioned, an apple of discord, cast down, in turn, to the competition and confusion of every important city in the province; which has convulsed parliaments, destroyed ministries, which yields only, and with reluctance, to the arbitrament of the Queen; and against which, even now, though the masses approve, each disappointed competitor exclaims, in the spirit of an epigram on the marriage of our Second Charles to Catharine of Braganza.

> Here's a health to Kate,
> Our Sovereign's mate,
> Of the royal house of Lisbon;
> But the devil take Hyde,
> And the Bishop beside,
> Who made her bone of his bone.

Here, in 1673, with the tact and foresight of a soldier, the Count de Frontenac, then Governor of Canada, established a fort, called, at first Cataraqui, and afterwards by his own name, which fell into the hands of the British in 1759-60. In 1787 the British abandoned their previous naval establishment, on Carleton Island, which happened to fall within the American boundary line, and, from that time, Kingston became their chief establishment on Lake Ontario, their best harbour, and the focus from whence radiated their future settlements on the shores of the lake, and the River St. Lawrence.

On the opposite coast of this northern Bosphorus, sheltered by large intervening islands, lies Sackett's Harbour—the American Cherbourg, as it has been called,—but with little to suggest the comparison, beyond a small and safe harbour, and defensible environs. Without comparing Kingston to Portsmouth, it was the only British naval establishment on Lake Ontario; and without exaggerating the strength of Sackett's Harbour, it had sheltered and equipped a fine squadron which, under Commodore Chauncey, had sacked York, and reduced Fort George.

Both Kingston and Sackett's Harbour had, for long, been objects of mutual apprehension. Enterprises had been planned on both sides for the destruction of either, as a sure means of naval supremacy, and ultimate conquest; but up to a very late period the opportunities of the Americans had exceeded those of the British. How far they had improved their chances has been already shown; but the arrival of Sir James Yeo at Kingston, early in the month, with about 500 officers and men, of the Royal Navy, and the completion of an additional vessel of war, the Wolfe, of 20 guns, justified the hope that the chances of war had at length turned in favour of the British.

These chances appeared to the popular eye to be reduced to a certainty when it became known that Chauncey and his fleet, and Dearborn with his soldiers, were in front of Niagara; that to supply the means of attack they had dismantled and disarmed Sackett's Harbour, and that the stores and ships in course of construction, and the arsenal, naval and military, had been left to the protection of the militia of the country.

Expectation, too, rose to the highest pitch when it was announced that the Commander-in-Chief was himself in Kingston; that an attack upon Sackett's Harbour had been planned; and that the combined forces would be commanded by Sir George Provost and Commodore Sir James Yeo, in person. The preparations made under the circumstances were such as to reassure the least sanguine. Sir George Provost, surrounded by able officers, had under his command 750 men, detailed from the following regiments: the 100th, the Royal Scots, the 8th, the 104th, the Newfoundland regiment, one company of the Glengarries, two companies of Canadian Voltigeurs, and two six-pounders, with their gunners. This force was conveyed in the Wolfe, 20 guns, the flag-ship of Sir James Yeo; the Royal George, 20 guns; Moira, 16 guns; Melville Brig, 16 guns; Netley schooner; and smaller vessels.

The expedition sailed from Kingston early on the morning of the 27th May, at the hour when, the first echoes of the American guns reverberated on the shores of Niagara, and Chauncey and Scott were engaged, hand-to-hand, with Myer and Harvey. The weather being favourable, and the wind fair, the flotilla arrived off Sackett's Harbour about 10 a.m.

The accounts of the subsequent occurrences, both American and British, differ in all but the result. The Americans exaggerate an irresolute resistance crowned by an undeserved success. The British, blind with rage and mortification, prove but blind guides to the confused enquirer. Sir George Provost, though an adept with his pen, upon this occasion, did not write his own commentaries; and the letter of his adjutant-general, Colonel Baines, affords but an imperfect explanation of this inexplicable transaction.

But the difficulty which clouded this page of the narrative, has been, to a great extent, dispelled, by an unexpected and friendly hand; and a light has been cast upon the movements and the men of this expedition, by private memoranda, which we have been most kindly permitted to use, and which command at once our respect and acknowledgments.

The witness, on this occasion, is well known to most men in Canada. To those who have attended, of late years, the numerous military gatherings on Queenston Heights, it is easy to recall one familiar face and figure. It is a tall and venerable form, of gentle aspect, but soldierly port—of grave costume, becoming the years of one

——— Whose age is like a lusty winter—
Frosty, but kindly.—

and whose left breast is decorated by a Canada medal* and an

---

* Since the above was in print, the writer has been informed that he is in error. There is no Canada medal; but let the error stand. If Dr. Richardson has no such medal, he ought to have one. And it would be well to know why this great boon has been withheld from the Militia soldier of Canada. Medals have been granted for services on the Ganges, and Sutlej, in China and in Kaffirland. A *post-obit* decoration has been tardily bestowed on the heroes of the Peninsula. Medals were given for Chateauguay, where there was some fighting, and for Detroit, where there was no fighting at all. Why is it that the men who fought and bled at Queenston Heights, on the Niagara and Detroit frontiers; at Frenchtown and Fort Meigs; at Schlosser and Black Rock; at Ogdensburg; at Lacolle mill; on the St. Lawrence and the lakes; should have been denied a guerdon, so highly prized, for services which cannot be ignored?

empty sleeve. To the enquiring stranger it would be replied, that the veteran who excited his interest was the Rev. Dr. Richardson, D.D., now Bishop of the Episcopal Methodist Church in Canada; and, in his youth, a gallant officer of the Provincial marine, who, in 1814, had, in action with the enemy, lost an arm in the service of his country.

This gentleman was the son of the brave Lieutenant Richardson, who, as before related, carried the Simcoe into Kingston harbour, in despite of the fire of the whole American squadron. Brought up from a boy in the navigation of the lakes, at the age of eighteen he followed his father's footsteps, and entered into the Provincial service. In 1812, being then twenty-one years of age, he received his commission as Lieutenant. At this time the Provincial Navy on Lake Ontario consisted of the ships Royal George, 20 guns; the Moira, of 16; the schooner Duke of Gloucester, of 8, and the Netley schooner, of 12 guns; with numerous small vessels, acting as gunboats and transports. The services of these vessels, in default of all other means of communication, were indispensable to the divisions of the army, both in the east and in the west of Upper Canada.

The officers of the Provincial Marine received their commissions from the Commander-in-Chief in British North America, and the whole force was attached to the department of the Quarter-Master-General. On the arrival of the first detachment of the Royal Navy, these gentlemen were informed that their commissions could not be recognized by the rules of a service, which subsequent intercourse with Turks and Frenchmen, Sardinians and Russians, has rendered far more cosmopolite. With a very suggestive show of reticence, the greater part of these officers retired from the marine, and took service in the militia, where they were permitted to risk their lives without offence to their feelings. While we appreciate the sensitiveness which shrank from an indignity, we admire the more the patriotism of those who cast aside every consideration which interfered with service to their country. Two of the number, Lieutenants George Smith and James Richardson, could not bring themselves to abandon their more natural element, and, to the great satisfaction of the Commodore, accepted rating as "masters," which gave them rank in the gun-room with the commissioned officers, and enabled them, as "masters and pilots," from their knowledge of their own inland seas, to render important services.*

We may feel satisfied in Canada, however, that the reign of martinet punctilio has long since passed away, and that a Canadian officer of the Queen, should occasion ever require his services, will receive at the hands of the army and navy of England the same share of respect which is freely awarded, in military intercourse, to a German "Felt-wacht-meister," or to a Turkish "Bim Bashi."

In the middle of May, Lieutenant Richardson had been despatched by Captain Barclay—previous to his own departure for the western waters—to escort, in the gunboat "Black Snake," the rear detachment of Yeo's blue-jackets, under Capt. Mulcaster, up the St. Lawrence to Kingston. On their arrival, the men had been distributed on board of the ships of the squadron. Richardson himself was appointed to the Wolfe, and was thus present at head-quarters on occasion of the descent of the 27th May.

The wind was fair, the weather favourable and propitious. About 10 a. m., on the 27th May, the squadron approached Sackett's Harbour. No enemy appeared at the landing place, and no ostensible show of resistance. All preparations were completed; the men embarked in the boats; the anchors ready to be dropped. The very spot indicated as the point of disembarkation had been reached, when, instead of proceeding to land and taking the place, which might then undoubtedly have been effected almost without loss of

---

* Mem. of Dr. James Richardson, D.D.

life, the troops were ordered to re-embark, the ships hauled to their wind, withdrew from the coast, and the enterprise was apparently abandoned.

The general amazement was controlled by the instincts of discipline, and by the belief that the retreat was a *ruse*—part of some preconcerted plan; and at this time an occurrence took place, which diverted attention, and caused some amusement. In the afternoon, as the Wolfe was working to windward, away from the landing place, and about six miles in the offing, a boat was discovered approaching with a white flag, from a low wooded point of land, which forms the entrance to a deep bay known as Henderson's Harbour. Commodore Yeo dispatched Lieut. Dobbs, in one of the ship's boats, to meet the stranger, and ascertain his business. After a brief interview, Dobbs proceeded on to the shore. The American boat continued its course, and discharged upon the deck of the flag-ship a gentleman, ostentatiously armed, with a belt bristling with weapons, who announced himself to be a captain of dragoons. He reported to the officer of the deck that he was in command of a detachment, which had, on an uncongenial element, been attacked by Indians, and had "concluded" forthwith to surrender. A part of his men were in the boat alongside, and Dobbs had proceeded to the shore for the remainder. It appeared that a party of Chippewa Indians, the occupants of about three canoes, had attacked the bold dragoon as he crept along the shore, seeking to reinforce the garrison at Sackett's Harbour, and had been, in reality, repulsed. One of the savages, badly wounded, had been taken on board of the Wolfe some short time before; but dread of the Indians had blinded the gallant officer to his own success, and, without further molestation, he had thrown himself upon the protection of the fleet. The remainder of his men were soon brought on board. At this time the commanders were at dinner. The officer was invited to the table, and, on being introduced, perceiving some twinklings of fun on the faces of the juniors, remarked: "Gentlemen, I confess that my appearance is uncouth, but my heart is as square as any man's."*

Whether the information given by this officer restored confidence, or that his deportment gave occasion for reflection, Sir George, in a few hours, made fresh dispositions. At midnight, in the dark—heavy rain had come on—at a distance of some miles from the landing, which they had all but gained some hours before, the men were put into the boats, and directed to the shore. Colonel Baines relates that the boats were assembled at 1 a. m., in compact and regular order, intending to effect a landing before the enemy could line the woods with troops; but the darkness of the night, ignorance of the coast, and a strong current had drifted the boats from their proper station. When day dawned they pulled for the proper point of disembarkation.*

In the meantime the enemy had not been idle. On the first approach of the British flotilla, the scant garrison of Sackett's Harbour consisted of a few American regulars, a small force of Albany volunteers, and the local militia. They mustered two field-pieces, and a long 32-pounder, on a pivot, surmounting Fort Tompkins. Colonel Baccus, of the United States army, was in command of the place. The general commanding the district, Jacob Brown, a respectable farmer, resided at a distance of about twelve miles from the harbour. He was immediately notified, and proved to be a man not unequal to the emergency. He took instant measures, alarmed the country, summoned the militia, and roused a spirit of resistance, which was not diminished by the abrupt departure of the British fleet. By daybreak, on the following morning, all his arrangements had been made.

The troops landed with little opposition. They first encountered

---

* Mem. of Dr. James Richardson, D.D.
* Report of Colonel Baines, Adjutant-General, May 30, 1813.

a body of militia, supported by a field-piece. This force was attacked and routed, their commander killed, and the field-piece captured. The advance, however, was enfiladed by the gun on Fort Tompkins, which inflicted loss; but the landing having been made, the front was forthwith cleared of skirmishers; and, divided into two detachments, under Colonel Young, of the King's, and Major Gordon, of the 100th, the troops, in excellent order and with perfect confidence, advanced to carry the place.

The works at Sackett's Harbour then consisted of two stockaded barracks, with block-houses and defences constructed of logs and cedar pickets; of Fort Tompkins, with its solitary gun; Fort Pyke, and the dockyard defences, denuded of artillery, employed in the attack on Niagara. The American garrison, in addition to the force first enumerated, consisted now of a swarm of militia, hurriedly assembled from all quarters, who, over-exultant the night before, were not a little disconcerted by the changed aspect of affairs in the morning. Little, had they thought—

> That upon night so sweet, such awful morn should rise.

The British advance was an uninterrupted success. The militia, in despite of appeal, remonstrance and objurgation, took to flight. The American regulars were broken and destroyed. The brave Colonel Baccus, their commander, was killed. General Brown resolutely, but hopelessly, struggled to retrieve the disaster. Dismay spread on every side. The officer in command of the dockyard set fire to the Pyke, a frigate on the stocks, two ships of war in the harbour, and the naval store-house, filled with the spoils of York. The stockaded barracks had been fired by our troops. General Brown, without disparagement to his personal conduct, was prepared to capitulate. The rough farmer, fresh from the plough, had displayed qualities which brave men admire, and older soldiers may have envied.

At this moment of undisputed triumph, came an order to retreat, issued by Sir George Provost himself. It is idle now to speculate on motives, to invent arguments, or discuss theories. The great fact is indisputable and irresistible. By all accounts, both British and American, the place was at our mercy, when, with the effect of a stunning and stupefying blow, the order to re-embark fell upon all hearts. The men sullenly and mechanically fell in, formed, and retired unmolested, from before a dispersed and demoralized foe. One of the brave colonels in command exclaimed, indignantly, in the hearing of Mr. Richardson, as he came up the ship's side : " If he would but give me my own regiment, I would yet land again, and have the place."

The expedition returned to Kingston, overwhelmed with indignant mortification. Brave men and gallant officers had fallen ; life and reputation had been sacrificed—honour itself imperilled, in the very wantonness of irresolution. The story told requires no further comment.*

---

* The personal courage of Sir George Provost in the field has always been extolled by those who were around his person, and who knew him best, and whom he inspired with strong affection. Colonel Macdonald, an officer who had served with great distinction and who subsequently acquired still more on the Upper Lakes in 1814, writes thus, on this head, dated Kingston, 29th May, 1813. "Sir George landed with the troops, accompanied by Mr. Brenton and myself. His Excellency was in the thickest of the fire, and of course had some narrow escapes in an action, the musketry of which was heavier than anything I ever saw, except the 21st March in Egypt."

CHAPTER XIII.

Return to Vincent at the Beaver Dam—Retires on Burlington Heights—Colonel Harvey—Stoney Creek—British retire from, and the Americans occupy their position—Harvey's plan for night attack—The Americans surprised—Desperate fighting—Americans dispersed—Generals Chandler and Winder taken prisoners—Present aspect of the ground—Old Lutheran Chapel—Burial place of the slain—No memorial stone—Why not? Americans fall back on Niagara—Abandon camps and supplies.

It is with a grateful sense of relief, that, following the natural course of events, we are now transported to the upper end of Lake Ontario—to General Vincent and the retreating garrison of Niagara—there to record how one resolute, thoughtful man, may control fate and restore fortune.

Vincent had withdrawn deliberately to the position of the Beaver Dam. Here his outlying detachments had joined him from the south. Bishopp, on evacuating Fort Erie, had blown up that work; and now the General, with the same deliberation, fell back upon the strong position of Burlington Heights.

Burlington Heights, situated about two miles to the west of the present city of Hamilton, was, in those days, a strong position. Modern artillery, however, has been very destructive to this sort of reputation. The area is too contracted to be of any value now. It is a peninsula, elevated about one hundred feet above the water of Burlington Bay on one side, and the extensive Desjardins marsh on the other. It was unassailable, except by the neck of the isthmus, which was defended by field works. Here the general covered and maintained his communications, with York on his left rear, and with Proctor and the western division of his army on his right.

General Vincent had the merit of appreciating merit in others. He discovered talent, made use of it, and did it ample justice. His despatches do honour to his soldierly honesty. He had by his side a man of rare military qualities—Lieut.-Colonel Harvey—in after years, Sir John Harvey, K.C.B., a general officer, and governor of Nova Scotia. He was at this time Adjutant-General to the forces in the field on the Niagara frontier. He had conducted the retreat of the troops from Fort George with marked skill and energy, and had aided his chief in taking up his present strong position. The force, however, was weak in one important particular. The ammunition was reduced to about 90 rounds per man, without resource or means of supply.

On the 5th June the American army, in pursuit, amounting to 2500 men, including 250 cavalry and eight guns, under command of generals Chandler and Winder, had reached Forty Mile Creek, one of the numerous streamlets which descend from the plateau of Niagara into Lake Ontario, and which, in popular parlance, indicate rather than define the distances between Niagara and Hamilton. The British advanced posts at Stoney Creek fell back before them, and the enemy occupied for the night ground well known to the late defenders. Vincent despatched Harvey with a small force to reconnoitre their position and strength. There is a tradition in the neighbourhood that Harvey himself, having borrowed the garb and the waggon of a Quaker, penetrated into the American lines, selling potatoes and "taking notes." Those who can recall the commanding stature and bearing of the gallant officer, maintain that this was the very last disguise in which he was likely to succeed. It is not impossible that some patriotic "friend" really found a good market for his produce, and valuable information for Harvey, who rapidly matured his plans, and laid them before the general, who approved of them at once, and promptly resolved on a night attack.

The force detailed for this, one of the most trying operations in warfare, consisted of five companies of the 8th, and the whole of the 40th regiment—numbering 754 firelocks—under the personal direction of the General, but led by Harvey, whose arrangements and conduct were admirable. The Americans slept in fancied security on the banks of Stoney Creek; the guns were posted on high ground on the left flank and centre. The generals occupied a farm house on their left flank, known as the farm house of old Jemmy Gap. Further to the left still, the ground rose higher gradually, until, at the distance of about a quarter of a mile, it struck the precipitous hill-side of the plateau, which borders the whole road from Queenston to Hamilton. It was near midnight when the British array reached the American watch-fires. "Sir," whispered a young Canadian cadet of the 49th (now Judge Jarvis, of Cornwall), "we are upon them."* "Hush!" replied Harvey, and, with a sign, sent forward a sergeant and a file of men. The first sentry, a careless watcher—perhaps sleeping—was despatched. A second found the same fate. The third fired; and with his shot came a shout and a rush, and the British stood among the American camp-fires. Some bayonetting took place, as the sleepers awoke, stumbling; but the surprised men were not dismayed. They rallied rapidly and well, and opened a destructive fire. Their guns, too, were unlimbered and manned. As was the practice in those days, on such a venture, the flints had been removed from the firelocks; and at this moment, standing out in strong relief, with the camp-fires around and behind them, the men were ordered to replace flints. One who was there declares this to have been the most trying moment of his life. The process is a slow one, and many a fine fellow fell without replacing his flint at all. But the pluck and steadiness of the men defied the trial. By degrees they were able to return the fire, to advance,

---

*Narrative of a "49th Man," given by Auchinleck, p. 175.

and answer the flashes of the enemy's musketry. In the meantime Harvey had despatched two companies to his right. Stealthily they crept along the slope at the foot of the plateau, among the beech woods, enveloped the farm house, and came down, with cheers, on the enemy's left. Surprised and staggered, the Americans still behaved bravely. Forming in small detached bodies, apparently without concert or command, they fought on, until forced by the bayonet to disperse. Generals Winder and Chandler were taken in their quarters. They had made themselves comfortable for the night. With the two generals, the British captured three guns, one howitzer, and three tumbrils, and about 100 officers and men.* The contest, though short, had been very sanguinary. The American loss in slain was large; but the withdrawal of the British made it difficult to ascertain numbers. That of the British, in killed and wounded, amounted to 160 men. Curiously enough, General Vincent himself was lost, in the bush, during the night, and was only picked up by a sort of military "hue and cry," in the morning. The American generals were lost irretrievably. Their army came back in the morning to recover them; but, finding that their antagonists had decamped with the "spolia opima," concluded to decamp too, and never drew rein, nor breath, until they found themselves safe within the works of Fort George.

The scene of their exploits was, in the year 1813, but little removed from forest and farm land, in the first stages of cultivation. It is now a garden. It is pleasant on an early spring morning, to saunter over the field of this midnight conflict, inhaling the incense of the apple orchards and peach blossoms, listening to the last cry of the whip-poor-will, retiring to its day dreams, and pausing to note each spot of interest, which the rustic *cicerone* may point out to stranger's eye. There, is still seen the old German or Lutheran place of worship, brown with age, and deserted now,

---

* Vincent's Despatch, June, 1813.

bearing on its wind-worn timbers, the bullet holes of the contest; and in an angle of the primitive fence, hard by, may be discovered, amid tall weeds and overhanging ottacas, a pile of stones, a hasty, huddled cairn,—all that exists to mark the spot where rest the remains of the brave men who perished in that midnight fray. There they lie, heaped together, friend and foe,

—in one red burial blent.

Surely this is a reproach to the land! Can neither men nor means be found to erect a simple monument to memories which belong to "*les braves de toutes les nations*,"* before the frail land-marks of the spot itself have passed away for ever? Can not the great omission be amended yet? Twenty dollars,—to reduce the proposition to its most practical bearing,—would suffice to supply a simple stone, in the style of the memorial placed to indicate where Brock fell. The date, and a brief recommendation to the pious care of the people of the surrounding country, would secure its maintenance and protection. Such a stone should mark every battle field in Canada; and all might bear the same truthful and noble motto:

Siste viator, herœm calcas.

On the withdrawal of the British troops the battle field at Stoney Creek was, as before said, for a short space, re-occupied by the Americans under Colonel Burns, a cavalry officer, upon whom the command had devolved. He merely remained long enough to destroy the tents which had been left standing, and to burn a quantity of stores. He then rapidly retired to the protection of the

---

* In a quiet corner of the churchyard at Gemappes, in the shade of a moss-grown buttress, is the simple tomb of General Duhesme, slain in the village, at the door of the " Three Kings," by a Black Brunswick trooper, on the evening of Waterloo. His widow and orphans record that they have erected this monument to the memory of a brave soldier and a good man, and leave it to the safeguard "*des braves de toutes les nations*." The hand would wither which could desecrate that stone.

lines of Fort George, though in executing this manœuvre he was intercepted, and suffered much. On their advance the Americans had been accompanied, along the lake shore, by a flotilla of boats, and batteaux. Burns fell back upon this support, and embarked his wounded, and such of his men as had not yet got under cover, and was slowly creeping down the coast to the place from whence he came,—when, on the 8th June, Sir James Yeo, who, by this time had become master of his own movements and had got out of Kingston, appeared in the offing; intelligence from the shore had apprized him of the state of things, and of the position of the enemy; and Richardson* dwells with sailorly impatience on the perversity of a calm which anchored every vessel of the squadron,

> As idle as a painted ship,
> Upon a painted ocean.

At length a breeze sprung up, and the squadron closed in with the shore, cutting off the twelve rearmost boats of the American flotilla, laden with valuable supplies and stores. Perceiving an encampment in the woods on the beach, the Commodore disembarked in the ships' boats two companies of regulars under Major Evans of the 8th Regiment. This active officer landed, and in the evening having been reinforced by two companies from Burlington Heights, under Colonel Bishopp, the second deserted American encampment was entered. It was in a state of conflagration at the time, but the captors saved from the flames 500 tents, 140 barrels of flour, 100 stand of arms, ammunition and other articles of a very acceptable character. Thus did this very gallant exploit of Harvey free the whole Peninsula from the invader, and threw them back upon the mere edge of the frontier, with a deep and dangerous river in their rear, between them and their supports and supplies.

---

* Mem. of Dr. James Richardson, D.D.

CHAPTER XIV.

New American Enterprise. Attempt on the Beaver Dam Post. Noble devotion of Mrs. Secord. Her Adventures—Reaches Decau's house in safety. Fitzgibbon. Bœrstler's Advance—Attacked by the Indians—Reaches Thorold. Present aspect of Thorold. Welland Canal. Hamilton Merritt. Col. John Clarke. Old Isaac Kelly—Militia attack on Bœrstler—He surrenders to Fitzgibbon. Mary Secord the real Heroine. Princely generosity of the Prince of Wales. Lieut. Fitzgibbon—His career—A Military Knight of Windsor. History of the Knights. A Reverie.

Nor was this all. One bold and successful feat of arms infused *morale*, and inspired another. On the retreat of the American force, Vincent had been followed up, and established his outposts at his old position, the Beaver Dam. Decau's house was occupied as a depot for stores. It was guarded by a small detachment of the 49th, about 30 men, under Lieut. Fitzgibbon. Fitzgibbon was one of the paladins of the war, a man of nerve and enterprise, of much vigour of character and great personal strength. An incident characteristic of the man had occurred on the spot. On taking up his ground at the Beaver Dam, he had driven out the American pickets. Attempting to intercept them he encountered alone at the back door of Decau's house two of the enemy, each armed with a musket and bayonet. Both charged upon him. Fitzgibbon grasped the musket of the more advanced man, and by main strength threw him upon his fellow, whose musket he also grappled with the other hand, and although both struggled desperately, he as resolutely held on, until his men came to his aid, and his antagonists surrendered.

Such was the man to whom on the night of the 23rd June there

came a warning inspired by woman's wit, and conveyed with more
than female energy. The commandant of Niagara, chagrined by
reverses, and anxious to reassure his own people, resolved to beat
up the British quarters, to attack Decau's house, and destroy the
depot of stores. The surprise of this outpost would have led to
further surprises; and to an officer, inspired with half the enterprise of Harvey, would have opened the way to Burlington Heights.
The outpost was within striking distance, and exposed. The
adventure was promising. He ordered, therefore, Lieut.-Colonel
Bœrstler of the United States Army to prepare for this service,
rapidly and secretly. He was in command of the 14th United
States Infantry, one 12 and one 6-pounder field guns, with ammunition waggons, &c.—a few cavalry and volunteers—amounting
altogether to 673 men.

In despite of all precautions, rumours of the intended expedition
eked out, and reached the ear of James Secord, a British militia
soldier, who resided at Queenston, then within the American lines.
He had been badly wounded the preceding autumn at Queenston
Heights, and was a cripple. He hobbled home to his wife with
the news. The pair were in consternation; they were loyal Canadians—their hearts were in the cause. If the design succeeded; if
Fitzgibbon was surprised; de Haren in the rear would follow.
Burlington Heights might be carried, and their country would be lost.
Mrs. Mary Secord, the wife, at the age of 88, still lives in the village
of Chippewa, to tell the story, and wakes up into young life as
she does so. What was to be done. Fitzgibbon must be warned.
The husband in his crippled state could not move, and moreover no
man could pass the line of American sentries. She spoke out, she
would go herself, would he let her? she could get past the sentries;
she knew the way to St. David's, and there she could get guidance.
She would go, and put her trust in God. He consented. At three
in the morning she was up, got ready the children's breakfast, and

taking a cracker and cup of coffee, started after day break. To have left earlier would have aroused suspicion. Her first difficulty was the American advanced sentry. He was hard to deal with, but she pointed to her own farm buildings a little in advance of his post, insisted that she was going for milk; told him he could watch her, and was allowed to pass on. She did milk a cow, which was very *contrary*, and would persist in moving onwards to the edge of the opposite bushes, into which both she and the cow disappeared. Once out of sight, she pushed on rapidly. She knew the way for miles, but fear rose within her, in despite of herself, and what " scared " her most was the distant cry of the wolf,—they were abundant in those days; and twice she encountered a rattlesnake,—they are not unfrequent even now. She did not care much for them, as she knew they would run from a stick or a stone, and they did not wait for any such exorcism. At length she reached a brook. It was very hot, and the water refreshed her, but she had some difficulty in crossing. At last she found a log, and shortly after got to the mill. The miller's wife was an old friend, and tried to dissuade her from going on. Spoke of the danger, spoke of her children; the last was a sore trial, for she was weary and thoughtful, but the thing had to be done, so she was resolute, and having rested and refreshed, proceeded on. Her next trouble was the British outlying sentry, but she soon re-assured him and he sent her on, with a kind word, warning her to beware of the Indians. This " scared " her again, but she was scared still more, when the cracking of the dead branches under her footsteps roused from their cover a party of red skins. The chief, who first sprang to his feet, confronted her, and demanded, " Woman! what you want?" the others yelled " awful." The chief silenced them with his hand. She told him, at once, that she wanted to see Fitzgibbon, and why. " Ah," said the Indian, " me go with you," and with a few words to his people, who remained, he accompanied her to Fitzgibbon's quarters, which she reached about nine on the evening of the 23rd. A few words sufficed to satisfy him. He sent off, forthwith, to his Major de Haren, in the rear and made his own preparations. She found friends in a farm house near, for in those days every body knew every body. She slept "right off," for she had journeyed on foot twenty miles, and safely, God be praised.

In the meantime the American expedition had silently assembled at Fort George, and within a few hours rapidly followed on her footsteps. At twelve of a fine night in June, they had taken up their line of march on St. David's, and at daybreak came upon Kerr and his Indians, already on their guard, and keenly expectant. They numbered about thirty warriors, Mohawks, chiefly of the Grand River; but Kerr saw, at a glance, the insufficiency of his force to resist, and had recourse to Indian tactics, to retard and harass the enemy and to spread alarm to remote posts. He threw himself therefore, at once, on the rear and flank of the Americans, and opened a desultory fire.

The Americans, throwing out sharpshooters in reply, still pressed forwards, but the Indians were neither to be repulsed nor shaken off. The track through the forest was narrow and broken. The guns and store waggons defiled slowly to the front. The yells and the rifles of the savages rang in the rear. A horror of the war-whoop hung then on the national conscience, and sensational stories, for the most part, had the usual effect of such stimulants on nerve and brain.

Bœrstler and his men had emerged from the forest into an open space, a clearing close by the present village of Thorold. Their guns, waggons, and other encumbrances, had reached a hollow in the road, overhung by a bank clad with beeches. This hollow forms now a basin of the Welland Canal. The spot, which then rang with the outcries of the combatants, now resounds with the hum of industry, and the working chaunt of the sailor.

From this point of view, at the present day, to the right and left, may be seen for miles—at the same season of the year—an uninterrupted line of lake craft—ships and brigs, brigantines and schooners, steamers and propellers—bearing testimony to the genius and perseverance of another of the men of 1812, who within the last few months has gone to his rest. Hamilton Merritt, U. E. L., commanded in his youth a corps of cavalry, distinguished in every fray on the Niagara frontier. In mature years he designed the Welland Canal, which unites Lake Erie with Lake Ontario. By dint of resolution he surmounted the prejudices and the difficulties which surrounded the undertaking; died at a good old age, full of such honour as Canada can confer; and will live in the gratitude of future generations.

Si monumentum requiris, circumspice!

It is a curious commentary on the proverbial versatility of the popular breeze, that the promoters and advocates of the Welland Canal were punished by their constituents for the part they took in advancing this great design, and at the next election lost their seats in parliament. Colonel John Clarke, of St. Catherines, one of those to whom this record owes much, relates with pride that he was honoured by this penalty. A few years—the progress of the enterprise, and the surprising increase of prosperity to which it gave rise, brought about the usual reaction, and the distinguished member was restored to his seat by triumphant acclamation.*

In the hollow, below the beech ridge, where the war-whoop of the Indian has now given place to the shriek of the steam-whistle,

---

* Colonel John Clarke was one of the early pioneers of the Niagara District. He died in 1862 at St. Catherines, C. W., at an advanced age. His surviving daughter is the wife of William McGiverin, Esq., M.P.P.

Bœrstler found a fresh foe. From the wood above, on the hill-side, came the ring of the militia musket; and the echoes of the forest multiplied the reports and the fears they created.

Old Isaac Kelly, born and *raised* on 48 Thorold, a septuagenarian, hale and hearty, who still lives not a mile from the spot, tells how, when he was a boy of 18, and was in the act of "hitching up" his horses for the plough, he heard the firing in the wood, and the outcries of the Indians; how he ran to his two brothers, both a-field; how the three got their muskets—they were all militiamen—home, to put in a crop; how, led by the sounds, they crossed the country to the beech grove, meeting eight or ten more by the way, suddenly roused, like themselves; how, from behind the trees, they opened fire on the American train, and on the guns, which were then unlimbering, to the rear; and how the Americans, more worried and bothered than hurt, changed their position, and took up ground in David Millar's apple orchard.

In the meantime, Fitzgibbon had taken rapid measures. Major de Haren, of his regiment, was at some distance in the rear, with three companies, cantoned near where St. Catherines now stands. An estafette, borne by James Cummings of Chippewa, one of the still surviving veterans of that day, had put this force in motion. Fitzgibbon himself was under arms, and on the way, attracted by the firing.

Suddenly he came upon the head of the enemy's column, and found all confusion. The men were scared out of their senses. The officer in command had lost his head. Fitzgibbon made the most imposing display possible of his 30 men; and advanced at once with a white handkerchief. He found Bœrstler ready for a parley. Fitzgibbon stated who he was—his rank; that he commanded a detachment of British troops; that his commanding officer, de Haren, with a large reinforcement, was close by; and by a judicious disposition of his men, and some passing allusion to his scarecrow Indians — like Robinson Crusoe, when he out-manœuvred the mutineers—he magnified his numbers in the imagination of his foe.

Bœrstler was in a "fix." The Indians yelled horridly; the militia-men fired without compunction; the red coats in front barred the way; a large reinforcement was in their rear—he was, in fact, surrounded and like wild beasts driven into an African corral; he and his men were bewildered by sounds and sights of fear. He took but short time to deliberate. He surrendered at once—himself and his whole force.

The surrender was embarrassing. Fitzgibbon was, in fact, nearly caught by his own captives. He did not dare show his weakness. He knew not the number of the Indians; but he did know that the militia force was scant indeed. "Why, sir," says Isaac Kelly, "when he gave in, we did not know what to do with him: it was like catching the elephant."

Fitzgibbon had presence of mind equal to the emergency. The American officers were called together, and a capitulation framed and penned. In the meantime de Haren hastened on, and scarcely was the capitulation signed, when he came up with 200 bayonets at his back.

The American force, which surrendered, consisted of 542 men, two field guns and ammunition waggons, and the colours of the 14th United States regiment.

The heroine of this achievement, under Providence, was Mary Secord, whose name is inseparable from the story.* When the

---

* "I do hereby certify that Mrs. Secord, the wife of James Secord of Chippewa, Esquire, did, in the month of June, 1813, walk from her house in the village of St. David's to Decau's house, in Thorold, by a circuitous route of about 20 miles, partly through the woods, to acquaint me that the enemy intended to attempt, by surprise, to capture a detachment of the 49th Regt., then under my command, she having obtained such knowledge from good

Prince of Wales was at Niagara, he saw the old lady, and from her own lips heard the tale ; and learning, subsequently, that her fortune did not equal her fame, he sent her, most delicately and most gracefully, the sum of one hundred guineas. God bless him for *that*, is the aspiration of every honest Canadian heart. He is his mother's own son.

The chief actor, on this 24th day of June, 1813, Colonel James Fitzgibbon, still lives at the advanced age of eighty-three; and demands some further notice.

He was the son of a farmer—had the advantage of a little early education, and acquired a fondness for reading. His passion for arms was irresistible. At seventeen years of age he enlisted ; and the same day, 25th Oct. 1798, was made a sergeant. At the age of twenty-one he was appointed Sergeant-Major.* He served in Ireland, and before Copenhagen, where the 49th acted as marines. He was appointed to an ensigncy and adjutantcy, and came to Canada. In 1809 he succeeded to a lieutenancy ; and resigned the adjutancy to command a small detachment in the field. His exploits at the Beaver Dam gave him his company. He thus rose by dint of meritorious service, at a time when commissions and

---

authority, as the event proved. Mrs. Secord was a person of slight and delicate frame, and made the effort in weather excessively warm ; and I dreaded, at the time, that she must suffer in health in consequence of fatigue and anxiety, she having been exposed to danger from the enemy, through whose line of communication she had to pass. The attempt was made on my detachment by the enemy ; and his detachment, consisting of upwards of 500 men, and a field-piece, and 50 dragoons, were captured in consequence. I write this certificate in a moment of much hurry and from memory, and it is therefore thus brief.

(Signed,)   JAMES FITZGIBBON,
Formerly Lieut. 49th Regt."

Given by Auchinleck, p. 175, but Mrs. Secord possesses the original, Dec. 1863.

* Morgan's Celebrated Canadians, p. 193.

promotion were not so freely given to deserving men as they are now. He was noted for his soldierly aspect, for shrewd wit, and for pluck which would take no denial. On this, and on all other occasions, during the war, Fitzgibbon made his mark. He was once authorized to raise an independent company — a corps of *enfans perdus*—fighting being looked upon as his especial privilege. It was to be composed from the line regulars. *All* volunteered; and the *embarras du choix* was the difficulty of the organization.*

At the close of the war he settled in Canada; and filled many offices of honour and emolument, under the government. His last appointment was that of Clerk to the Legislative Council. He retired on a pension, and returned to his native land, where, in just appreciation of his services, he was made a Military Knight of Windsor. The career of Fitzgibbon is the counterpart of numberless others in Canada. Soldiers, from the ranks, stud and embellish, and enrich the soil; their sons are the most honoured in the land; the exertions of the fathers have become the inheritance of the children; and their success is an example of what the honest, earnest British soldier, true to himself and his Queen, may achieve, and add, thereby, to the long list of useful citizens and good men who have " risen from the ranks " of their incomparable service.†

It may be pleasing to his surviving contemporaries—it may be profitable to Canadians generally—to know something of the haven the old soldier came to. It is natural that men in these remote regions should be curious about the " Military Knights of Windsor." The enquiry is often made. This institution is as old

---

* A " Green 'Un " (presumed to be Judge Jarvis), given by Auchinlech, p. 178.

† Since the above was written, our old friend has gone to his rest. An English paper briefly announces "on the 12th Dec. 1863, at his residence in the Lower Ward, Windsor Castle, at the advanced age of 83 years, Colonel James Fitzgibbon."

as that of the Knights of the Garter—indeed it is one year older—for it was founded by King Edward the Third, in the twenty-second year of his reign. The Order of the Garter was created in the next year, A.D. 1349; and was inaugurated on St. George's day, 23rd April, at Windsor Castle, as declared by the Black Book, or Statutes of the Order, "for the reward of virtue and the improvement of military valour."* The same chivalrous spirit inspired the inferior order of the Military Knights. In the days when a complete lance consisted of the panoplied knight and his five men-at-arms; in the days of *esquires* and *bas chevaliers*, (now dumped into "bachelor,") endowments were made by monarchs and mighty men for the support of retainers, whose age; whose services, and whose wounds demanded that provision which their own means could not supply. Such are British institutions. "*Date obolum Belisario*," was the doctrine of the mongrel descendants of republican Rome. The Order of the Military Knights of Windsor was instituted in 1348, by our Edward the Third, for the support of twenty-four worn soldiers, "who had distinguished themselves in the wars, and had afterwards been reduced to straits." On death, or vacancy, the appointments are supplied by the crown. The mailed warrior has been succeeded by the veteran of modern days. In unchangeable England, the change is only one of costume. Each member enjoys a small annual stipend, and the advantage of a residence in the Towers of the Lower Ward, and in the connecting curtains, which, in modern parlance, might be called casemates. These residences are peculiarly suited to old soldiers with small means. The only service required, is the attendance of a certain number daily, at the religious offices in St. George's Chapel, where they occupy stalls at the feet of the Knights of the Garter, wearing long, dark blue cloaks, with a scarlet collar, and a Maltese

---

* Windsor and Eton, by Edw. Jesse, 1841, p. 44.

cross, of like colour, on the left shoulder. Here, amid the sights and sounds of modern warfare (for the Guards of the Sovereign parade daily before their windows); surrounded by all the associations of feudal grandeur, with the corbeills and machicolations of the Norman Conqueror above them; under shadow of that massive keep—the old Round Tower—from whence floats daily the royal standard of England; with the quaint carvings and florid tracery of St. George's Chapel before their eyes, exists still a noble institution of olden days, well worthy of the imitation of younger countries, more abundant in resources applicable to such endowments.

And lo, at the moment, as if before the wand of an enchanter, rises, by slow degrees, struggling with the mists of memory, a vision of the past. Forty years and more a-gone, when life was young and fresh as morn,

———the dewy morn,
With breath all incense and with cheek all bloom,

we can well recall now the figure of an aged man, who daily led by one who loved him well, took his seat in a sunny nook of the wall, hard by the Winchester Tower, on that noble terrace which commands the finest view in all England. Alas! to him, the winding river, and the Brocas clump, and the spire of Clewer; or nearer still, the busy town, and the bridge, and the angler on the end of the "Cobler," tussling with some reluctant barbel; or the shadowy Slopes below him, or the antlered deer beyond; or further still,

Those distant spires, those antique towers,
Which crown the watery glade,

Eton in all its monastic pride—was but as a sealed book, a picture turned to the wall. For, at the storming of Fort Erie, some wild Indian fortress, away in the back woods of Canada, years before, he had lost his precious sight, blasted by an exploding magazine,—

here, in the glad sunshine, day after day, did the old soldier love to sit and tell of savage sights, and scenes of fiery fight " 'mid antres vast and deserts idle," while we boys—we were two then—listened with gaping delight to the fine veteran, who " raising his sightless balls to heaven," poured forth the gratitude of his heart to his God and to his king, gathering from the fulness of that gratitude, light and gladness, when all else was dark around him.

> Ah! happy hills! ah! pleasing shades!
> Ah! fields beloved in vain!
> Where once my careless childhood strayed,
> A stranger yet to pain.
>
> * * * * *
>
> Some bold adventurers disdain
> The limits of their little reign,
> And unknown regions dare descry.
> Still, as they run they look behind;
> They bear a voice in every wind.

Vale.

CHAPTER XV.

General de Rottenburg succeeds General Vincent—Dearborn retires—Boyd in command at Fort George—American Frontier exposed to attack—Colonels Bishopp and Clark—Clark's career—Hazardous and successful foray on Fort Schlosser—Bishopp, emulous of gallant deeds, attacks Black Rock—Black Rock, now and then—Bishopp lands—Defeats the enemy—Captures the place—General Porter rallies the Americans—The British attacked in turn—Bishopp wounded to death—His worthy career in Europe and Canada—Influence over the Volunteers—The Americans enlist the Indians—Lake Ontario—Commodore Chauncey attacks Burlington Heights—Fails—Again sacks York. Sir James Yeo provokes the Commodore out of Niagara—Two American schooners foundered—Two taken—More expected from Yeo very inconsiderately—Yeo did his duty thoughtfully and well—From Ontario to Lake Champlain—Escapade at Gore Creek on the St. Lawrence—Death of Capt. Milne—Supplies how furnished—How transported in winter and summer—Value of the Commissariat—Sir William Robinson—Commissaries in Canada—Isaac Winslow Clarke—His career—Bateaux Brigades.

Shortly after the affair of the Beaver Dam, and early in July, Major General de Rottenburg succeeded Major General Sheaffe as Lieut.-Governor of the Upper Province; and as such took the command of the troops from the hands of Major General Vincent. About the same time General Dearborn, harassed in mind and body, withdrew from the command of the American army; and the defence of Fort George and Fort Niagara, and of so much Canadian ground as the American soldier stood on, devolved on General Boyd.*

An American army of 4000 men was in fact cooped up within the lines of Fort George, on the British side of the river, constantly on the *qui vive*, a mass of dissatisfied, harassed men, difficult and

---

* James, Vol. I, p. 219.

costly to feed and supply, and cut off from their own shores by the River Niagara. As has been before said, they held but a selvage of the coast, and were unsafe beyond their advanced sentries; the upper portion of the frontier, on the river, was occupied by the British, and the impolitic concentration of troops below, denuded the coast above, and invited incursion. From the Falls of Niagara up to the village of Buffalo, the, then, line of defence was open to attack by small parties, who could select their point of landing, and who were handled by enterprising officers. Chance had thrown together on the frontier two such men, congenial spirits, Lieut.-Colonel Bishopp, of the British Army, and Lieut.-Colonel Thomas Clark, of the 2nd Lincoln militia. Clark, a Scotchman by birth, was an Indian trader, and forwarder of goods to the western hunting grounds, a member of the firm of Street & Clark. The Indian trader is a soldier half made. The conductor of a brigade of boats into the Indian territory must be able to command men. In lawless and remote regions that command is only yielded to personal character. Like the baron of feudal days, the leader to be obeyed, must possess strength, must display prowess, must show that he has nerve as well as brain; and yet the highest qualities of brain are taxed to counteract rival traders, and defeat the deadly wiles of the capricious savage. Promptitude, watchfulness, patience, of cold, fatigue and hunger, foresight and forethought — qualities essential to the success of an Indian trader—constitute an amalgam which moulds the soldier. From the first outbreak of the war, Clark was foremost in frontier fray. He had acquired the confidence of his men, and obtained the cordial co-operation of those who, like Bishopp, understood volunteers, and could appreciate the merit of the extemporaneous soldier. On the night of the 4th July, while the Americans were celebrating the anniversary of their independence, Clark, who had noted their weakness or their improvidence, collected about 40 of his militia, and crossed the river from

Chippewa to Fort Schlosser, celebrated in after years as the scene of the capture of the Caroline steamer. To the fate which befel her, these brave men were exposed, for an accident, an unlucky shot, or a disabled oar, might have doomed boat and crew to the boiling rapids and the unsparing cataract. They landed, however, unobserved, surprised the work, called a fort, and captured the guard there stationed. They secured several stand of arms, a quantity of ammunition, one brass 6-pounder, and a large store of provisions, and with this booty and fifteen prisoners returned in safety to the Canadian side. James Cummings, of Chippewa, also engaged in the Indian trade at that time, accompanied the expedition. It is pleasant to receive from the lips of one who took part in these occurrences, and who at 73 enjoys all the vigour of middle age, a relation of the exciting incidents, and hair-breadth escapes, over which horror and wild glee cast a strange and ghastly glamour, when men laughed and cried in the same breath, and forgot in the passing struggle with boiling eddy or desperate foe, both the past and the future. It is necessary to hear these recitals before we can realize, or indeed understand, the imminence and extent of these dangers, or the indifference with which, when past, they were regarded. But Bishopp fired up when he heard of the exploit. "Hang the fellow, he has got before me. By Jove, it was well done—we'll try it again;" and he did try it again.

At 2 a.m., on the morning of the 11th July, accompanied by Clark, and by Cummings the narrator, and backed by about 240 men, 200 regulars and 40 of the 2nd and 3rd Lincoln, Bishopp swooped down upon Black Rock, the American naval depot on the River Niagara.

Black Rock is now a large manufacturing village about three miles below Buffalo, at the embouchure of the Erie Canal. The furnace and the forge and the fitful flashes, and the roar of uninterrupted industry, have succeeded to monotonous earthworks, to the shout of battle and the red artillery. The great breakwater, which now divides the still canal from the seething river, did not then exist. The river was wider, the shore more open than it is now, and the silence of the summer night was scarcely broken by the muffled oar. The party had embarked a little below the present village of Waterloo, and, overshooting their mark, reached the shore below Black Rock. Bishopp landed at once, almost without a sound, and dashed into the encampment of the American Major, Adams, dispersed about 300 militia, and captured three heavy guns. These were turned instantly on the Block-house, which, with its garrison of regular artillerymen, gave in incontinently. General Porter, who commanded on the frontier, lived hard by. He escaped out of a window, took to horse, and rode to Buffalo. Bishopp and his friends repaired to his house, courteously asked for breakfast, and were hospitably entertained. In the mean time the work of destruction went on. The Blockhouse, and the barracks, and the naval arsenal, and a fine schooner, were destroyed by fire. All the public stores which could be removed, were transferred to the boats, and some conveyed across the river; but private property was scrupulously respected. The *Buffalo Gazette* of July 13, says " while the main body was thus employed in disposing of the public property, a party entered the houses in the village, but we have not ascertained that they committed any outrages on private property."*.

While the British were thus employed, General Porter had made the best use of his time. He had roused the people of Buffalo, and brought down strong reinforcements of regulars, militia and Indians. Time had crept on, and Cummings, who knew the people best, and felt much as if on a hornet's nest, remonstrated with Bishopp, but the gay and gallant fellow laughed, and "poked fun at him." He had come to destroy those stores and guns, and

---

* James, Vol. I, page 229.

meant to do it. Now, anchors and chain cables, and heavy iron guns, were not toys to be lightly handled nor easily destroyed. The most that could be done was, to sink them in the Niagara, from whence they could be fished up with no great trouble. At length the work was completed, the men re-embarked unmolested, and Bishopp was the last to retire. Scarcely had they left the bank when the Indians, who, snake-like, had crawled to the top, commenced to fire. Part of the men were disembarked, and drove the enemy back into the woods and upon their supports, while they in turn, uniting, forced the small detachment back to their boats. Bishopp was everywhere, commanding, directing, getting his men off. In the confusion of the moment, some of the oars of his own boat were lost, and she drifted, helplessly, down the stream, exposed to an increasing fire. "Here the gallant Bishopp, the darling of the army, received his death wound. Never was any officer, save always the lamented Brock, regretted more than he was."* He was borne back to his quarters, where in a few days, he expired at the early age of 27. His remains lie beneath a modest monument erected to his memory by the pious care of his sisters, the Baroness de la Zouche and Mrs. Pechell, in the churchyard at Lundy's Lane.

Colonel Cecil Bishopp was a son of Sir Cecil Bishopp, Bart., afterward Lord de la Zouche. He was an accomplished gentleman. He had served in the Guards. Had represented Newport in the Isle of Wight in Parliament. Had been attached to a Russian embassy. Had served with distinction in Flanders, in Spain and in Portugal, and died full of hope and promise in Canada, gallantly "doing his duty" and not without avail, for his example lives.

Bishopp had been appointed Inspecting Field officer of militia on the Niagara frontier. He won all hearts. He was possessed

---

* Letter of a "Green 'Un" (Judge Jarvis, Cornwall), given by Auchinleck, p. 178.

of that indescribable fascination of manner and character which, apparently without an effort, acts like a charm. It was a gift. His influence over the militia was supreme. He knew that he was not dealing with raw recruits, with mere children, who have to be taught and treated like children, but with men, for the most part of a certain age, reasoning and reasonable men, who are willing, nay eager, to learn anything conducive to the defence of all they hold dear, and who accept the restraints of discipline as indispensable to that end. With an instant and intuitive perception of what was due to himself and to them,—without departing from his own dignity, he won their affection, commanded their respect and "could do with them just as he pleased." Those who can remember the present Sir George Wetherall, when in command of the volunteers in Montreal, some twenty-five years ago, will recall a reproduction of the same character. With such an officer at their head, the militia of Canada, on their own soil, are equal to any troops this continent can produce, and are content that they should take the odds of their great name and estimation, and will try fortune with them. The following epitaph is inscribed on a tablet erected to the memory of Colonel Bishopp, at the family burial place, Parham, Sussex, and ascribed to Sir James Macdonald:

> His pillow—not of sturdy oak;
> His shroud—a soldier's simple cloak;
> His dirge—will sound till time's no more—
> Niagara's loud and solemn roar.
> There Cecil lies—say, where the grave
> More worthy of a Briton brave.*

These incursions on the part of the British had, as we have just

---

* The incidents in the early career of Colonel Bishopp, and the epitaph, have been borrowed from Morgan's Canadian Celebrities, p. 225. For the residue, I am indebted to those who knew him, and who still live near where he died.

observed, led the Americans to have recourse to the assistance of the Indian tribes who still adhered to the American soil. They were called " The Six Nations," but consisted chiefly of Mohawks, from the Mohawk Valley, in the state of New York, and a few relics of other nations, whose names may possess interest, but afforded no strength. This Indian alliance has given rise to much useless comment. By enlisting savage mercenaries in their service, and by denouncing the British for doing the same thing, the American government became liable to the charge of great inconsistency; but, as we hold that the child of the soil, whether savage or civilized, is justified in resisting an invader, we have certainly no right to complain that the Americans should have defended their country with the same weapons we ourselves employed. The savage, as an instrument of warfare, is not more repugnant to humanity than is war itself in any shape,—not more repulsive than mines and torpedoes, and the thousand hideous forms which war assumes at the hands of refined man. The savage may be inspired, may be taught, may be bribed, to pity and to spare. Bomb-shells and spherical case discriminate less, spare less, and are less placable. If, as is stated in the *Buffalo Gazette*, of the 13th July, 1813—" Our savage friends expressed a desire to scalp the dead, but were prevented,"—we may admire the precaution which restrained an instinctive propensity; but British writers certainly cannot exclaim, if the savage, assailed in his lair, should defend himself in a savage manner. But, without scolding at others, let us transpose the position; let us show what we did to humanize and mitigate the horrors of the war. It has been already shown that the employment of the Indians on the western frontier, was justified by necessity. The savage could not be neutral: his services were sought by the Americans, and secured by the British, simply because the hatred, engendered by years of wrong, was not to be appeased by bribes or cajolery. It will be seen hereafter, how earnestly and how effectually the British commanders, Brock, Proctor, and St. George, labored to neutralize the rancorous animosity of the Indian, and to divest of its venom the weapons which, in self-defence, they were compelled to use. On the Niagara frontier similar expedients had been employed. Early in 1813, a committee of officers, headed by General Vincent, had resolved to pay ten dollars for every prisoner brought in alive by his Indian captor. The Prince Regent subsequently approved and confirmed the proceeding. A Boston paper of the time noticed the resolution, in defiance of the " *anathema maranatha* " of the democratic press; but from among the number saved, not one voice appears to have been raised in generous recognition, or in reply to the Thersites of the time, whose tongues, wherever England or Canada were concerned, " coined slanders like a mint."

We will now, for a brief space, return to Lake Ontario, on our way down to the province of Lower Canada, and to the scene of war on Lake Champlain. On the 26th July, Commodore Chauncey again appeared on Lake Ontario, in the new ship General Pyke, which so narrowly escaped destruction by Provost's retreat from Sackett's Harbour. With a fleet consisting of 14 vessels, mounting altogether 114 guns, and manned by 1,193 seamen, and having on board 300 regular troops, under Colonel Scott, he made an attempt on the position of Burlington Heights, which was defended by Major Maule, and 150 rank and file. The troops were disembarked and embarked again. It was understood that the demonstration on Burlington Heights had attracted thither the Glengarries, which defended York; and

Ut canis à corio nunquam absterrebitur uncto,

the Commodore and the Colonel determined to revisit the helpless scene of their former exploits. On the 31st July, they disembarked, without opposition, at the point termed the " Garrison;" took quiet possession of the town; broke open the gaol, liberated the prisoners; and took out of the stores of the inhabitants (called "public stores" in the despatch), several hundred barrels of flour and provisions. They destroyed barracks and other buildings, eleven boats—magnified into transports; and having heaped mischief on misery, returned to their safe harbor at the mouth of the Niagara River.*

While Chauncey was thus marauding at the western extremity of the lake, Sir James Yeo, after having destroyed the American camp at Forty-mile Creek, on the 13th June crossed the lake, captured two schooners and boats with supplies; then secured a depot of provisions on the Genessee River. On the 19th he captured more stores and more provisions at a place called Great Sodus; and on the 29th June returned to Kingston. On the 31st July, Sir James sailed from Kingston with supplies for the army; and having landed them at Burlington Heights, steered for Niagara, and "looked in"—in nautical phraseology—as a challenge to Chauncey, who was not slow in accepting it. The British squadron consisted of six vessels of war; the American amounted to fourteen. A great deal of manœuvring took place on both sides—" bearing down" and "bearing up," "getting to windward" and "falling to leeward," on the "larboard tack" and on the "starboard tack,"—scientific evolutions quite beyond the lubberly ken of landsmen; which ended, however, intelligibly and in stern earnest. Two fine American schooners, the Scourge, of 8 guns, and the Hamilton, of 9, were upset in a squall, and all hands lost, except 16 saved by the British; and two vessels of the same class, the Julia and the Growler, were cut off and captured. Chauncey, though still by far the stronger, retired into Niagara. But these results were not conclusive, nor were they satisfactory on our side of the lake; and landsmen, who did not know the difference between a caboose and a marlinspike, and who can

---

* James, Vol. II, 231.

hardly be blamed if they could not stomach such matters, took upon themselves to pass very hard and very unjust comments upon Sir James Yeo. A British sailor was expected to do many impracticable things; and among the rest, to catch an adversary who, being a quicker sailor, would not be caught, and whose long guns, at long distances, made it dangerous to follow. The fact is, that Sir James did his best to close with his adversary, but unavailingly. And we have here the evidence of Dr. Richardson, who was then "sailing master" on board the flag-ship. The armament of the two squadrons governed, to a great extent, the movements of the commander. Sir James was provided, for the most part, with carronades,—excellent for rapid firing at close quarter, but unavailable at long range; while, on the other hand, Chauncey had long guns, which gave him a decided superiority at a distance. Thus, while Yeo sought to "lay alongside," the other disapproved of these familiarities; and, as with sailing vessels, the closing in action depends on the weather gage, Chauncey's superiority in sailing enabled him to decline coyly all delicate attentions of this sort. "I heard him once remark," says the venerable narrator, "to an observation from Captain Mulcaster, 'If we were on the high seas, I would risk an action at all hazards; because, if I were beaten, I could only lose the squadron; but to lose it on this lake, would involve the loss of the country. The salvation of the western army depends on our keeping open their communications.'"* Thus spoke out the man of thought as well as action; thus spoke the man of head, with courage to do what his brain dictated,—indifferent to disgrace if incurred in the service of his country. As a brave seaman, he was beyond reproach.

We now leave the blue Ontario for the picturesque shores of Lake Champlain; and, on our way down the St. Lawrence, pause

---

* Memoirs of Dr. Richardson, D.D.

for a moment at the scene of one of those daring and sometimes profitless adventures to which seamen are prone. It befell at a place called, not inappropriately, Goose Creek, lying on the opposite side of the river, a little below Gananoque. On the 20th July, the enemy, lying *perdu* among the rocks and channels of the Thousand Islands, had pounced on a brigade of batteaux, conveying provisions and supplies from Montreal to Kingston, and had spirited away the whole convoy into the difficult and romantic recesses of the creek before named. Three gun-boats, under Lieutenant Scott, and a detachment of the 100th, commanded by Captain Martin, were sent from Kingston, to intercept the American return to Sackett's Harbour: a very sensible plan, which was unfortunately spoiled by a rush into his stronghold. They had reached the spot as evening fell, and were compelled, by the darkness, to defer the attack until morning. In the night came up Major Frend, of the 4th Foot, with an additional gun-boat, and a small reinforcement. On his way he had encountered Captain Milnes, a promising young officer, and Aide-de-Camp to Sir George Prevost. Milnes volunteered, of course; and at 3 a.m., before dawn, the whole force felt its way forward. They found the enemy fully prepared. The channel became narrow; the banks rocky and precipitous; and large trees felled across the stream, brought them up in front of a log fort. The woods were filled with riflemen; and the American plied well his national weapon. The seamen and troops leaped into the water—carried the heights, and drove the foe into their fort. But the odds and the difficulties were too great. Frend ordered the re-embarkation of the men, and fought his way out; but with twenty-one casualties— among them the gallant Milnes, who was mortally wounded, and died shortly after, much deplored by his brothers in arms.

The capture of this brigade of store-boats by the enemy—no unfrequent occurrence on both sides—will convey some idea of the danger and difficulties surmounted in supplying a military force scattered from Quebec to Michilimacinac, along an exposed frontier of upwards of a thousand miles. It taxed talent, and energy, and foresight of no ordinary calibre to anticipate and provide for all wants—to evade or surmount all obstructions, in a climate which admits of but six months of water conveyance, and at that season, and on that line of communication, invites and aids attack; and in a country where the roads in winter, though practicable, are so narrow, and at times so cut up, as to make the movement of weighty articles very slow and protracted. The baggage and daily supply of a regiment on the march, conveyed in a long single line of *traineaux*, would occupy miles of road, from which to diverge one foot is to plunge into three feet of snow; and where a "break down" interrupts the advance of the whole line. The troops had to be supplied for the present, and in anticipation of the casualties of the future. It will surprise men, living in the abundance of productive and overflowing Canada, to learn that in 1818 the soldiery, the militia, and the Indians, were fed upon Irish mess-pork, and on "pilot bread," or ship biscuit, manufactured at Portsmouth. In a new country, where population was scattered and cultivation sparse—where the produce barely sufficed for the support of the husbandman—and where war disturbed both sowing and harvest, it became necessary, in providing for the troops, to consider the wants of the whole population. It is, therefore, easy to imagine the arduous duties—the responsibilities—the mental labour which devolved upon the commissariat. What the belly was to the members, according to the fable of Æsop, the brain was to the belly in the story of Canadian warfare. Shoes and bread were the real *pabula belli*. These essentials were regularly and plentifully supplied; but to secure this supply, demanded great administrative talent; a thorough knowledge of the country, the language, the means of conveyance, channels of communication, and of the means and resources, however limited, which could be appealed to upon an emergency.

Sir William Robinson was the commissary general, an experienced officer of the department, and an excellent link of connection between the expenditure of the war and the British treasury; and he was well supported. It must be evident that, in such a scene of scattered warfare, waged at the same time on remote frontiers, much was necessarily left to individual responsibility, and that much depended on the local knowledge and capacity of subordinate officers. Fortunately, Sir William found in the country a class of men, made to his hand, who possessed these requisites. Many of them were U. E. Loyalists—men who, for opinion's sake, had abandoned their counting-houses in Boston, New York, and Philadelphia, and who had applied their commercial talents and habits of business to the improvement of a new field of enterprise, and, in some cases, to the acquisition of a new tongue. Among the names of the officers of the commissariat department in Canada, returned in July, 1811, by Sir Gordon Drummond, will be found those of Isaac W. Clarke, Montreal; James Crookshank, York; James Coffin, Fort George; William Stanton, York; John Coffin, Quebec; William Ross, Kingston; Robert Reynolds, Amherstburg. All these gentlemen were U. E. Loyalists—living witnesses of the gratitude of the crown, which never ignores or forgets fidelity; but visits and rewards it from the father to the children. They proved, all, to be valuable officers in a branch of the service which can never be sufficiently estimated; and among them no one more so than Isaac Winslow Clarke, Deputy Commissary-General of Montreal.

The career of this gentleman is characteristic of the times. He was one of the sons, and a partner in the business of Richard Clarke, a loyal Boston merchant,— consignee of the tea, which, destroyed by the violence of the mob in Boston Harbour, is noted as the first outbreak of the revolution. As in all popular convulsions, the weaker and the obnoxious party was treated mercilessly.

The Tory was knocked down, and talked down, and written down; and, like in the fable of the lion, the man who put him down, gave his version of the exploit. The Clarkes were obnoxious to the men and the opinions of the day. The father took refuge in England, with his son-in-law, Copley the painter, and was written down and proscribed, without trial, in the "Boston Confiscation Act."* Isaac, the son, endeavouring to collect some debts due to the firm, at Plymouth, in Massachusetts, was paid in full by a mob at midnight. He executed a mutual discharge, saved his life, and followed his father to the fireside of his talented brother-in-law, where, with his sister, and her since celebrated son, the late lamented Lord Lyndhurst, he remained until appointed to the commissariat in Canada. In this country he served his Sovereign for fifty years. In 1812 he was regarded as an officer of great trust, of long experience, and indefatigable zeal. The organization of the *batteaux*

---

* In an excellent American work "Biographical Sketches of the American Loyalists," published in Boston, 1847, and in a well-digested Preface, entitled an Historical Essay, the author, Lorenzo Sabine, admits, philosophically enough, that the process of "tarring and feathering" was not one likely to reclaim an offending brother. What "brother," he exclaims, "who saw only with the eyes of a British subject, was won over to the right, by the arguments of mobbing, burning, and smoking." He cites many instances of the cruelties of mob law, and closes with the following: "Did it serve any good end to endeavour to hinder Tories from getting tenants, or to prevent persons who owed them from paying honest debts? On whose cheek should have been the blush of shame, when the habitation of the aged and feeble Foster was sacked, and he had no shelter but the woods; when Williams, as infirm as he, was seized at night, dragged away for miles, and smoked in a room, with fastened doors and a closed chimney top? What father who doubted whether to join or fly, determined to abide the issue in the land of his birth, because foul words were spoken to his daughters, or because they were pelted when riding, or moving in the innocent dance? Is there cause to wonder that some who still live, should yet say of their own, or of their father's treatment, that " persecution made half of the king's friends."—*Vide* pp. 76, 77.

brigades was due to him. These boats — flat-bottomed, of light draught, but carrying heavy cargoes — were partly towed, partly punted, partly dragged by ropes up the rapids of the St. Lawrence. The crews were supplied by a levy or *corvée* of French Canadians. Several thousands of these men were devoted to a service, for which they were peculiarly qualified by a hardihood, activity, and cheerfulness,—undaunted by fatigue. From five to seven *voyageurs* were assigned to each *batteau;* but at certain difficult points the united strength of the whole brigade forced the boats, one by one, up the stream. But the progress was slow, and the opportunities of attack many; still, the precautions taken and the bold front shown, for the most part defeated these attempts. John Finlay, the executive officer at Lachine, distinguished himself by acts of vigour and devotion, which, in the sister service, would have been fame. The commanders in the field, and especially Sir Gordon Drummond, repeatedly expressed their obligations to Mr. Clarke. Few but men in these high positions can appreciate the value of such unpretentious services.*

---

* In 1824 Deputy Commissary General Clarke, then 76 years of age, was on his way to England, where his friends had reason to expect that he would receive from the Crown the same marks of favour which had been bestowed on others. He died at sea, leaving one son, who was for many years private secretary to Lord Lyndhurst, when Lord Chancellor of England; and two daughters—one the wife of the Hon. Charles R. Ogden, at one time Attorney-General in Lower Canada, and now Attorney-General in the Isle of Man; the second sheds light and happiness on the hand which traces these lines.

CHAPTER XVI.

Montreal the centre of supply—Description of Montreal—View from top of the Mountain—Montreal of 1840 or 1864, not the Montreal of 1812—Montreal viewed as the Military Key of Canada—Country around—View of Belœil—Canadian scenery—Canadian people—The *Habitants*, their progress, improvement and characteristics—Strong temptation to invasion—Approach to Montreal and the Richelieu country—Description of Lake Champlain—American force on the New York frontier available for invasion.

Montreal was the source and centre of supply. It was then, as it is now, the commercial emporium of the Canadas. In population it exceeded any other settlement on the St. Lawrence. Situated on an island in the combined embrace of the Rivers Ottawa and St. Lawrence, it possesses, partly from its latitude and partly from the great area of water with which it is surrounded, a mildness and softness of climate unknown to any other part of Lower Canada. The Island of Montreal is longer, but not so wide, as the Isle of Wight; and the St. Lawrence equals, in varying width, the strait which divides that island from the coast of Hampshire.* In the rear of the city, running parallel to the river, at the distance of a mile and a half from the water's edge, rises a long ridge of rocky and precipitous hill, some 550 feet above water-level, from which is derived the original name "Mont Royal." The summit of this mountain commands a view, extensive and diversified. The city, with its towers, and spires, and public buildings, covers at the feet of the

---

* Montreal Island, - - 30 miles long, 10½ miles broad.
   Isle of Wight, - - - 23   "   13   "

spectator, an area of three miles, by one and a half. In midriver lies the umbrageous island of St. Helen's—half park, half arsenal, glistening in the morning sun, like an emerald set in gold. The St. Lawrence, a mile and a half wide at the narrowest, extends east and west as far as the eye can reach, covered with ships fresh from the ocean, and by steamers numberless, leaving on the wind their murky trail. In mid-landscape, that architectural marvel, the Victoria Bridge, spans the river, in all its strength and beauty; and the ear can detect the roar of each passing train which rushes through its iron ribs. Beyond, the rail-tracks wind through a champaign country, settled for two centuries, where farm houses and farm buildings line the roads like streets, rich in population and rustic wealth; while in the distance the twin mountains of Belœil and Montarville, sites even more picturesque than their names, rise from the plain, *insulæ* of beauty amid a sea of verdure. But the eye can hardly tear itself from the scene of cultivation close around. The slopes of the mountain, and the rich alluvial soil at its foot, are one entire garden. Villas and pleasure-grounds cover the hill-side. A beautiful reservoir, cleft out of the rock, glitters in the sunlight, with all the formal beauty of a *paysage* by Watteau—the costumes and gay colours of the present day heightening the illusion—and imparts health and freshness to the city spread beneath. In the distant valleys, the agricultural skill of the English farmer combines with the minuteness and precision of the old French style of gardening to create a scene

> Ever changing, ever new:
> When will the landscape tire the view?
> The fountain's fall; the river's flow;
> The woody valley, warm and low;
> The windy summit, wild and high—
> Roughly reaching to the sky;
> The pleasant seat; the ruined tower;
> The naked rock; the shady bower;

The town—the village—dome—and farm :
Each gives to each a double charm—
Like pearls upon an Ethiop's arm.

But the spectator from the hill-top, or the frequenter of St. James Street, or of the Rue Notre Dame, must not suppose that in 1812 things were as they are now. Not for twenty-five years later, did a civic government provide for the wants of advancing civilization; not for twenty-five years, did gas-lights, or pavements, or hydrants exist. The long line of banks and stately edifices which now adorn St. James Street, rise from an abandoned graveyard, which in 1812, was bounded by the crumbling city defenses. Fortification Lane was the foot of the town wall; Craig Street was the town ditch; beyond, on the upland, were country houses and orchards. In 1812 the Rue Notre Dame, now flashing with plate-glass and piled stores of jewelry and brocade, was a narrow street of low, cozy Canadian houses, one story and a half high—the *sancta* of much genial grace and of unbounded hospitality. The nocturnal reveller —and there was a good deal of revelry in those days—who slipped off the disjointed stones, mis-called *trottoir*, plunged mid-leg in mud, in the palpable darkness, without hope of refuge in a street-railway car, or of help from a sleepy policeman. The modest old Catholic parish church, which in early days gave a Catholic welcome to the houseless Protestant congregations,*stood lengthwise in front of the present

---

* The Hon. Samuel Gerrard, who at the age of ninety years, retained a vivid recollection of events coeval with the conquest, was wont to dwell with pleasure on the catholicity of the Catholic population and Priesthood of that time. Under the terms of the capitulation, if they had had any ill feeling to gratify, they might have been as exclusive as they pleased; but obeying a noble inspiration they offered the use of their church to other Christian denominations, and it received all members of the Christian family, until other provision was made. The benevolent influence of their first impulse has descended to the present generation, and pervades a whole community. There is not in

noble church of Notre Dame—grand in design, though somewhat marred by a too great severity of style. Those splendid wharves, faced with miles of cut stone, unequalled in America, and rivalled only in Europe by the docks of Liverpool, or the quays of St. Petersburg, have replaced a nauseous bank, heaped with filth and garbage; and a muddy islet, the receptacle of drift-wood and drowned animals; and a turbid stream, from whence the strongest swimmer never rose. Montreal of the present day, with its palatial residences,—its places of public resort,—markets numerous, convenient and ornamental,—with its cathedrals, churches, colleges, and convents,—with its multiplied institutions and social improvements,—with a population of 100,000 souls, is as superior to the Montreal of 1840, as the Montreal of 1840 was in advance of 1812; and yet at that time Montreal was the commercial heart of Canada; the fountain of supply; the focus of mercantile energy and wealth; and was regarded as the grand end and aim—the promised prize of—American conquest.

It was then universally believed in the United States that the fall of Montreal would entail the subjugation of Canada. This opinion may be questioned. Situated at the head of navigation from the ocean, and at the foot of all the channels of communication with the upper country, the temporary occupation of Montreal would doubtless have compelled all the western garrisons to fall back upon Kingston; but the force concentrated at the latter point, would have sufficed to keep at bay the American army then in the field, reduced, as it must have been, by detachments.

Christendom a community more devoid of the vices and bigotry of sectarianism than that of Montreal. It is not that men of different persuasions tolerate each other—they unite in kindly and cordial feeling, socially, and in all matters of public concern. In matters of faith all claim liberty of conscience; and, without derogating from their own opinions, respect the liberty they claim, by not interfering with those of others.

And it may be doubted whether the army from Western Canada, descending the St. Lawrence, might not have invested the invader, in a false position, on the wrong side of a wide river—which they could not bridge, and British gun-boats would soon command. The possession of Montreal would, no doubt, facilitate an attack upon Quebec. It had offered this facility to Amherst, in 1759-60; and to Montgomery, in 1775-76. And yet Quebec would have never fallen but for Wolfe's triumphant daring. Montgomery failed. And so long as the climate in winter, and the British navy in summer, command the St. Lawrence, Quebec is safe.

Montreal was, indeed, in dangerous proximity to the American frontier, at a point where a large force could easily be placed within striking distance. Forty-five miles from Montreal, *à vol d'oiseau*, is the line which divides the State of New York from Lower Canada. It is commonly known as the "Line Forty-five," being on that parallel of latitude, established by treaty as the frontier of the two countries. This line intersects the head of Lake Champlain at Rouse's Point, where the lake narrows to a river, which, assuming there the name of the Richelieu, passes through the most fertile district of French Canada, and disembogues into the St. Lawrence at Sorel. The territory fertilized by this river is rich as the Delta of the Nile. It is a wide alluvial flat. It was long regarded as the garden of Canada. It was seized upon, at once, with instinctive appreciation, and settled by the first French settlers of the country. The tourist, who will scale the top of Belœil, sees around him a striking panorama. The main roads appear to radiate from the foot of the mountain. The farms, on the old seigniorial system, are laid off, right and left of these roads, with a front of three acres by a depth of thirty. The farm-houses and buildings on every lot, for convenience and mutual assistance in winter, front on the road. These houses—red-roofed, delicately whitewashed, kept with remarkable neatness—surrounded by gardens and foliage, and well arranged fields, chequer the whole country. For miles and miles extend these vistas of dwellings, with a village church, its steeple glittering in the sunlight, and a modest *presbytère* interpolated on the landscape, every three leagues. The character of the population is in keeping with the scene. The French Canadian is eminently a gregarious animal, attached to his *habitats*. He hopes to live and die within sound of the bell which rang at his baptism. He is attached to his fellows, to his institutions, his language, his religion; he is attached to his priesthood—who by their exemplary lives and their care, temporal as well as spiritual, deserve all his love. He is social and hospitable; courteous and courtly. The manners of the *vieille cour* are still to be found among the *habitants* of Canada, and invest the females of the race with an indescribable charm. But his attachment to the past makes him indifferent to the future. He is slow in improvement; and in the great race of human progress is exposed to be left behind. And yet, those who have known these people for twenty years, can bear witness to an advance, which, although it might be accelerated to their advantage, promises much. Education has made great strides. That which was regarded as an imposition, is now esteemed a privilege. In the small towns and villages, and even in the farm-houses, is seen a manifest increase in the comforts, the conveniences, the elegancies, and luxuries of life; and with them, an increased independence of character. Men think more for themselves, and are less easily led. Time was, when they were docile to a fault; but upon occasions, they have shown all the *vivida vis* of a gentle nature. When roused they are stern to savageness.

The possessions of such a people were inviting to an invader—as the flesh-pots of Egypt. The government of the United States had, for long, honored this part of Canada with special attention. To Mr. Secretary Armstrong, Montreal was as the apple of his eye. It was argued pertinently enough—Why waste men and money upon distant frontiers? strike at the vitals, and paralyze the extremities. Capture Montreal, and you starve de Rottenburg and Proctor. In Montreal your troops will find winter quarters and English Christmas cheer. As the Cabool prince remarked at Calcutta, rubbing his hands with the leer of a freebooter—"A splendid place: ah, yes! a splendid place to plunder." The fields on the Richelieu would forage and feed an army, more plentifully than the plains of the Low Countries.

These counsels carried with them great weight; and it will be seen that for the remainder of the campaign, the capture of Montreal was the grand end and crowning object of American strategy. In furtherance of this scheme the cabinet of Washington assembled a large force on Lake Champlain. This lake runs due north and south; and divides the State of New York from the State of Vermont. It is in length 130 miles, by a width of from one to fifteen. It is one great link in the chain of communication between the city of New York and the banks of the St. Lawrence. The Champlain canal, which connects the southern extremity of the lake with the River Hudson, was not commenced until 1818; nor could the proverbial ingenuity of the race in its wildest imagination have conceived then, the network of American railroads which now converge on Rouse's Point. But, long before the introduction of the rail, the internal channels of communication had greatly improved. In 1812 the country between Albany and Whitehall, about 80 miles, was open and cultivated; the roads the best in America; the Hudson afforded 140 miles of uninterrupted navigation, and Lake Champlain supplied the rest.

What Loughrig tarn is among the lakelets of North Britain, such is Lake Champlain to the lakes of North America. It is a perfect gem. The coast scenery of Erie and Ontario is comparatively tame: though undulating, it is in general aspect flat—a rich alluvial margin, acquired to the land in the course of ages, by the gradual retrogression of the water. But the coast of Lake Champlain rises rapidly into upland, backed on both shores by mountain peaks, which, if of no great altitude, are most beautiful in shape and grouping. The waters are pure and deep, and studded with lovely isles. The alternate coasts, never lost to view, are dotted over with villages, and homesteads, and farms; and teem with flocks and herds, and elaborate cultivation. The cities of Burlington and Plattsburg adorn its shores; and Ticonderoga and Crown Point, associated with tales of Indian stratagem, and of the old French wars, impart pictorial beauty and historical interest to the *Horican*, immortalized by the pen of Cooper.

At the time when General Dearborn retired into winter quarters, in 1812, he had under his command, on Lake Champlain, an army of at least 12,000 men. This fine force was partially moved to Sackett's Harbor; and frittered away in the spring in the raid upon York and the empty acquisition of Fort George, to the great dissatisfaction of the Government at Washington. But on the retirement of this officer, the commander in the field concurred with the cabinet. In the summer of 1813 about 6,000 men were collected at Burlington and Plattsburg; and extensive barracks were prepared for the reception of troops at these points—at Champlain in New York, and Swanton in Vermont. Commodore Macdonough, with a force of seamen from the seaboard, was actively engaged in fitting out a naval armament on the Lake. These preparations bespoke their object. The aspect of affairs on this frontier was very menacing.

CHAPTER XVII.

Sir George Prevost and Sir James Craig—Sir James a good man but obdurate—Sir George politic and useful—He identifies himself with the people—They support him and British rule—The Legislature legalize the issue of army bills, and vote additional militia forces—Exchequer Bills—Sir George prepares for defence—English Volunteers—French Militia—The two people incline to different systems of enrolment—Both readily unite against common enemy—Isle aux Noix—Attempt made to surprise this post—Capture of American schooners Growler and Eagle—Reprisals—Officers and men of H. M. brig of war, Wasp, transferred to Lake Champlain—Plattsburg, Swanton, Champlain, destroyed—Burlington challenged—Blockade of the seaboard by the British—Increased American strength on the Lakes.

Sir George Prevost, necessarily resident at Quebec, the seat of Government, retained the chief military command in Lower Canada. In 1811 he had succeeded in the government a man of great talent and energy—eminent for his services in Europe, Asia, Africa, and America; but unsuccessful in Canada. Sir James Craig was an honest man and a brave soldier; but he had governed soldiers all his life, and his ideas of government squared with the rules of discipline. He had none of the flexibility of character which constitutes a successful administrator under a constitutional system. He came at once into collision with the legislature. And in those days there was no responsible council to fend off the blow of the battering-ram. The assembly humbly prayed to be allowed to defray the expenses of the civil list. The prayer had doubtless a double object: the privilege to pay inferred a right to discharge and the alternative was ominous to some of Sir James' advisers. But the request was reasonable; and Sir James was wrong in refusing to lay it at the foot of the throne. His acts were maliciously, and perhaps, seditiously reviewed. He seized on the newspaper, and sent the editor to gaol. This might have been the usual practice at Cape Town or Madras, at Gibraltar or Messina, but it was not suited to the climate or constitution of Canada. These acts brought him in direct antagonism with a majority in the assembly, which being French Canadian, fastened upon him at once the imputation of hostility to the Canadian people. This, no unusual *ruse* in politics, was nothing but a *ruse*. As Sir James said, with much pathos, " For what should I oppress you ? Is it from ambition ? What can you give me ? Is it for power ? Alas ! my good friends, with a life ebbing not slowly to its period, under pressure of disease acquired in the service of my country, I look only to pass what it may please God to suffer to remain of it, in the comfort of retirement among my friends. I remain among you only in obedience to the commands of my King."* The fact is, that he was an honest, earnest man ; but too much of a martinet to be a useful civil governor. He returned home and died.

Sir George Prevost was made of more malleable material ; and happily so, for the country and for the empire. Not all the power of England could, of itself, at that conjuncture have saved Canada, had not Canada been true to England and to herself. The preservation of the country depended on the support of the legislature, and on the good will of the masses. He identified himself with the masses ; and, at a most critical moment, secured their cordial co-operation. The acts of the legislature—their ready contributions to the conduct of the war, bear witness to his success as a civil administrator. He was politic as well as just. But under a form of government which rules by parties, he could not please both, and in his turn he incurred an hostility which was neither blind to his faults nor kind to his errors. There can be no stronger

---

* Morgan, Celeb. Can., p. 160.

proof of the influence he exercised and of the earnest loyalty of the people than the liberality of the Legislature. At this time it was all important to provide a currency as a substitute for gold, which, if put in circulation, would have found its way rapidly to a better market in the United States. It was desirable to be prepared with an expedient to counteract an accidental dearth of gold. Banks and Bank notes were unknown in Canada. To many of the inhabitants a paper currency was unintelligible—to some obnoxious,—the recollections of the paper currency of French rule—the *ordonnances* or assignats of Bigot and his compeers were yet rife. In the face of these popular prejudices the Legislature legalized the issue of a paper currency. They authorized the issue of what was termed an Army Bill, analogous to the Exchequer Bill in England. It was a bank note bearing interest. These notes were made a legal tender. They were more than legalized, they were popularized by the example of the Legislature. The issue amounted to $2,000,000. The Legislature provided for the expense of the operation and the temporary payment of interest. These Bills were redeemed by the Imperial treasury at the end of the war, but the action of the Legislature of Lower Canada at this critical time was declaratory of confidence in British rule and of a determination to uphold it.

---

* In 1658 the people of Canada were informed that the Royal Treasury of France was in no condition to repay the advances the Canadians had made to the Government. That the payment of Colonial Bills drawn upon it was suspended for a time. Vaudreuil and Bigot were apprized of this measure by an official circular. * * * This news startled those concerned, like a thunderbolt; there was owing by France to the Colonists more than 40 millions of francs (say £1,600,000 stg.) and there was scarcely one of them who was not a creditor of the State. " The paper money amongst us" wrote M. de Levis to the Minister " is entirely discredited and the people are in despair about it. They have sacrificed their all for the conservation of Canada to France ; now they find themselves ruined, resourceless, but we do our best to restore their confidence.'
—Garneau, History of Canada, Vol. II, p 68.

If Great Britain had failed in the contest, the Legislative endorsers of these notes would have been responsible for the paper.*

The example of the Legislature was worthily sustained by the exhortations of the Catholic clergy. In no Catholic country in christendom does the clergy exercise a stronger or more healthy influence than in Canada. They are the domestic chaplains of every farm-house. In devotion and loyalty to the British Crown they are second to none. It has been shown on all occasions which justified their interposition. In 1775 Sir Guy Carlton declared publicly, that if the Province of Canada had been preserved to Great Britain, it was owing to the Catholic clergy.

In 1812 the Catholic church in Canada was under the guidance of the Rev. Joseph Octave Plessis, Bishop of Quebec. This able Ecclesiastic was contemporary with the treaty which ceded Canada to England. He was a native of Montreal, born in 1763. He became Bishop of Quebec in 1806. His services, in the protection of his church, and in the promotion of the best interests of his people, were most honourable; but, among them all, none do greater credit to his heart and head than his constant adherence to the British Crown.

---

* Exchequer Bills—Macaulay explains what they were. "Another and at that conjuncture, a more effectual substitute for a metallic currency owed its existence to the ingenuity of Charles Montague. He had succeeeded in engrafting on Harley's Land Bank Bill, a clause which empowered the government to issue negotiable paper bearing interest at the rate of three-pence a day on a hundred pounds. In the midst of the general distress and confusion appeared the first Exchequer Bills, drawn for various amounts from a hundred pounds down to five pounds. These instruments were rapidly distributed over the kingdom by post, and were everywhere welcome. The Jacobites talked violently against them in every Coffee House and wrote much detestable verse against them, but to little purpose. The success of the plan was such that the Ministers at one time resolved to issue twenty shilling Bills for the payment of the troops. But it does not appear that their resolution was carried into effect. History of England, vol. iv. p. 608.

Nor was the Prelate a blind or an unreasoning adherent. He gave good ground for the faith that was in him. " In considering the system of vexatious tricks organized against the church and people of Canada, by chiefs and subordinates who were sent from the Court of Louis the XV., at that time under the sceptre of Madame de Pompadour, he admitted, frankly, that under the English Government the Catholic clergy and rural population enjoyed more liberty than was accorded to them before the conquest;" and after having praised the English nation, " which had welcomed so generously the French Ecclesiastics, hunted out of France by the Republicans of 1792," he added, " that the capitulation, as well as the treaty of 1763, were so many new ties of attachment to Great Britain, and that religion itself would gain by the change of domination."*

It was in the spirit of this manly avowal, that he issued his *mandement* or episcopal proclamation, read in every church in his diocese, and concluded in the following eloquent language: "*Guerriers,*" said he,, " it is to you that belongs the task of opposing yourselves, like a wall,† to the approach of the enemy. They will cease to be formidable when the God of battles fights on your side; under his holy protection, march to combat as to victory: sustain that reputation for obedience, for discipline, for valour and for intrepidity by which you deserved your first success. Your confidence will not be vain, if in exposing your lives for the defence of your country and your hearths, you take care before all things to make your peace with God."

These sentiments of the Bishop were enforced by his clergy with a quiet undemonstrative earnestness, which is energy, without the pretence it often assumes. It pervaded, encouraged, emboldened

---

* Life of Mongrandeur Plessis, by L'Abbé Ferland. Translated by D. B. French, p. 14. Vide ibid., p. 23.

† The expression of Stonewall Jackson was here anticipated.

all men. A remarkable incident, hereafter, on the battle-field of Chateauguay will exemplify its influence.*

Sir George Prevost applied, vigorously, the resources at his command to the protection of his threatened frontier. He had, at this time, cantoned in the districts of Montreal, Laprairie, St. John's, and Chambly, about 3,000 men; two-thirds of which were Voltigeurs and embodied militia. It is curious to observe the varying characteristics of the races, in the terms of service most acceptable to each. The French Canadian preferred to be a conscript; the Anglo-Canadian insisted upon being a volunteer.†

---

* Human story reproduces itself. Let us take the testimony of Burke, given twenty years before. "When the English nation seemed to be dangerously, if not irrevocably divided—when one, and that the most growing branch, was torn from the parent stock, and ingrafted on the power of France, a great terror fell upon this kingdom. On a sudden we awakened from our dreams of conquest, and saw ourselves threatened with an immediate invasion, which we were, at that time, very ill-prepared to resist. You remember the cloud that gloomed over us all. In that hour of our dismay, from the bottom of the hiding-places into which the indiscriminate rigour of our statutes had driven them, came out the body of the Roman Catholics. They appeared before the steps of a tottering throne with one of the most sober, measured, steady and dutiful addresses that was ever presented to the Crown. It was no holiday ceremony, no anniversary compliment of parade and show. It was signed by almost every gentleman of that persuasion, of note or property in England. At such a crisis nothing but a decided resolution to stand or fall with their country, could have dictated such an address; the direct tendency of which was to cut off all retreat, and to render them peculiarly obnoxious to an invader of their own communion. The Address showed what I had long languished to see, that all subjects of England had cast off all foreign views and connections, and that every man looked for his relief from every grievance at the hands only of his own national government.—Burke, Speech before the Bristol Election, Sept., 1784.

† It was the boast of the soldiers, as we find it recorded in their solemn resolutions, that they had not been forced into the service, nor had enlisted chiefly for the sake of lucre; that they were no janzzaries, but free-born Eng-

Both Briton and Gaul made good soldiers in the field; but the one stood on his independence, and accepted bounty-money; the other eschewed soldiering *en amâteur*, yet cheerfully obeyed the draft. Both acted in accordance with their traditions. Since the days of Cromwell, the Englishman has been free to fight for whom he pleases. He enlists for reasons best known to himself; and "takes the shilling," because he chooses. The Frenchman has been a feudal follower of his lord and of his king from his earliest to his latest history. The terms of his tenure in Canada revived a system not then extinct in France, and perpetuated habits of thought and action derived from his ancestors. He obeyed with the same devotion with which he would have followed a Montmorenci or a Condé; and with an inborn recollection of the discipline of Royal Roussillon or Guiènne. It was necessary to devise and adapt a system suited to the genius of both races of the population; and Sir George Prevost did so.

In no part of Canada have the two peoples so much amalgamated as in the district of Montreal. It would be more correct, perhaps, to say assimilated: each race still retains its distinctive features;

> Each gives to each a double charm,
> Like pearls upon the Ethiop's arm.

But commerce and constitutional government have exercised their influence; and we see that tendency to a union of the Norman and Saxon elements which, in the course of ages, has made England what she is. On this occasion, as ever since, in questions of national defence, a generous rivalry animated both races. The Frenchman bore no love to the puritanical "Bostonnais," whose previous visits were not held in pleasant recollection. The Englishman rankled in the face of a nation which heaps upon him and his

---

lishmen, who had, of their own accord, put their lives in jeopardy for the liberties and religion of England, and whose right and duty it was to watch over the welfare of the nation which they had saved.—Macaulay, Vol. II, p. 94.

country, contumely and vituperation. Hard words may break no bones, but they offer a poor salve to old sores. Thus, with the cordial aid of an united population, Sir George made vigorous arrangements for the defence of this frontier.*

About ten miles below the outlet of Lake Champlain, barring the channel of the Richelieu, stands the military post of Isle aux Noix — now a fortress, then a swampy island, protected by rude breastworks and a wooden block-house. In 1812, when the only means of communication was by water, Isle aux Noix was regarded as a bulwark of the frontier. The country on each side of this fortalice was, for many miles, an impenetrable forest. It is now cleared and cultivated; traversed by roads, and seamed with railways. In those days it was regarded as the portal of the district. Here was stationed a small regular garrison. Here, not long before, Sir James Craig had caused to be conveyed three gun-boats, built at Quebec. In the summer of 1813 the garrison consisted of detachments of the 13th and 100th regiments, and a small party of artillery, under command of Major Taylor, of the 100th.†

The Americans, shortly after the commencement of the war, had, on their part, built and equipped a small flotilla, to watch the entrance to the lake, and protect its waters from insult. This object is now secured by a strong but small work, called Fort Montgomery, which, on the verge of the frontier, and at the margin of the river, prevents the British from getting out, as effectually as Isle aux Noix prevents the Americans from getting in. It may be questionable if, in the event of a war, either work would, under the present

---

* In September was embodied another battalion of militia, called the *Fifth Battalion*, afterwards Canadian Chasseurs; while the merchants and traders of the 1st Montreal Sedentary Militia organized themselves into four companies of volunteers for garrison duty, and field service in case of emergency.— *Christie*, Vol. II, p. 41.

† James, Vol. II, p. 239.

circumstances of the frontier and conditions of warfare, prove aught else than a mere man-trap, in which soldiers are confined alive, to be disposed of at leisure. A few scows filled with stones and sunk in the muddy channel, would probably answer the purpose, at a less expenditure of men and money.

Little apprehension was entertained at Isle aux Noix of an attack from the lake, when at day-break on the morning of the 1st June, a sentry on the southern rampart discovered trucks, and streamers, and the masts of tall vessels rising above the mists, which at early morn, and at that season of the year, settle down upon the marshy banks of the river. The alarm was given—the garrison was roused—the gun-boats manned, and got under weigh; and, feeling their way through the fog, came upon two armed sloops, of from 90 to 100 tons each, armed each with 10 guns—eighteen-pounder carronades and long sixes; and each mounting on a pivot an eighteen-pounder Columbiad. The object of the incursion was never made intelligible. It was venturesome, but indiscreet. Without the co-operation of a land force nothing could have been effected. The armed vessels could only have approached the works to their own assured destruction. From the nature of the channel they could not bring their broadside guns to bear: following in file, the fire of the one impeded the fire of the other. As it was, the gun-boats had them at their mercy, and raked both. Major Taylor, perceiving his advantage, landed men from the boats and *batteaux*, and lining the bushes on either side of the stream, kept up a galling fire of musketry. After a contest of three hours and a half, they struck their colours; and proved to be the Growler and Eagle, armed sloops, with a complement of fifty men each, and commanded by Captain Sidney Smith, late of the Chesapeake. The Growler was brought to the garrison in safety; the Eagle was so mauled by her puny antagonists, that she was run ashore to save her from sinking, but was got off, afterwards, and repaired.

This unexpected attack and its results, exposed the hospitals, barracks, and stores in preparation on Lake Champlain for "Montreal service," and encouraged the British to attempt their destruction. Sir George Prevost, in a despatch to Brock, in July, 1812, had remarked most justly, that " our numbers would not justify offensive operations, unless calculated to strengthen a defensive attitude." There can be no doubt but that, at this moment, the best defence was to be found in disarming further attack.

Preparations were made accordingly. The prizes were re-equipped; the three gun-boats put in the best order; a flotilla of row-boats and *batteaux* provided for the conveyance of troops. But the movement was paralyzed for the want of mariners. Fortunately, there was then lying at Quebec H. M. brig of war, Wasp. Her gallant commander, Everard—Pring, his second—and their whole crew volunteered to man the vessels on Lake Champlain. The service was readily accepted—the men transported to their destination—and on the 29th of July, the expedition left Isle aux Noix for Lake Champlain. The military force consisted of detachments of the 13th, 100th, and 103rd regiments—about 1000 officers and men, under command of Lieutenant Colonels Williams, Taylor, and Smith. A small artillery force, under Captain Gordon, and a few embodied militia were added; and the whole placed under Lieutenant Colonel John Murray, of the 100th, one of the most prominent officers of the war. On the following day the flotilla reached Plattsburg—landed—dispersed the militia under General Moore—and destroyed the barracks on the Saranac, which were preparing for the reception of 4,000 men.* They upset Pyke's encampment, burned the arsenal, hospital, store-houses; and removed a large quantity of naval and military stores. Everard then stood across the lake to Burlington, in the Growler—now re-named the Broke—accompanied by one gun-boat. He was close in on the 2nd August: found two

---

* Murray's Despatch, 3rd August, 1863.

sloops, one of 11 and the other of 13 guns, ready for sea ; and a third, somewhat larger, lying under protection of a battery of 10 guns, mounted on a high bank, while two floating batteries and field-pieces, on the shore, strengthened the position.* Everard captured and destroyed four vessels under the eyes of this very superior force, which he very wisely abstained from attacking. The barracks and stores of Swanton, on Missisquoi Bay, were destroyed, as were also the barracks, block stores, and buildings at Champlain town ; the contemplated mischief was frustrated for a time, and the expedition returned to Isle aux Noix. This irruption, which was essentially a military movement of great importance, was denounced by the American press as an outrage. The British were stigmatized as " faithless ruffians, unprincipled invaders."† They forget that on the following day was perpetrated the second descent by Commodore Chauncey on York, a place already plundered, half depopulated, and where there was, at the time, no military establishment.

This bold stroke, on the part of the British, disconcerted for the time the American project to invade Lower Canada by the most natural and accessible channel, and with the aid of a naval force ; and it now becomes necessary to explain the circumstances which had about this time much facilitated their naval preparations on the northern lakes. The Government of Washington had made the best use of adversity. Driven to bay upon the sea-board, they devoted their energies, their men, and material to their inland waters, and from a new stand of vantage dealt forth strenuous blows.

---

* Everard's Despatch, 3rd August, 1883.
† James, Vol. II, p. 244.

CHAPTER XVIII.

Stung by reverses the British Admiralty acted with vigour—Ships were equipped of a calibre to meet the Americans—Americans blockaded in their own harbours—Commerce destroyed, revenue ruined—Seamen useless on the ocean, transferred to the Lakes—Naval engagements—Dominica and Decatur—Pelican and Argus—Boxer and Enterprize—Cruise of the President under Commodore Rodgers—Detroit frontier—Unpleasant vicissitudes—Story of the Frontier—Squire Reynolds—His narrative—Early state of the Detroit Frontier—Building of Fort Miami—Who paid for it—Surrender of Michigan Territory and Detroit to Americans under Jay's Treaty 1796—British war-vessels on the Upper Lakes allowed to rot—Brock's interview with the Indians—June 1812—First scalp taken by the American McCulloch—Indian exasperation—Resolution to retaliate—Declaration of war received 28th June, 1812—Capture of the Cayuga Packet by Lieut. Rolette.

We will, therefore, return to the ocean, which we left on the 1st June, after the successful issue of the contest between the Shannon and the Chesapeake. Long before this event occurred—early in the year—the British admiralty, stung into activity by previous reverses, had despatched to the coast of America vessels of a class, and in such strength, as to sweep the sea of the American cruisers, and compel the best and bravest of their ships and officers to take refuge in their own harbours. In Feb. 1813, Sir John Borlase Warren, having established a vigilant blockade of the American coasts, intercepted their carrying and coasting trade, and ruined their commerce.* The public revenue sank from $24,000,000 to $8,000,000. The Bays of the Chesapeake and Delaware were scoured by Admiral Cockburn and a light squadron; great damage inflicted on naval stores and arsenals, and the towns on the coast kept in a continual state of harassment. A few comments which it is proposed to make on the occurrences of this naval campaign, and on the atrocities charged

---

* Alison, Vol. IV, p. 462, Am. edition.

against Cockburn and his crews, are postponed to a later and more opportune occasion in the course of this narrative. The effect of the blockade was to shut up the American frigates in the ports of the Atlantic, and to transfer their officers and crews to Lakes Champlain, Ontario, and Erie. Thus it was that Captain Sidney Smith, late of the Chesapeake, was found and captured at Isle aux Noix. Thus it was that Commodore Perry, on Lake Erie, and later still, Commodore Macdonough, on Lake Champlain, were enabled to do such good service to their country.

But, not to interrupt the even tenor of our inland way hereafter, it may be as well to note here a few remarkable events of maritime war which signalized the summer. On the 5th August, the Dominica, a British schooner of twelve guns, 67 men, and nine boys, was captured by the American privateer Decatur, Captain Dominique Diron, mounting half the number of guns; but one, an 18-pounder, on a pivot, of more value than all the guns engaged, and supplied by a complement of 120 men. The American, confident in his numbers, carried the Dominica by boarding. The obstinacy of the contest is best shown by the list of casualties. The Dominica lost her captain, Lieutenant Barété, purser, two midshipmen, and thirteen men killed, and forty wounded. Out of a crew of seventy-six souls, fifty-seven were *hors de combat* before she surrendered.

On the 12th of the same month, the Pelican, a British eighteen gun brig, just in from a cruise, was despatched from Cork before she furled sails, to encounter an American war schooner, known to be committing depredations in St. George's Channel. She proved to be the Argus, of 20 guns. After a sharp action of forty-five minutes, the American was carried by boarding. Her captain, Allen, was killed in the action. The Pelican was the superior vessel of the two. She was heavier in tonnage, and threw a broadside 34lbs. more than her adversary, but the Argus had the advantage in crew by about 20 men.

Later in the year, on the 5th September, the British brig of war Boxer, of 14 guns, lying at anchor off Portland, Maine, discovered a sail in the offing; weighed, and brought to action the American gun brig Enterprize, of 16 guns. Here the advantage in tonnage and weight of metal was on the side of the Americans. In men they were 120 to 60. The usual sanguinary scene ensued. The fighting on both sides was desperate. Both of the captains, Blythe and Burrows, were killed, and the British ship was surrendered when her crew was reduced to 27 men. Her colours could not be hauled down; they had been nailed to the mast. Greeks may have met Greeks in a manner worthy of all imitation, but it may be doubted if they ever surpassed British or American sailors at the close of an action.

These were the most remarkable events of this naval campaign: Commodore Rogers, in the President, made a long cruise, prolific in despatches, during which he was always running away from somebody, or somebody running away from him. He made a few prizes, and a great escape, and successfully got home, which appears to have been the greatest success of his expedition.

We will now retrace our steps from the ocean to our own inland seas—from the sea-board of the Atlantic to the Detroit frontier. Here, in the extreme West, the war had undergone many vicissitudes. The scenes there enacted have, to a certain extent, been already recorded as they befell; but for a clear understanding of the catastrophes of this campaign, it is well to recapitulate some of the early occurrences of the year. It is not a pleasant tale to tell which terminates in disaster, but a great nation looks upon reverses as the true test of prowess, and whether on the banks of the Canadian Thames, or in the rocky fastnesses of Cabool, encounters the decree of fate with dauntless front. From these, and a thousand such ordeals, England has emerged, purified, and strengthened. All that men of British lineage wish to know upon subjects such as these is the truth. The wisdom, which truth inspires, has long since taught, that we can never be told the truth too often, or too emphatically, and we are permitted on this occasion to draw it from a source beyond all peradventure.

All men who know Amherstburg, or Malden, as it is often called, know Squire Reynolds. There is not in all the Western Counties a man better known or more respected. He is in fact an institution—one of the oldest and earliest in the country. At the age of eighty-three, he unites the mental vigour of middle age with a wonderful amount of bodily activity and buoyancy of spirits. His vitality is Palmerstonian. This gentleman exercises in his part of the country the functions of a patriarchal Rhadamanthus. He is the universal arbitrator and referee. If you want safe law or intelligible logic; if you want counsel for the present, advice for the future, or an inkling of the past, you are handed over at once, and as a matter of course, to Squire Reynolds. He lives in a snug homestead, more villa than farm-house—low, with extended wings—embedded in a grove of fine old pine trees. In front flows the Detroit, literally seamed with long lines of schooners, tugged and towed by little ungainly steamers—the "Black Dwarfs" of the river, small, ugly, but possessed of giant strength—and which scare up from the surrounding waters, flocks of innumerable wild-fowl. Around him are the inclosures and gardens, and the indescribable mass of out-buildings, which the protection of his cattle in winter imposes upon the Canadian farmer—with an eye, in early days, to the wolves—perhaps to the Indians. We are reminded in the long low irregular building, in the court yards and out-stedings, and even by the relics of a former "stockade," of "Rotherwood, the dwelling of Cedric the Saxon."

With this introduction, the kindly old gentleman may be left to speak for himself. Seated in his rocking-chair, before a cozy log fire, at his own hearth-stone on the shores of the Detroit, on this misty November morning,—he jerks himself back from before the blaze, and exclaims—

"Know something of the country! Why, I think I do. I knew it before it was made, and have seen it grow, every inch, since. I remember when, with the exception of this little strip of settlement, hardly wider than the Beach Lots where we now are, there was not a house between Huron and Ontario. No man but the hunter traversed that wilderness, of which London is now the centre. Our communications from 'below' were all by water. The Courts of Law were transported by water. Well do I remember when, in 1802, the Brig Speedy, Thomas Paxton, master—father of Major Paxton, of Fighting Island—was lost on the Lake, and the Judge and the Jury, Crown Offices, and litigants—all went down in her.

"My father was Commissary to the British troops at Fort Detroit —at that time the chief trading port and military settlement in this part of the world. I was born there in 1781. At this time the whole State of Michigan was British Territory—the river Miami divided it from the State of Ohio,—and we were often and much disturbed by quarrels, and bloody fights at times, between the Indians of our territory and the frontier settlers, who could not be kept back.

"At length, in 1794, Governor Simcoe, with the authority of the British Government, caused a Fort to be built at the mouth of the Miami, for the protection of our frontier. Pilkington, late General Pilkington, of the Engineers, planned it and superintended the construction. Colonel England was in garrison there with part of the 24th Foot. In 1795, by Jay's Treaty, a new line of frontier was established. The Americans persuaded the British Government that the Line of the St. Lawrence and the Lakes, was the safest frontier between the countries, and so, for the sake of a quiet house, they gave up all the frontier posts—Oswegatchie, Oswego, Niagara, Miami, and Detroit. I saw the British flag hauled down from the flagstaff of Detroit at noon, 11th July, 1796. I saw it again hoisted by Brock, at noon of Sunday, 16th August, 1812.

"When we gave up Detroit, the river was wider than it is now in front of that huge city. It must have been at least 1,000 yards wide then, but the wharves on both sides have much encroached on the waters. The fort stood back on a rising bank about 700 yards in the rear of the river. We left it in capital order. The troops were withdrawn and quartered at Sandwich and Fort Malden. We had at that time the entire control of the waters of the upper Lakes. We had a flotilla, composed of two large brigs, 16 guns each; one schooner of 8 guns; and three gun-boats of one gun each. They were all allowed to rot.

"Thus England abandoned Michigan, a territory as big as Spain—with its coal mines and other resources—and our Indian allies were left to the tender mercies of the Ohio trappers, who invaded their hunting grounds, and drove them to desperation. Lord Dorchester went home in disgust, remarking that Canada was a new 'Arcady the Blest,' to be protected, thenceforward, by catch-poles and javelin men. Well did Lord Chatham exclaim, before this time, that the diplomatists of England threw away, with a dash of the pen, what her soldiers had won at the point of the bayonet.

"There was a gentleman of your name residing at that time in Newark. He was in the Commissariat. Ah! an uncle. Well, I can tell you something about him in relation to the surrender of this territory. In 1797, the year after the evacuation, I was sent down by my father to Newark, on a mission of which I was proud. I was only 17 years old then. It appears that Governor Simcoe, who had built Fort Miami, and had defrayed the expenses out of the Military chest, had further resolved that the expenditure should be refunded from the revenue of the Province, and I was sent down with an order on Peter Russell, President of the Council, for the amount. Mr. Russell honoured the order and gave me the money, which I handed over to the Imperial Officer, Commissary James Coffin, and took his receipt. We became great friends in after years.

"I cannot say whether the Province actually paid the money or not. The revenue was very small then. The amount paid over was somewhat about £4,000 specie, sealed up in canvas bags. Lord Dorchester and General Simcoe might have had to raise the money themselves—Simcoe had left the Province. All I do know is, that the money was refunded to the Imperial Treasury. If Canada paid for Fort Miami, it was given up without much regard to her interests. I don't know that she paid in like manner for any other places surrendered on the frontier.

"I was here in 1812. I was myself a commissary to the forces; and, in those days, to feed a force, and provide in advance for the supply, was an arduous task: of course our main dependence was on the regular line of supply from Montreal. The troops, and the Indians, too, were supplied from our stores. The chief rations then consisted of Irish mess pork; but pigs had begun to be plentiful; and, when our communications were interrupted, I contrived to supply the deficiency from the farms which were springing up over the country, with most of which I was familiar. While I had charge, the troops never wanted, though they had often but little to spare.

"Before the war broke out—I think early in June, 1812—Brock paid us a flying visit. He was then Governor, during the absence of Governor Gore. When at Fort Malden, the Indians asked Brock for powder and guns, to go back into Michigan, and get back their lands. The General told them, that to give them ammunition, would be to make war on the United States; 'but,' said he, 'I am very sure that they will make war upon us before long. So wait a bit, and you shall have all you want;' 'but,' added he very solemnly, ' if I supply you, you must abstain from scalping the dead, and ill-treating your prisoners. Promise me that, and then you shall have all you want.' They did promise. Colonel Elliott, the Indian interpreter, was present, and translated.

"You would like to know how that promise was kept. I can tell you something about that, too. When Hull crossed at Sandwich, 12th July, 1812, he despatched scouting parties to the Canard River, only seven miles from Fort Malden, under Cass, and one McCulloch, a Kentucky man.* They encountered at the Canard Bridge an Indian scouting party of fifteen warriors and two squaws. The Indians opened fire on the Americans, who fell back. One of them crossed the river, fool-hardily, and was shot. McCulloch scalped him, and the body was abused by those with him.

"McCulloch bared his arm, and attached the trophy to his left elbow, a way they have of drying such things. On his way back he stopped at the Park farm, near Sandwich, and asked Widow Park for a drink of water. She observed what hung from his elbow, and remarked on it. 'Yes,' said he, 'it is the scalp of a d—d redskin we killed below there.' 'I am sorry for it,' said she; 'the Indians would not have done the like. I guess you'll suffer for this.'

"And so they did. When the Americans retired, the Indians went over and found the body of their comrade, scalped, and his skull beat in. They wrapped it in a blanket, and bore it back to Fort Malden, went right to the door of Colonel St. George, the commandant, and laid it down at the threshold. They called out the Colonel. 'Look!' said they, 'our great father not long ago told us not to scalp, not to kill. Look at our brother; the long knives not only scalped him, but killed him over again. Look at his skull! Our promise is wiped out.'

"This was but the beginning—more by and by. But in a day or two the Americans came back to the river Canard—the Ta-ron-tee,

---

* McCulloch (Captain McCulloch) was, it is to be presumed, the person killed by the Indians, at the head of a scouting party, in the subsequent affair of Van Horne. *Vide* James I. p 62.

as the Indians call it,—which by this time was better protected, by more Indians and a small party of the 41st. Again they had a fight, and were again repulsed. A fine fellow of the 41st lost his life here.* He was advanced sentry in the plain on the other side of the river. They came upon him suddenly, and called to him to throw down his arms, and surrender. He replied that he was there to defend his post, and fired, killing one man. They fired, too, and mortally wounded him, and, on their retreat, left him to die in a shed. He died, and was found, scalped, and the Americans were at first accused of the deed; but that was soon proved to be wrong. It turned out that one Main-poche, an Indian of ours, had stealthily followed the Americans in hopes of picking up a scalp, in revenge for the act of a few days before. He did not succeed; but on his return, alighting upon the dead body of the soldier, he thought that any scalp was better than none. He brought it in, and, both from the colour and cut of the hair, was detected at once by the comrades of the dead man, who gave him a good thrashing for his pains.

"We heard of the declaration of war on the 28th June, 1812. Brock sent up the news from York. He had arranged before with Proctor, to go over and take Detroit, at the first outbreak of war. Hull had not yet reached this post, but was on the way with reinforcements from Ohio. On the 2nd of July all arrangements were made, and we were on the point of starting, when, below Bois Blanc Island, on the Canada shore, appeared a fleet of boats. We made up our minds at once that it was the Americans coming to attack us, and manned our works. It was all a false alarm. It turned out to be a brigade of trading boats and canoes from Montreal to Macinaw. Next day orders came from Prevost to make no offensive movements, and nothing more was done.

Vide p. 42 *ante.*

"But upon this day, the 3rd, a gallant feat was performed by Lieut. Rolette, a plucky little French Canadian from Quebec. He was Lieutenant in the Provincial Marine. He was out in a boat with eight men, when he saw a vessel approach under American colours He went right alongside, and boarded, and found himself among American uniforms. Without a word, he put a sentry on the arm-chest, one on the companion ladder, and one at the wheel, and then gave loud orders to shoot any man resisting. The Americans knew nothing of the declaration of war. Independent of the crew there was on board a guard of thirty-three soldiers. Shortly recovering from their surprise, the Americans, remarking the number, began to cast ugly glances on their captors; but it so chanced that the vessel was close off a windmill on the Canada shore, around which had been thrown up a breastwork of logs, which gave it a military look. Rolette, with presence of mind, ordered the helmsman, in loud tones, to put the vessel under the guns of the battery. This had its effect for the moment. Fortunately a batteau came down the river at this time, with men and an officer, and enabled him to secure the prize. She proved to be the Cayuga Packet, containing Hull's military chest, extra baggage, military and medical stores, and all the correspondence of the army.

CHAPTER IX.

Squire Reynold's narrative—Arrival of Brock—Interview with Tecumseh—Affairs on the Frontier 1813—Ball at Malden—From the dance to the field—Colonel St. George—Attack on French Town—Capture of General Winchester—Retreat of Proctor—Wounded abandoned—Rolette hit—Brownstown and the scalps—Fort Meigs—British engineers—Colonel Gratiot—Major Reynolds at the Raisin—Defeat of Green Clay—Retaliation of the Indians—Retreat from Fort Meigs—Council of war—Recriminations—Proctor, Elliott, Tecumseh—Proctor's treatment of the Militia—Second attack on Fort Meigs—A failure—Fort Stevenson attacked—Bravely defended by Major Croghan—Col. Short killed—Stormers repulsed—Proctor retires—Barclay at Malden—Efforts to equip squadron—No men nor material—The two 24's—Calibre and character of guns in the squadrons respectively.

" This exploit of Rolette's was of great value to Brock when he arrived on the 13th of August. I was with Col. Elliott, Superintendent of Indians, when news came that a boat had reached the beach with officers on board. Tecumseh was in the room. Elliott got up and spoke to Tecumseh in Shawanee, and we went down together to the water-edge. We found the General and others disembarking. Among the first was John Beverley Robinson, and a lot of York volunteers. We were told more wanted to come than the General could bring; and he put them off by saying that he wanted some to remain to defend York.

" Tecumseh was presented to Brock. I observed him looking narrowly at the General. On our way back to the house, he remarked to Elliott that the General was a brave man, deserving of all confidence.

"And now, with respect to the occurrences on this frontier in the spring and summer of 1813. I was present at them all. The troops could not move without the Commissary; and I am proud to feel that whatever was left to me was done satisfactorily. A little of the early fighting, when told, explains the rest.

"On the 18th Jan., 1813, being the anniversary of old Queen Charlotte's birthday, all the young fellows on the coast side—*les jeunes gens de la côte*—combined with the military to give a ball. We had assembled at Mrs. Draper's Tavern, here in Amherstburg, and the lads and lasses were full of dance and fun, when in walked Colonel St. George equipped for the field. "My boys," said he, in a loud voice, "you must prepare to dance to a different tune; the enemy is upon us, and we are going to surprise them. We shall take the route about four in the morning, so get ready at once." Of course there was some confusion and surprise, but I believe the fellows liked the fighting as much as the dancing. The ball broke up at once, and every man was at his appointed post at the proper time. It had been very cold, but no snow had fallen. The river had taken across, and we started for Brownstown, four miles distant, on the ice. It was not considered strong enough to bear more than small 4-pounders. The men marched in extended order.

"It appears that the General had got intelligence that General Winchester was advancing rapidly to attack Fort Malden or Detroit, and had resolved to anticipate him. The American Generals, Winchester and Harrison, were at loggerheads. Winchester, an old revolutionary officer, did not like to be superseded by Harrison, and aimed at a great blow, on his own account, before the other could come up to share the glory. We took the wind out of his sails most completely. It was just dawn of day when our columns got out of the forest on an open space in front of the house of a Canadian named Jerome, which the Americans had stockaded. The place was called French Town, on the River Raisin. The Americans must have arrived on the ground the night before. The stockaded house was quite insufficient to receive them. Part were encamped or bivouacked on the outside. As we got out of the wood, the *reveillé* was beating inside the stockade, and it seemed as if the advanced sentry was attracted by the rattle of the drums, for he did not perceive us, in the mist of the morning, until they had ceased. Then he heard the rumble of the gun-carriages, and turned and fired, and hit Gates, the leading grenadier of the 41st, right through the head. The ball went in at one ear and out at the other. Our people deployed rapidly to the right and left, in the open, and commenced to fire. Proctor made a strange disposition of his line. He put a gun on each flank, and advanced one gun in front of the centre, so that every ball of the enemy, which missed the gun, struck the men in the rear, and some of our own musketry hit the gunners. I'll tell you a story about this presently. In the mean time the fire from our line was so heavy, that it drove the enemy who were outside the stockade down the bank on to the frozen stream below, and into the woods beyond, where numbers were killed by the Indians. The stockaded house still held out, when, to our surprise, General Winchester was brought in a prisoner. He had slept away from his men at the house of a Frenchman named Lasalle, about two miles off, and, aroused by the firing, had mounted his horse, and was riding down in haste, when he was intercepted by a drunken Indian, known by the soubriquet of Brandy Jack.* His captor had despoiled the poor General of his cocked hat, coat and epaulets, and had donned these insignia of rank, and cut a most ludicrous figure with his vermilion cheeks and painted face and pompous aspect. The General, in his shirt-sleeves, on a bitter cold morning, was in a sad plight. Brandy Jack described how the General had fired his small gun (pistol) at him—' no good,'—and gave the captive of his rifle to Proctor, who received him with all kindness. The transition

---

* James and Christie attribute the capture of Winchester to Round Head a Wyandot chief. He may also have enjoyed the soubriquet of " Brandy Jack" but the squire maintains the latter denomination to be the true one.

from peril of instant death to assured safety warmed the heart of General Winchester. He felt, at once that, the British were not the monsters they were painted, and he offered to surrender the stockaded house and garrison, if promised quarter. The promise was, of course, made, and the garrison laid down their arms. This led to a catastrophe which was deeply deplored by us all.

"But I promised you a story about Rolette. He came up to me on the ice, and said he was very sick—that he had a racking headache. I recommended him to return. The brave little Frenchman turned upon me as if I had insulted him. He was detailed to take charge of a gun, he said; to go back would be eternal disgrace. 'Look here,' said he, producing a heavy Bandana handkerchief, 'tie this tight round my head.' I rolled it up thick, and did so. 'I am better already,' he remarked, and pushed on. After the action he came to me. 'That handkerchief,' said he, 'saved my life; look here;' and in the folds of the handkerchief was a musket-ball, which had partly cut through the silk, and had flattened, one side of it, on his skull. That cranium of his must have been substantial. It was all swollen and blackened where the ball had struck. He was in front of our line in the centre, and had been wounded by our own men. Irvine, of the navy, a Lieutenant, who commanded the other gun, was also wounded in the heel.

"I have spoken of the catastrophe. I will tell you, now, how that came about. Scarcely had the prisoners surrendered, and been marched off to the rear, when news came that General Harrison was only eight miles distant, and was rapidly advancing with large reinforcements. Proctor got alarmed, and ordered a retreat. This was all right, but there was no need to hurry about it. The prisoners and many of the wounded were removed safely; but some of the wounded, too much hurt to be moved, were left in the stockaded house, where there was also a store of liquors. The Indians—not Tecumseh's people, but Indians of the Lake, under Dickson—

prowlers and plunderers, who, it is believed, did not fight at all, got at the liquor, and, when mad with drink, assailed the prisoners. The guard was insufficient. It is feared that some of the wounded were murdered, too. It was a sad affair, and caused intense feeling in our camp. Proctor was greatly blamed by us, though he was made Major-General, and got the thanks of the Lower Canadian Parliament. He need not have retired so precipitately. Why, he left his own dead and wounded, including Colonel St. George, hit in three places.

"I had under my order at this time a number of sleighs and drivers for the commissariat transport, and I had taken possession of a Frenchman's house at Stoney Creek Landing, and used it for a depôt. When Proctor retired with his men, it was reported that the wounded had been left behind. We discharged the sleighs there and returned, bringing down from eighty to a hundred wounded and twenty-three corpses. The wounded were made as comfortable as possible on straw spread on the floor of the Frenchman's house. The dead were conveyed to Amherstburg, and buried, all in one pit, here in the church-yard; I can show you the place. I found poor Col. St. George, a brave old officer, who had been sent out from England to instruct the militia, lying where he fell, badly hurt. I brought him back in his own sleigh, having knocked the seat out, and filled it in with straw. He would have died else; as it was, he did not get off his bed before July. The Americans followed us from French Town to Brownstown, an Indian village, at a cautious distance, it is true; for we never saw any of them. But they boasted that the 'heroes of Brownstown returned, bringing on their bayonets the scalps of their enemies as trophies of war.'* This was published and printed;

---

* James quotes a paragraph from the *National Intelligencer*, the American Government paper of that day, which stated that "when the Americans returned to Detroit from the battle of Brownstown, they bore triumphantly on

but it is not added whether the scalps were those of the wounded, or of the Indians, or of their own people. It is believed that with them a scalp was a scalp, from whatever skull it came, and that it was a cute Yankee trick to carry off the spoil, and credit the Indians with the act.

"The next affair in the campaign was that of Fort Meigs, on the Miami, which occurred in the month of April, 1813. General Harrison, after the capture of Winchester, occupied himself in strengthening Fort Meigs, as a depôt and starting point for future attacks on Detroit. It is about 40 miles distance. Proctor determined to beat up his quarters, and sent for my brother, Major Reynolds, of the 2d Essex. My brother was highly praised by Proctor in his despatch of the 26th Jan., for his conduct at French Town. Proctor asked if he could depend on the services of the militia. The answer was, that, for a few days and prompt action, undoubtedly; but that at that period of the season, longer delay would destroy all hope of crops, and bring starvation on the settlement and the troops. Proctor despatched, at the same time, two British engineers, disguised in Canadian costume, grey capôts and sashes, to inspect the ground on the British side of the Miami, opposite to Fort Meigs. These gentlemen were so imprudent as actually to stake out the ground where they proposed to erect the British batteries. There happened to be then in the American service a Swiss colonel named Gratiot, a very clever engineer, and he chanced to be at Fort Meigs. He detected at once the meaning of the stakes on the opposite shore of the Miami; and, before the British got down, he had run out an *epaulement*, or some such sort of thing,

---

the points of their bayonets between 30 and 40 fresh scalps, which they had taken on the field." James, I, p. 66. But this evidently bore reference to Muir's affair at Maguagua, 12th August, 1812. Still, "scalps are scalps,' whether taken in 1812 or 1813.

with a brass eighteen-pounder behind it, and our people were caught in their own trap.

"After Hull's surrender, my brother had been sent with two companies of militia, about 100 men, mostly French Canadians of the Côte, to occupy French Town, on the Raisin. He was backed by some Indians—how many can hardly be said, they were so uncertain,—one day, 20; the next, 100; the next, 50; the next, none at all. One Colonel Lewis, with about 700 American regular troops, attacked him there. Our people fought most bravely, retired slowly from log to log, from morning till night. When night came, the Americans thought better of it, and gave up the pursuit, returning to the quarters our people had occupied at French Town. This affair was the subject of Proctor's despatch of the 26th Jan.

"Proctor embarked at Amherstburg, here, on the 23rd April, with a considerable force, convoyed by gun-boats.* He took with him two long 24-pounders, to arm the work his engineers had planned against Fort Meigs. It took some time to get into position, and then the 18-pounder began to show its teeth. It commanded our guns, and was well served and aimed. It soon dismounted one of the 24's, and disabled the other, killing a fine boy of the Newfoundlanders, who was serving the vent. Still our people were not to be beaten that way. They got things right at last, when Harrison planned a sortie under Miller, aided by an attack from without. A reinforcement of 1200 Kentuckians, under General Green Clay, was within striking distance. Clay came down the river, crossed to the British side, and, aided by Miller's vigorous sortie, drove our people out of the battery upon their reserves, who were in camp further down the stream. The Americans followed in confusion. Our people rallied upon

---

* Force 23d April, 1813.—Regulars.................. 520
    "   "   "   "   Militia..................... 460
    "   "   "   "   Indians.................1500—2480

their own advanced rear, consisting of 300 militia, who opened fire at once, and then charged with a cheer, which brought up the regulars still further in the rear. Reynolds and Capt. Laurent Bondy, of the Côte, led up to the muzzles of the American rifles, which, once fired, are no match for the bayonet. Bondy was shot through the body, and fell against a tree. 'Don't stop for me,' he said, to some of the men who paused. 'Don't mind me—I'm done for. Do for those fellows.' And they did.*

"The Kentucky men ran, the sortie was repulsed, the battery recaptured, a large number of prisoners was taken, and again occurred some of the same scenes which had caused so much horror at French Town. The Indians of different tribes, scattered through the woods, were beyond control; they overpowered the escort. One man, Russell, of the 41st, was slain in defending his charge. Tecumseh rushed up, and drove his tomahawk into the skull of a truculent ruffian who would not hold his hand. Some of the prisoners were murdered, and among them Colonel Dudley, the second in command. I call it murder, because I won't call murder by any other name. There is no doubt those Indians were shocking implements of war, though perhaps not much worse than bomb shells or Greek fire, and why could not the Yankees leave the devils alone? Who scalped the red skin at the Ta-ron-tee?† The Indians were fighting for their lands, and avenging their own wrongs. If you

---

* 5th May, 1813.

† James, in his Military Occurrences, Vol. I, p. 62, gives the following version of the same occurrence: "In the pocket of Captain McCulloch of the American army, killed in this affair (Tecumseh and Van Horne) with the Indians, was found a letter addressed to his wife, in which this humane individual states that on the 15th July he had killed an Indian, and had the pleasure of tearing the scalp from the head of the savage with his teeth." That the Indian was scalped is an undoubted fact. We may be allowed to question the operation in dental surgery.

want the skin of a wild cat, you must take the scratching. We did all we could to stop the Indians. We gave five dollars for every prisoner brought in. Hundreds were brought in, and paid for by the Commissaries. I have paid numbers of such certificates myself.

"Another word on these scalping stories. They have been the stock in trade of American writers ever since the war, only they grow a little as they get on. Have these people forgotten the 'heroes of Brownstown, with the scalps on their bayonets,' borne home in triumph? Now if the boast was true, where did the scalps come from? Not from our dead, for I removed them all myself. Not from our wounded, for I helped to remove most of them, and know that none were left. Did they scalp their own dead? or did they scalp the Indians? If they scalped the Indians, what right have they to complain that the Indians scalped them?

"But the defeat of Green Clay had no effect on the place, which still held out. Proctor opened fire from his 24's, and Gratiot gave him shot for shot. We were getting back to the old slow work, and I knew that the supplies were running short. I despatched orders for more, and got them, but we wanted 'push.' Proctor did not go at it in a way to satisfy any one. At last he dismounted his guns, put them on sleds, and let them down the steep bank under the fire of the enemy. It was done, by the men, as if on parade, but it was clear that a retreat was intended, and all began to talk. Tecumseh, through Colonel Elliott, demanded a council. It was held. I was present, but came in after Proctor had spoken. Tecumseh was up, calm, cool, deliberate, thinking in look, very hard in what he said. Elliott translated. 'Our father has brought us here to take the fort, why don't we take it? If his children can't do it, give us spades, and we will work like beavers; we'll eat a way in for him.' Other and harder words followed, until suddenly Proctor, in a passion, turned on Elliott with, 'Sir, you are a traitor.' Elliott instantly, half drawing his sword, answered, 'Sir, you ——— short, and not sweet.' Proctor put his hand on his sword-hilt. Tecumseh, who had sat down, Indian fashion, on his hams, and who was filling the pipe on his tomahawk, rose slowly, and shook the tobacco out, saying to Elliott, 'What does he say?' 'Sit down,' says Elliott, putting his hand on Tecumseh's arm, "never mind what he says." Other officers present moved up at once, and without a word stepped between; all felt it was wrong. Not long after, Elliott resigned his place as Indian Superintendent, and called Proctor out, but no meeting took place. Proctor was right; a commander in the field holds his life for the safety of others; he can't toss it away for the fun of a personal fight.

"Next came the militia. It has been said they deserted Proctor. Nothing can be more untrue, unfair, ungenerous. Who had they to speak for them? He was their mouthpiece. His despatch was the only record—praise others; say nothing about them; and the brave man who fought for all he loved, had nothing to look to but the love of those he fought for. Proctor treated the militia badly. When they saw his guns on skids, and knew the siege was over, they sent respectfully to ask leave to go home, only to put in a crop for the benefit of his men and their own children. He sent them home and disarmed them. He tried to disgrace them, but they would not be disgraced, because they knew they did not deserve it. Brock was another sort of man. He thought, and felt, and spoke for othe men, and other men loved him, and fought for him, and died for him.

"About the middle of July, Proctor planned another attack on Fort Meigs. He only took with him the regulars, and a few Indians. He refused the services of the militia, and, as I before said, took away their arms. How much of his future ill success is to be credited to this piece of policy, you will see. I went with the troops on this second expedition to Fort Meigs.* The plan was to inveigle

---

* 25th July, 1813.

the enemy out of the fort, and to get in with them; but they would not come out, and as the place could not be taken with two six-pounders, the British retired with all the discredit of a defeat. What Proctor could not do at Fort Meigs, he tried to do on a more distant and more defensible work on the Sandusky river, Fort Stephenson, defended by Major Croghan, a brave Irishman, in the United States army. Proctor sent Major Chambers, with a flag, to demand the surrender of the fort.* Croghan came out on the drawbridge of the ditch, and said to Chambers,—'Tell your General he may blow the fort to hell, but it shan't be given up by me.' He was as good as his word.

"Fire was opened on the work from the six-pounders, and on the evening of the 2nd August, Colonel Short, of the 41st, led on the storming party. They rushed through the smoke, down into the ditch, up against the palisades, but neither ladders nor fascines had been provided; the tools they had were bad, some of the axes had no handles. The attempt to tear down the palisades failed. The men then tried, desperately, to clamber over, and while doing so, the enemy opened from a concealed gun, which flanked the ditch, and which, charged with grape, did deadly execution. Lieut. Gordon and Colonel Short were both killed; about 100 men were killed and wounded, and the recall was sounded. The storming party was brought off; the Indians, who don't understand storming, covering the rear. The next morning Proctor left the river.

"Croghan made a gallant defence, and deserved all praise. His number was under 200 men. We had 500, and about 200 Indians. Croghan found in the magazine many boxes of muskets, meant for the militia. He opened them, and provided every one of his men with four or five, loaded ready at his side, so that the musketry fire was tremendous and incessant, and at close quarters, in open day-

---

* 2nd August, 1813.

FORT MEIGS AGAIN—CROGHAN AND FORT STEPHENSON.

light, most fatal, and the masked gun did its work just in the nick of time.

"While these fights had been going on on the west shore of the Detroit, we had been preparing at Amherstburg for a contest on the lake, which we knew must determine who should be master on the western frontier. It was supremacy on this lake, or starvation. The party who held the lake cut off all means of supply from the other, and the more the mouths, the greater the danger. Now, the British had to feed the Indians, and their whole families, as well as their own people, and from the absence of the militia, no crop had been put in.

"Since June, Captain Barclay, of the Royal Navy, had been hard at work, fitting out his small squadron. We had a good harbor and dockyard between Bois Blanc Island and Fort Malden. We were preparing the Detroit, the Queen Charlotte, and other smaller vessels, but Barclay had neither guns, nor men, nor marine stores. The guns from the fort were put on board of the Detroit. I heard Captain Finnis ask Proctor to let him have two 24-pounders, the same that had been withdrawn from before Fort Meigs. Proctor said he must keep them to cover his retreat, should it take place 'General,' said Finnis, 'if we are lost, you are gone. Give me the guns, and, mayhap, you won't have to retreat at all." Finnis was right; the guns might have saved all. As it was, they were taken without a shot fired, at Dalson's farm. Poor Finnis, who was a brave officer, was killed at the second broadside. The same ball killed Garden, of the Newfoundlanders, acting as marines, another brave officer. I was not in the sea fight of course, but I know that when the ships were supplied, our stock in store was reduced very low.

"Perry's squadron were all armed with 32's and long 24's. His two best ships, the Lawrence and Niagara, were brigs, armed each with 20 32-pounder Columbiads. The best of ours had only a motley complement of 24's, 16's, and 12's ; one brig, the Hunter, had 10, 4-pounders. The men told me that when engaged with the American schooners, their 32's crashed through her; while, in return, our balls stuck in the side of the American, like currants in a pudding."

CHAPTER XX.

Captain Barclay and Commodore Perry—Resources of each—Perry's difficulty—Crosses the bar at Presqu'Isle—Description of Barclay's crew and armament—10th September—Battle of Lake Erie—Desperate contest—The Lawrence surrenders—Perry's personal exploit—Changes his ships—Renews the contest—The British squadron captured—Officers all killed or wounded—The resistance of Barclay and his crews—Barclay's heroic character and conduct—Appearance before a Court martial—Honourably acquitted—Barclay's defeat, Proctor's doom—Position of Proctor—Nature of country—Supplies exhausted—Alternative of retreat or surrender—Retreats—Line of march—Difficulties—Followed by Harrison—Kentucky Mounted Riflemen—Tactics in the battle—Character of forest—Not impracticable to horsemen.

We take leave of Squire Reynolds, and his store of incidents, at the time of this great disaster. While Barclay had been occupied at Amherstburg, Commodore Perry had been equally busy at the port of Presqu'Isle, in Pennsylvania, on Lake Erie. He had the great advantage of being near to his supplies, and abounding in them. From the sea-board he had received excellent crews. Military and marine stores had been furnished to him at great cost and trouble, but neither cost nor trouble could supply Captain Barclay.

For some time Perry labored under this disadvantage: Presqu'Isle was a bar harbour, across which he could not take his ships with their guns on board. In consequence, Barclay lay off the harbour, and, with a very inferior force, kept him at bay. He could not venture into deep water in disarmed ships, but a gale at last drove Barclay away. Perry slipped out, took his guns on board from lighters, and was, from that moment, master of the lake. Not, however, without a desperate struggle. Barclay retired to Malden, and pushed on his preparations. The Detroit was fitted for sea with guns of all calibres. Fifty able bodied seamen came up from Kingston, and were divided among the five vessels of the squadron, the remainder of the crews was composed of Canadian lake seamen, some of the amphibious Newfoundlanders, and marines from the 41st foot.*

At length, when, as Barclay writes,† " there was not a day's flour in the store, and the squadron was on half-allowance of many things," and " it was necessary to fight the enemy to enable us to get supplies of every description," the British squadron took to the lake. The distance from Malden to Put-in-Bay, where the American fleet lay at anchor, was about sixty miles. On the morning of the 10th September, 1813, at sunrise, the two squadrons sighted each other, and prepared both for the battle. At a quarter before twelve, noon, the British, having the advantage of the wind, commenced the action. Barclay, in the Detroit, engaged the Lawrence, Commodore Perry; and for two hours the battle raged. The Lawrence was utterly disabled, and reduced to an unmanageable hulk. At this critical moment Perry did a daring feat. He left

*ENGLISH FLEET.	AMERICAN FLEET.
Detroit,..............19	Lawrence,...............20
Queen Charlotte,......17	Niagara,................20
Lady Provost,.........13	Caledonia,.............. 3
Hunter, ...10	Ariel, ... 4
Chippewa,............. 1	Trippe, ... 1
Little Belt,........... 3	Tigress,................ 1
—	Somers,................. 2
63	Scorpion,............... 2
	Ohio,................... 1
	Porcupine,.............. 1
	55
Weight of metal: British, 459lbs.	American,.........928lbs.
Number of men,........ 345	Number of men,....580

† Barclay's Despatch:—Put-in-Bay, Lake Erie, 22nd September, 1813.

the Lawrence in a small boat, and, passing through the midst of the fire, gained the deck of his consort, the Niagara, and re-hoisted his flag. The Niagara was uninjured. Before, however, he could take part in the fight, the Lawrence struck her flag to Barclay. Then came a reverse. The wind had changed, and gave Perry the advantage. The Niagara bore up, and passed through the British line, engaging the Detroit and Queen Charlotte. The Detroit had been severely handled in her contest with the Lawrence, and had become since a special object for the raking attentions of the gunboats. Finnis, of the Queen Charlotte, had been killed early in the action; his first Lieutenant, Stokoe, had been struck senseless by a splinter. Irvine, of the Provincial Navy, who succeeded, with equal courage, may not have had the experience of these officers. He either fell on board of the Detroit, or the Detroit fell on board of him. Garland, first Lieutenant of the Detroit, was mortally wounded, and Barclay himself was at last shot down, and compelled to leave the deck. At this moment Lieut. Buchan, who commanded the Lady Prevost, and Lieut. Bignall, who commanded the Hunter, were both wounded. "Every officer, in fact, commanding vessels, and their seconds, were either killed, or wounded so severely as to be unable to keep the deck. Never in any action was the loss more severe."*

In this condition, without officers to direct or men to fight—for the slaughter, from the superior weight of metal of the enemy, had been dreadful,—and so wrecked, that, in a heavy sea on the next day, both the Detroit and the Queen Charlotte lost their masts,—after four hours of desperate fighting, the whole squadron was compelled to surrender.

Writers more addicted to sound than sense, have thought fit to ascribe their misfortunes to the "mixed crew of Canadians and

---

* Barclay's Letter:—Put-in-Bay, Lake Erie, Sept. 22nd, 1813.

soldiers" who manned the British squadron. Barclay might well be proud of the "Canadians and soldiers," who, with vessels ill-fitted and half-armed, with guns of all calibres, and insufficient ammunition, had enabled him for five hours to maintain this unequal contest; who had compelled the Lawrence to strike her colours, and who yielded at last to nearly double strength of men, and more than double weight of metal. It may be questioned if the best seamen who fought under Rodney or Collingwood could have done more.

Cooper, in his Naval History, remarks, in the right spirit of an American sailor: " Stress was laid at the time on the fact that a portion of the British crews were Provincials; but the history of this continent is filled with instances in which men of that character have gained battles, which went to increase the renown of the mother country, without obtaining any credit for it. The hardy frontier-men of the American lakes are as able to endure fatigue, as ready to engage, and as constant in battle, as the seamen of any marine in the world. They merely require good leaders, and these the English appear to have possessed in Captain Barclay and his assistants."

Barclay was the type of a British sailor. He had served under Nelson. He was noted for personal courage, and for that moral courage which, at the call of duty, defies despair. He was one of those sea-dogs which looses its hold only in death. He expected more from human nature than could be found in any other nature than his own. Defeat disturbed a temper which death could not daunt. His despatch on this occasion does not do justice to the brave men who stood by him so truly.

Some months afterwards, he tottered before a court-martial, like a Roman trophy—nothing but helm and hauberk. He had lost an arm at Trafalgar; the other was rendered useless by a grape shot through the shoulder. He was further weakened by several severe flesh wounds. Little wonder, that men not given to such weakness shed tears at the spectacle. Little wonder, that the president of the court, in returning his sword, told him, in a voice tremulous with emotion, that the conduct of himself and men had been most honourable to themselves and to their country.

Barclay's disaster was a knell of doom to Proctor. The possibility of such a result and its consequences had not been unforeseen. Salvation would have been the issue of success. Barclay had gallantly risked his "forlorn hope" to save his friends, and had failed,—retreat or ruin alone remained.

Proctor's position should be fairly understood. Winter was not far before him—Autumn was upon him. The forest tracks called roads, were, by the rains of the season, made almost impassable. Soon they would be impracticable. The only feasible communication, that of the river and lake, was intercepted by the American fleet. Fort Malden had been divested of its guns, its ammunition, and its spare food to supply Barclay. The garrisons on the line of the Detroit river could only be victualled from the scanty stores in hand, or be supplied from Burlington Bay. This resource was distant 200 miles from the nearest post. It was clearly more wise, and easier to march his troops to find supplies—than to bring supplies to find his troops,—prisoners, perhaps, in the hands of an enemy. But, whether for advance or for retreat, the by-paths of the forest, intermediate, were such as the macadamized and locomotive imagination of the present day cannot encompass. A backwoodsman, laden with his axe, wading here, ploutering there, stumbling over rotted trees, protruding stumps, a bit of a half submerged corduroy road for one short space—then an adhesive clay bank—then a mile, or two, or more, of black muck swamp,—may possibly, clay-clogged and footsore, and with much pain in the small of his back, find himself by sundown at the foot of a hemlock or cedar, with a fire at his feet, having done manfully about ten miles for his day's work ; Apart from the fire, and the blessed rest, practice deducts woefully from the poetry of bush life. But what could be done by the unaccustomed soldier, from long garrison service, out of training, with his pack and his blanket, canteen and haversack, with his musket and full supply of ammunition—a weight calculated by Napier, at his day, to exceed sixty pounds. What could the best and most enduring man, so laden, be expected to do, amid the sloughs of this unmitigated wilderness. But what was to be done with the impediments—the guns, the ammunition waggons, the daily and reserve supplies *de guerre et de bouche?* The man might carry enough to support life from day to day—but what was to provide for the morrow ? How were the women and children,—the rapid accumulations,—the *flotsam* and *jetsam* of a fluctuating force, to be conveyed away, protected and fed, for at least twenty marches ? And yet the alternative of ruinous retreat was hopeless surrender. Hull might have been exchanged on his own ground.

Proctor preferred at once the wiser part—rapidly he called in his outposts on either side of the river Detroit ; he dismantled Malden, Windsor, Sandwich, destroyed such stores as could not usefully be removed,—and then, having destroyed all public buildings, in the fort at Detroit, and transported all the guns across the river to the Canadian side at Windsor, he commenced his retreat upon Burlington Heights. It was deliberately organized and judiciously planned. The retreat being necessary, it was presumed that the Americans would not follow the British and their Indian allies far into the depths of the forest. A protracted advance would equalize the difficulties of either party—the American, removed from his base of supply, would certainly not find in the track of his adversary, improved means of transportation. So Proctor collected his people at Windsor ; sent off his heavy baggage, reserve supplies, women and children, in advance, and on the 28th Sept. finally relinquished Detroit, and fell back upon British territory. His route was well chosen to assist him as far as possible into the interior.

On Lake St. Clair, thirty miles due East of Detroit, is the embouchure of the Thames, emulous in its turbid tide alone, of its British prototype. It is navigable for small vessels, some seventy or eighty miles on the line of the proposed retreat. The road, such as it was, followed the North shore of the sinuous and sluggish stream, at places on the bank, at others, and where "cutting off bends" at some distance from the river. The direction of the stream, ascending, of the line of road, and of the line of retreat, were generally the same, due East. The boats having been despatched with the *impedimenta*, the troops following, covered the advanced retreat. The force at this time, with Proctor, consisted of about 830 men, including the 41st Regt., about 540 strong. The residue consisted of men of the Royal Newfoundland regiment and militia. Tecumseh, the Shawanee Chief, with 500 warriors, and the invariable incumbrance on the Indian war path, a large number of squaws and papooses, all of whom had to be fed by the British commander.

The American force under Gen. Harrison, which had been thrown on the Canadian shore of the river Detroit, amounted to 5,000 men. Deductions having been made for the occupation of Malden, Windsor, and the Fort at Detroit, had left a force at Harrison's disposal of 3,500 men, of whom 1,500 were Kentucky Mounted Riflemen, of whom this officer says in his despatch to his own government, " the American backwoodsmen ride better in the woods than any other people,—a musket or rifle is no impediment, they being accustomed to carry them on horseback from their earliest youth."* It is well known, too, to those who have had any experience in the bush, that horses used to this work, acquire an

---

* Despatch :—Detroit, 9th October, 1863.

instinctive facility for dodging difficulties and surmounting obstacles, —they become singularly sure-footed and steady; however deep they may plunge, they rarely stumble. Horses so trained, thread the mazes of the forest at a rapid walk, and can only be checked by a wind-fall or black swamp.

It is also worthy of remark, that the whole of this part of Canada is a rich alluvial deposit reclaimed in the course of ages from Lake St. Clair. The forests are of prodigious size. Here is found in luxuriant growth,—six feet in diameter at the base,—the noble black walnut, now so favourably known for purposes of domestic ornament and use; and here the wild turkey, weighing from 20 to 30 lbs., displays in large flocks, its lustrous plumage, rich with metallic tints, and frights the solitude with its unearthly gobblings. These noble overtowering trees intercept the light, and to a great extent destroy the undergrowth—between the huge trunks the space is clear; you may ride between them as freely as through the aisles of a Gothic Cathedral. The trees which would neutralize and disturb the regular formation of infantry, offer but little impediment to a bold irregular cavalry, each horseman fighting " on his own hook."

CHAPTER XXI.

Proctor falls back to Baptiste Creek—General Harrison with Perry's assistance follows—5th October—British force halts at Dalson's Farm—Colonel Maclean of Scarborough—His reminiscences—Warburton in command at Dalson's—Proctor retires personally to Moravian Town—Roused before daylight—Intelligence—Troops attacked and retreating—Warburton followed by Shelby and Kentucky riflemen—Description of these troops and mode of attack—Proctor halts his men—Nature of ground and position—Tecumseh—His last words—No abattis made—American attack—Defeat and surrender of the British.

Proctor had drawn off on the 28th of September. His baggage-waggons and store-boats had been sent on in advance. Many of his men had already marched 18 miles through a country deep as the worst marsh in Holland. They fell back leisurely for about 30 miles to Baptiste Creek, near the mouth of the Thames. They crossed on a bridge which, when passed, was most unaccountably left by the troops undestroyed. They then took up their line of march on the north shore of the Thames. They still covered the rear of their boats and convoys.

From the Bridge to Dalson's farm, near where the town of Chatham now stands, was a distance of about 16 miles. Dalson's was a small clearing, one of those scattered Oases which were then found, at long intervals, in the wilderness. Here, the uninterrupted level was broken by a rising ground, probably pitched upon by the pioneer and bush ranger, as possessing the recommendation of dryness.

Here, upon the 5th of Oct., Proctor had halted with his whole force. He had been retarded by the state of the roads, and by the necessity of not leaving in the rear, supply-boats—delayed by the tortuous course of the river—by mud banks, and all the obstructions which accident heaps upon ill-fortune. The rains, though sufficient to destroy the roads, were insufficient to swell the river.

Harrison followed by the same route, supported by Commodore Perry, with three gun-boats, and a flotilla of smaller craft—manned from the American fleet, buoyant with success. The retiring army, laden with an unnecessary amount of baggage, and weighed down by moral depression, was pursued by lusty arms and light hearts, in boats lighter and more swift, from the smaller requirements of an army in pursuit.

It is embarrassing to encounter, at this point, the conflicting and angry statements, and harsh comments on the ensuing events.— Happily, however, at this moment of deep and painful embarrassment, there has come to our aid a living eye-witness of these events, whose opportunities and whose fidelity are beyond cavil.

In the township of Scarborough, and within a few miles of Toronto, still lives Colonel Maclean, who was a lieutenant in the 41st, at the battle of the Thames. He was on the staff of General Proctor. He is a son of the brave Clerk of the Legislative Assembly, who, as a volunteer in the ranks, had fallen by the side of McNeil, at York. He had obtained a commission in the 41st, and had seen service in all the varied affairs in Michigan, and on the river Detroit. He was present at the battle of the Thames. After the war of 1812, he served his Sovereign with his old regiment in India—before the stockades of Rangoon and Prome ; had occupied the temples of Ava, and had witnessed the subjection of the Court of Ummerapoora. At mature age, he returned to his paternal farm; and under the lowly roof of one of those old-fashioned, wide-spread Canadian dwellings, which looks like a gigantic mushroom, or the wide and black expansion of an Arab tent, he dispenses a homely, yet frank and soldierly, hospitality, which an Arab might envy. Here, on the advanced side of 70, he presents the remains of a giant form, and an intellect which compels us to own, that the men of 1812 were the mastodons of our formation. It may seem hypercritical, but it is not less observable, that the exuviæ of a race fast passing away indicate that the natural development of the present generation does not equal that of their grandsires.

Maclean was on Proctor's staff, saw all that one man could see, and knew more than most around him. The story of the fight is given almost in his own words. Proctor, on the afternoon of the 4th Oct., had taken up a good defensible position at Dalson's Farm, and had left his force under his second in command, Major Warburton. Proctor did not anticipate an immediate advance of the enemy. He knew that the difficulties of his own movements must still more embarrass theirs, and it was believed that the American commander would prefer rather to bridge the quagmires with gold, than plunge into them to provoke an encounter with such a foe, desperately at bay.

With the heavy baggage in advance was the wife and family of the General. They had shared with him, for many months, in the hardships of a frontier campaign, and had been despatched some days before, with other helpless impediments to the march, in the direction of the retreat. They had reached the Indian village known as Moravian Town, from certain missionaries of that persuasion who had devoted themselves to holy labors among the savages in that part of Canada. This mission was about 16 miles from Dalson's Farm. The General, having made his arrangements, proceeded with his staff to Moravian Town to meet his family. Maclean offered to remain and watch events; but the General, confident in the security of the position, smiled at the proposal, and directed his young Aid to accompany him.

Before daylight they were aroused from their sleep by hurried intelligence from the front, that the enemy had reached and attacked the position at Dalson's Farm, and that the troops were falling back. The rapid strides of exultant pursuit had overreached the leaden footsteps of unwilling retreat. An early frost had suddenly set in, hardening the roads and bridging the morasses, and offering one of those chance combinations of ill-luck which persecutes the unfortunate. Thus favoured, the American Mounted Rifles had pushed on, and, about an hour after midnight, were in the British bivouac.

Warburton retired at once, and was perseveringly followed by Harrison and his men. These men, styled by Harrison "mounted infantry," were for the most part Kentucky trappers and hunters—men like the leather-stocking of Cooper, inured to the wilderness, and between whom and the Indians there existed a constant warfare and chronic hatred. Hardy, daring, keen, ruthless, admirably clad in a leathern hunting-frock and trowsers, decorated with tasselled fringes, a handkerchief of red, or blue, or yellow, wrapped tightly around the head, with tomahawk and scalping-knife in his belt, and his trusty rifle in his hand, the Kentucky pioneer presented an appearance as redoubtable as it was picturesque. As a cavalry soldier, in the European acceptation of the term, he was useless; not a man among them bore a sabre; but as scouts or videttes, and for the purpose of rapid advance or retreat, they were invaluable. The usual tactics of these horsemen, however, were to follow up and harass the retreating foe, and, dismounting from their docile steeds, plunge among the trees, and ply the fatal rifle. Upon this occasion, profiting by the unexpected improvement in the roads, they had recourse to a further expedient. Every man, like the Templars of old, brought on a foot-soldier behind him, so that in actual conflict a line of skirmishers, thrown to the front, covered and concealed by their smoke, the approaching cavaliers. This dangerous force was under the immediate command of an ex-governor of Kentucky—Shelby—a veteran of the revolutionary war, who, at the age of 66, still showed all the fire and vigour and energy of youth.

Such were the men who now tracked down the retiring British soldiers. Proctor, roused from his sleep, took to horse, and with his staff rode to the front. He encountered the retreating force about three miles to the west of Moravian Town. Day was breaking. He instantly ordered the whole force to halt, and face right about. The order was most gladly met. The men, after a wearisome night's march, seemed to be reinvigorated by the prospect of a fight. The position thus accidentally taken up was very favourable. The Thames, not wide, but deep, covered the left flank; the road cut the line perpendicularly at about 200 yards from the river; from the road the line of front continued for about 300 yards, until it struck an impassable cedar swamp, which effectually covered the right flank. Upon this narrow front Proctor disposed his small force. They had contrived to bring up with them a single gun, a six-pounder, on a travelling-carriage. This piece of artillery was planted on the road, in what may be termed the centre of the position. The men were deployed to the right and left from the river to the swamp, their formation being dislocated and broken by the intervening trees. In front of the position was a continuous, but open, forest. The swamp on the right was occupied by the Indians. This disposition was excellent. The left flank was secure, the centre strong. The right flank, more extended, was covered by the swamp, which, extending lengthwise in the direction of the road, flanked the American attack on the main position. Here Tecumseh, in a morass, of which the mere name alone can convey no idea to the uninitiated—amid moss-hung trees and twisted trunks, and trees fallen and rotten, overgrown with a vegetation tangled and thick, smothered by too much moisture and too little air, knee-deep at the best, and often deeper—was unassailable by the Kentucky horsemen, while he could sally out upon their flank, and wage a hand to hand conflict, in which the lithe Indian on foot, with rifle and tomahawk, was more than a match for the individual horseman.

These dispositions were made at about six o'clock in the morning. Two hours elapsed before the enemy appeared. In that interval, Tecumseh had conference with Proctor. On parting, he shook hands with his chief, with a fearless look. His last words were, "Father! have a big heart!" It was believed that Tecumseh had retired to his people in the swamp with the understanding that he was to await the discharge of the gun as a signal for his onset. The gun was never fired.

Two hours elapsed. In that interval the men sat down and rested, and partook of such scraps of food as remained in their haversacks. But no precaution was made against surprise, or to notify an advance. No pickets were thrown out, nor videttes to the front, though a small force of militia cavalry was at the General's disposal. MacLean rode down the front track for about a mile, and saw nothing, but heard the American bugles ringing in the woods around him.

Another precaution—the one most naturally suggested and easily executed—was incomprehensibly omitted. A dozen axes—and with the force, there must have been one hundred—would, in an hour, have cut down an *abattis* impassable to men on horseback, clearing also the front to musketry fire. This simple expedient never occurred to Proctor; at all events, it was never put in practice.

The enemy, by their scouts, had reconnoitered and saw clearly the British position. About 8 A. M. they first showed the head of their advance. They came on slowly, carefully covering themselves with the trees. The riflemen on foot crept on stealthily in front, and soon troubled the British line. The horsemen followed, dodging behind trees, but still maintaining a disconnected formation. They approached nearer and nearer. On a sudden, they clustered together, and made a rush forward. They were met by a volley, which daunted them for a moment. In another, they again clustered together, and, before the men could reload, charged again. The men broke, and in one moment more, all was over.

The chief attack was on the right of the road and line. The men here threw down their firelocks. The gun and the left flank, taken in reverse, broke and surrendered in detail. Proctor and his staff, stunned by the sudden disaster, and overborne by the irresistible tide of fugitives, retired upon Moravian Town, and found their way ultimately, in wretched plight, to Burlington Heights. One officer and twenty or thirty men, who were on the extreme right of the line, next to the Indian ambuscade, withdrew unobserved, and joined the other fugitives at Ancaster.

The whole effective British force engaged on that 5th of October, was 476 men, of whom 12 were killed and 22 wounded. The American army on the field amounted to above 3,000 men.

This great catastrophe, unparalleled in the annals of the British army, requires some further investigation. It may be said, in extenuation, that the men were worn out, and borne down by harassing and irritating service, and that, from the nature of this service, all regimental pride, all *esprit de corps*, had been lost. They had been detached on outpost duty for months, in the most exposed places. Fever and ague, and the depressing symptoms of this disease, were rife among them; 170 men were then in hospital. They had not received pay for months; they had no great-coats; their food had failed. They knew that on the preceding day their supply-boats, fallen to the rear, had been taken by the enemy. They had 180 miles of wilderness behind them; they were exhausted by the night's march. They knew that there was no hope of successful retreat. The expressions used by them, when faced about in the morning, showed that they were ready to strike a last blow; but they felt that it was the last.

But there was another element of disintegration at work. Proctor was on bad terms with his regiment. He was the General commanding on the frontier. He was also Lieut.-Colonel of H. M. 41st Infantry. There is not in the whole social fabric a more beautiful or more delicate piece of machinery than the internal structure and economy of a British regiment. What a main-spring is to a watch, such is harmony among the officers. While they pull well together with the good taste and good feeling which characterize the service, the same manly, cheery, cordial spirit prevails in every barrack-room. The men, with intuitive tact and feeling, without knowing how, nor caring how, imitate that which recommends itself to their best instincts. Discord among the officers disconcerts good men, and makes bad men licentious. Discontent and dissatisfaction corrode discipline. It did so in the present instance. The fact and the effect were both known. The bands of discipline were relaxed, and broke at the first strain, and the result was ruin.

To this unhappy combination of causes must be ascribed the want of energetic unanimity, and the absence of that mutual confidence, which begets self-reliance, and is the foundation of all military coherence in the hour of trial. The men had ceased to rely on one another—to regard " shoulder to shoulder," as the bulwark of strength and maxim of salvation. To these causes must be ascribed the fall of a corps, to that hour distinguished for martial conduct, and which, on fifty stricken fields since, has washed out, with the best blood of its bravest, that one, solitary, spot on an honoured escutcheon.*

Proctor was tried by a court-martial. It is not for the Canadian

---

* To this holocaust of expiation Canada has contributed its victims. Montizambert, Major, a member of one of the oldest and most respected families in Quebec, served in this regiment in India—at Candahar, at Cabool, in the Kyber Pass—and was slain while gallantly leading his men on the 12th Sept., 1848, in Mooltan. Lieut. Evans of the 41st, son of Gen. Evans, was killed while storming a hill fort in Affghanistan, subsequent to the fall of Cabul in 1846.

chronicler to add one word to the decision of His Royal Highness the Prince Regent, dated Horse Guards, 9th Sept., 1815, by which so much of previous service, and perhaps of future promise, were extinguished for ever.

CHAPTER XXII.

Tecumseh—His character—Origin—Tribe of the Shawanese—From Virginia—Driven into Ohio—Thence into Michigan—The Brothers Elksottawa and Tecumseh—Influence of Tecumseh over Indian tribes, due to his personal qualities—Anecdotes—Haughty conduct towards the "Long Knives"—His disinterestedness—Indian skill as draftsman—His personal appearance and costume—Stern adherence to England—Last words to Proctor—Attack of the American riflemen—Tecumseh slain by the hand of Col. James Johnston—The four heraldic supporters of Canada—Outrage offered to his remains.

But the great episode of this fatal field has yet to be related. Here fell Tecumseh. Here fell the untaught Shawanese, the friend and comrade of Brock. It is difficult to do justice to the memory of this worthy compeer of Spartacus, of our own Caractacus, and of that noble Æthiop, Toussaint L'Ouverture. No braver barbarian ever graced Roman triumph. Here he fell—

Butchered, to make a Roman holiday!

We have but few of the *notabilia* of his early career. He was chief, or chief-conjoint, of the Shawanese, a tribe originally of Virginian stock, but which, in the slow but sure progress of European cupidity and aggression, had been driven back from the sea-coast, and had established their hunting-lodges in .the Scioto country, in what is now the State of Ohio. This was in 1730. In 1812 they were estimated to number about three hundred warriors.* They were designated the "fierce Shawanese," and have been denounced for their ferocity; but men and the descendants of men familiar

---

* Schoolcraft. Indian Tribes. Vol. I, p. 301.

with the Inquisition, the *auto-da-fe*, the fires of Smithfield and of the Grenelle,—with the rack, the wheel, the red-hot pincers, and the boiling pitch,—with

> Luke's iron crown, and Damien's bed of steel—

have no pretence for fastidiousness on this score; nor should they use hard words towards their fellow-men, frenzied by acts of cruel and often wanton wrong. Their contact with the whites had not tended to abate this fierce characteristic. Year by year, and inch by inch, had they been forced back, from camp-fire to camp-fire, from the Atlantic to the Wabash, appealing in vain to a Christian doctrine since known as the "Monroe," and which, being done into plain English, apparently means—

> That they should take who have the power,
> And they should keep who can.

Hunted and harried, in course of time they receded until they found themselves in the territory of Michigan, under British protection. In 1812 they obeyed the counsels of the Prophet Elksottawa, and followed to the field his more warlike brother Tecumseh. From his youth up he had shown himself to be a remarkable man. Devoid of education, in the European acceptation of the term, he had yet learned to control himself. Instinctively he had risen above the instincts and passions of his race. He despised plunder; he abjured the use of spirits; he had overcome a propensity strong within him, and had, for years, renounced "fire-water." His conduct in the field was only exceeded by his eloquence in council. This combination of head and hand won the hearts of his tribe and of their savage allies. The influence of the chief extended over the warriors of many other Indian nations. With the skill of a statesman he appeased all dissensions, reconciled all interests, and united all minds in one common alliance against the hated Americans. This was due to his personal qualities alone.

He had little respect for the superstitions of his people. "Totems" and genealogies he treated with indifference. As a specimen of his eloquence, may be related his reply to Governor Harrison of Indiana. On the 12th August, 1810, he appeared, at the head of 400 warriors, at Vincennes, in front of the Governor's residence, and was invited "*in*." He replied: "Houses are built for you to hold council in; Indians hold theirs in the open air." When the meeting was over, one of the governor's aides-de-camp said to him, pointing to a chair: "Your father requests you to take a seat at his side." Standing erect, and in a scornful tone, the chief answered: "My father! the sun is my father, and the earth my mother. On her bosom I will repose;" and then seated himself upon the ground.

He hated the "Long-knives" with an intensity of hatred. In battle, in actual conflict, he was unsparing. To the wounded he was pitiful; from the conquered he turned with contempt. At the capture of Detroit, to a remark from Brock, he replied, haughtily: "I despise them too much to meddle with them." Not an act of violence could be charged against the Indians on that occasion. Brock, admiring the control he possessed and exercised, took off his silken scarf, and wound it round the waist of the chief. Tecumseh was, in despite of his stoicism, evidently gratified; but, to the surprise of all, appeared the next day without the decoration. To an inquiry, he answered that he could not wear such a distinction, when an older and an abler warrior was present. He had given the sash to the Wyandot chief, Round-head. Before crossing the Detroit, to attack Hull, Brock had sought from him topographical information. Tecumseh threw himself on the ground, took a sheet of bark, and with his knife traced a map of the country—its woods, hills, rivers, roads, morasses,—which the best officer in the army could not have surpassed. He was taciturn by habit, after the manner of the Indians; but when roused, his intellect and his imagination gave utterance to a flood of impassioned oratory.*

The American delineator delights in depicting Tecumseh in a red coat, with a pair of tinsel epaulettes, such as append to the shoulders of unhappy British officers on the American stage. He has even been mustered into the service as a Brigadier-General. Without disrespect to his memory, it may be said that he did not hold a rank which he would have adorned. Contrary to the Indian nature, he had an aversion to external ornament. His invariable costume was the deer-skin coat and fringed pantaloons; Indian moccasins on his feet, and an eagle-feather in the red kerchief wound round his head, composed his simple and soldierly accoutrements. Richard, Cœur de Lion, himself was not more contemptuous of spoil, or avid of glory. He was about five feet ten inches in height, with the eye of a hawk, and of gesture rapid; of a well-knit, active figure; dignified when composed, and possessing features of countenance which, even in death, indicated a lofty spirit. He was in the forty-fourth year of his age when he fell.

He had, under severe trial, adhered with stern fidelity to the British arms. He did not assimilate with Proctor. Still, in prosperity and in adversity, with his counsel, or against it, to the last hour he was true as steel. True to King George, true to British men,

---

* The greater portion of the facts relating to the career and character of Tecumseh, have been drawn from "Tupper's Life of Brock," and from the spirited sketch of the chief given therein, and drawn by Colonel Glegg, afterwards Military Secretary Lord Aylmer in Canada; but, in the temporary absence of the book, and, in addition, recourse has been had to one of a series of papers on the war of 1812, which have lately appeared in a popular periodical—*Harper's Magazine*. It is to be regretted that these papers, cleverly written and artistically illustrated, should, in an attractive form, pander to the worst prejudices of an obsolete time, and should disseminate, near to our own firesides, and in the year of grace 1863, the most unjustifiable statements with respect to Indian violence and British complicity.

true to his faith in a cause and in a people of whom he had but an indistinct idea, he died fearlessly in that faith, true to the last. His death sheds a halo on the story of a much abused and fast departing race. May the people of England and their descendants in Canada never forget this noble sacrifice, or the sacred obligation it imposes. It should be held as the seal of a great covenant. "And Jonathan said to David, the Lord be between thee and me, and between my seed and thy seed for ever."

The last words of Tecumseh to Proctor, had been: "Father, have a big heart!"—and with his own big heart on his lips, he withdrew to direct his own people in the swamp on the left of the battle-field. The American horsemen in their advance divided into two bodies. The right division, under Lieut.-Colonel James Johnston, advanced upon the British line, threw out their dismounted riflemen, and charged with the effect related. The left division, under Colonel Richard M. Johnston, the elder brother, attacked the Indians in the swamp. An account given by a fair American writer is intelligible enough.* Richard Johnston and twenty of his men devoted themselves to draw the Indian fire. Nineteen out of the twenty-one fell, but the Indians, elated by their success, sprang from their covert and met, on even ground, a portion of the rifles who had been providently dismounted, and who, now pushed forward into the fight. Johnston, himself wounded in four places, but still in the saddle, was attacked by a prominent warrior, who wounded him a fifth time with a rifle shot. At the same moment, his horse, also wounded, stumbled forward, but did not throw his rider. Johnston had at his side a pistol loaded with four buckshot and a bullet. He saw the Chief rush at him with upraised tomahawk—levelled his pistol and fired. He remembered no more. He could discover nothing through the smoke—faint from loss of blood, he reeled out of the

---

* Army and Navy of America, by Jacob K. Neff, M.D., p. 566.

saddle, and was borne almost lifeless from the spot. He was told afterwards, that he had killed Tecumseh. The Colonel gave his story simply and not boastfully, but others scrambled for credit where a brave man found cause for pain. There is every reason to believe that Johnston did slay Tecumseh. On his body was found the marks of four buckshots and a bullet. These wounds had caused his death. From their direction they must have been inflicted from above—as from a man on horseback. Johnston was the only man on horseback in that part of the field.*

And so died as brave and as true a soldier of England as ever trod the heather of the Highlands or the wealds of Kent. He completes the tale of the immortal four, who, to the end of time, will hold up in the face of all nations, the young escutcheon of Canada. Four more chivalrous supporters of a national trophy have never before adorned the pages of History or the triumphs of Sculpture, than Wolfe and Montcalm—Brock and Tecumseh.

It is painful to be compelled to record the disgraceful fact, that the body of the Indian hero was treated with foul indignity. It is believed, that the inanimate corse was scalped, and it was braggishly asserted by the Kentucky men, that strips flayed from his skin had been used as razor straps.† Scotchmen of the present day blush

---

* Battle of the Thames. "This action fought in October, 1813, was the last and most complete defeat of the Savages of the North-Western Lakes. Tecumseh was supposed to have fallen by the hand of Colonel Johnston, of Kentucky; but that veteran soldier has himself said, that all he could say, was: when attacked by the Chief, he fired, and when the smoke cleared away, the Indian lay dead before him. The popular account attributes the deadly aim and wound to one Mason, a native of the county of Wexford, Ireland, who though a grandfather, aged four-score, volunteered his services on that expedition. He had been an old revolutionary soldier, and fought in the ranks with his own sons—themselves men of middle age."—*History of the Irish Settlers in North America*, by Thomas d'Arcy McGee.

† "The Indian hero, Tecumseh, after being killed, was literally flayed in part by the Americans, and his skin carried off as a trophy." *Vide* Appendix—Bishop Strachan's Letter.

when told, that after the battle of Sterling—five centuries and a a half ago,—their countrymen made whip-thongs of the hide of Crossingham, the English Treasurer; and generations of Americans will remember, with greater shame, an act of equal barbarism, committed, in a refined age, by a Puritan people, with even less show of provocation.

CHAP. XXIII.

Battle of the Thames—Its effect—In the States—In Canada. Sir George Prevost. Demonstration on Niagara. Vincent concentrates at Burlington Heights. American projects on Montreal. Generals Wilkinson and Hampton. Plan of attack from the West and from Lake Champlain. Hampton advances to Odelltown—Encountered by De Salaberry—Retires—Followed to the Four Corners. Career of De Salaberry—Attempts to surprise the Americans—Discovered—Falls back on the line of Chateauguay. Preparations for defence. Reports on the battle by the American Adjutant-General, King.

The catastrophe of the Thames was a source of intense exultation to the American government and people. "Io triumphe" resounded through the land. It had obliterated the disaster of Hull. It had restored the Western country, the territory of Michigan, and the Fort of Detroit, to the American arms. It had cowed the Indians. Cannon, the trophies of Burgoyne and Saratoga, which had been re-captured by Brock, were re-taken and paraded, crowned with flowers. The remnants of a British regiment were marched with triumphal pomp through the *bourgades* of the West, and though entitled to the treatment usually accorded to prisoners of war, had been ignominiously herded with the inmates of a local Penitentiary.* British officers, confined in the cells at Frankfort in Kentucky, had leisure to study the philosophy of institutions, which award the same penalty for shooting a wife or stealing a negress. To crown all, it elevated Shelby and Johnston to the rank of heroes, and, in after years, made General Harrison President of the United States.

---

* James, Vol. II, p. 299.

It fell as a heavy blow upon the British, but it caused no discouragement among the people of Canada. It roused much indignation, and caused a renewed outburst of dogged resolution, but the immediate advantage to the Americans was immense. It gave them undisputed possession of the waters of Lake Erie and Lake Huron. It relieved them from all apprehension on their Western frontier, and enabled the Cabinet of Washington to concentrate their energies and their forces on the long contemplated project against Montreal.

In retracing our steps from West to East, we may be allowed to express surprise, that Harrison had not followed vigorously in the same direction, and treading with his Kentucky horse on the retreating footsteps of Proctor, reached, simultaneously, with him his refuge at Ancaster., The position of Burlington Heights might thus have been assailed on all sides, by land and lake, for speedy means of communication with Chauncey and his fleet at Niagara could easily have been found, and the British force advanced on the Niagara frontier, would have been placed between two fires; and cut off from reinforcements and supply, would have been exposed to the fate which had just befallen the army of the West, or the Right Division.

For, be it remembered, that after the successful actions at Stoney Creek and the Beaver Dam, the British advanced posts had occupied the latter position, and the American forces on Canadian soil, though they held no more than the ground they stood on, still fringed the whole Niagara frontier between Fort George and Fort Erie, and that Commodore Chauncey occupied the safe and convenient refuge of the harbour mouth of the River Niagara.

In the interval between the engagement at Stoney Creek, and the battle of the Thames, Sir George Prevost had made a tour of inspection in Upper Canada, and had made bold to attempt a demonstration, as it was afterwards called, on the works held by the Americans at

Fort George. If this demonstration meant anything it must have contemplated the storming and the capture of Fort George, for the idea of a purposeless demonstration cannot be entertained. And yet the capture of this work would have resulted in exposing the town of Newark and the captors themselves, in an inferior position, to the powerful fire of Fort Niagara; while the occupation of Fort George by the Americans weakened the American army in the field, and kept a large detachment of good troops uselessly entrapped upon the Canadian frontier. Nevertheless, on the 24th August, Sir George made a formal attack upon this post, drove in the pickets, looked the defences in the face, and retired, as Veritas says:—

> The King of France, with forty thousand men,
> Walked up the hill, and then, walked down again.

Sir George appears to have been afflicted with a strange infirmity of military purpose. His error consisted, not so much in the failure of the attempt, as in attempting at all, either without plan, or without resolution. To woo a Queen, or to command victory requires a daring spirit:—

> "Fain would I climb, but that I fear to fall,
> If thy heart fail thee, climb not at all."

The Governor General returned to Kingston and to Montreal, taking with him De Rottenburg,—the Lieutenant Governor,—in his train, and having done little to infuse courage and confidence, or prepare the minds of men to encounter the trials to come.

On receipt of the intelligence of Proctor's disaster, General Vincent prudently withdrew from St. David's and the Beaver Dam, and again concentrated his forces at Burlington Heights. He also called in his outposts from Long Point on Lake Erie and made every preparation for a desperate struggle with Harrison. The universal feeling at this moment was "no surrender," and yet there can be no doubt, but that fears which acquired strength as they flew, had magnified the danger to such an extent at Quebec, that orders were given at this critical moment, for the complete evacuation of all Canada, west of Kingston. Officers of rank and zeal, among whom the most conspicuous was Sir John Harvey, interfered to avert a measure pregnant with ruin, but so sure was the American Government that Vincent would save the " kernel " and Harrison only find the " shell " that they ordered their successful General back to Detroit, and by the aid of Perry's fleet threw the " Conqueror of the Thames " and his army on the Niagara frontier, in support of the combined operations planned from Sackett's Harbour and Lake Champlain on Montreal.

Thus, by degrees, Montreal became the grand centre of American strategy. Immense preparations had been made for a *coup de foudre* which was to terminate the campaign in a blaze of red lights with melodramatic effects. In the words of an American writer of no mean rank, the Hon. B. Gardinier of New York, once a Member of Congress:* " The Democrats concerted a grand campaign. The whole season was employed in tremendous preparations. Public expectation was perpetually on the stretch. The Secretary of War was in the vicinity of the armies. Perry had secured Lake Erie. Chauncey had hemmed in Yeo. Wilkinson sounded his bugle. Hampton rose in his strength. From East to West was nothing heard but the dreadful note of preparation and the easy capture of Montreal. From both armies came letters teeming with assurances of victory. Victory was the cry of a thousand trumpets."† And again, from the same writer, we have an enumeration of the forces prepared for the invasion. " When Wilkinson lay at Grenadier Island, the army of the North amounted to

---

* From the " Canadian Inspector," being an answer to Veritas, pp. 24, 25.
† Examiner, p. 317.

10,000 men. Hampton had 5,000, which with 6,000 militia augmented the force destined to reduce Lower Canada to 21,000 men. Opposed to this army were 5,000 regulars—2,000 of which were in Upper Canada." *

This writer was not far wrong in his estimate of the relative strength of the British and American forces. The original plan of the American campaign, as enjoined on General Wilkinson, had embraced the surprise and capture of Kingston and the seizure of Prescott—as a whet to a growing appetite, only to be appeased by the conquest of Montreal.† General Hampton having assembled his strength at Plattsburg was directed to penetrate across the Seigniory of Beauharnois, emerge on the shores of the St. Lawrence, and occupy the coast of Lake St. Louis between the mouth of the Chateauguay and the Indian Village of Caughnawaga. From hence he could at any time unite with Wilkinson on the Island of Montreal, between St. Ann's and Pointe Claire. The Isle Perrot was regarded as a *point d'appui*, and intended so to be held, and the flotilla which had transported Wilkinson was prepared to aid in effecting the junction. This conjoint operation followed in the footsteps of its military predecessors. Like Amherst in 1760, and Montgomery in 1775, Wilkinson and Hampton manœuvred to attack Montreal on its most accessible side. Then, as now, Montreal was not to be assailed in front with impunity. From Lachine down to the Island of St. Helen's, the rapids of the River St. Lawrence—a stream, very wide—in some places, very shallow, abounding in rocky reefs, and in rapid currents—and impassable, except in a class of vessels which can not be extemporized—present obstacles which, with a little precaution, may be made insurmountable.

---

* Examiner, p. 91, Vol. II.

† Armstrong. *Vide* Letter, dated War Department, Sackett's Harbour, Sept. 22, 1813. Appendix, Vol. II, p. 201.

Now, as then, no enemy can cross the River St. Lawrence below the Island of St. Helen's, until he has subjugated the South shore, and has scuttled the gunboats of England. These are some of the conditions precedent of a passage of this great river in summer. In winter the navigation will take care of itself. The American War Department was well aware that if, by a sudden irruption, they could occupy the fertile and inviting valley of the Richelieu, seize Sorel, and cross the St. Lawrence, they would, hazardously, place an immense river between themselves and their supplies; expose their army to attack both from Quebec and Montreal, and invite every available war-ship of England to interrupt reinforcements and intercept retreat. They eschewed therefore any line of advance which would put them on the St. Lawrence below Montreal. To assail the city in front was impracticable without the aid of boats of a description which is not portable, and the last, and, perhaps only, practicable, expedient, was a descent on the Island from the West and an advance upon the city by the olden route of Lachine. It is not necessary to dwell further here, upon what, when occasion serves, will be shown hereafter, that, such being the unavoidable conditions of an advance on Montreal, the facilities of defence, developed by the necessities of the attack, if rightly improved, render Montreal a military position of great strength, resembling to a certain extent Vicksburg on the Missisippi—but in many respects superior.

These considerations, perfectly well understood by every instructed officer in the American service, led to the only feasible scheme of attack, had the execution been equal to the plan.

The combined operation was well designed, and the better, that either force, under Hampton or under Wilkinson, was in itself, more than sufficient in numbers and equipment to have attained the object in view. Wilkinson's force was 10,000 men—infantry, cavalry, and artillery, admirably supplied and transported by water. The men landed and fought in light marching order—the very knapsacks were cared for in the boats. Hampton by his own account had with him " 4,000 effective infantry and a well-appointed train of artillery." * And then, without speaking of cavalry, by which we know that he was accompanied, and without taking into account the 6,000 militia which, from the best American authority, we also know, that he had at his disposal, there can be no question, but that the American invading force from the Plattsburg frontier came up to the strength assigned to it by Sir George Prevost in his Despatch of the 30th October,—that is to say, to 7,200 combatants.

To encounter these combined forces, were dispersed below Kingston, on the line of the St. Lawrence, and in the District of Montreal, over a surface of at least 300 miles—in garrison, in camp—on outpost and in hospital some 3,000 troops, regular and militia. Of this force 1,600 men were in line on the South of the St. Lawrence, to repel Hampton's invasion. The advanced column, watching the frontier, consisted of 350 men.

The renewed preparations at Burlington in Vermont, and at Plattsburg in the State of New York had, from an early period in the season, attracted attention in Lower Canada. These preparations could have no other object in view than an irruption on Montreal, through that part of the District of Montreal lying west of the river Richelieu. Isle aux Noix—St. John's and Chambly—were the garrisoned points directly menaced—but garrisons can rarely do more than protect the posts they occupy; and it was necessary to provide for the observation as well as the defence of an extended frontier. To this advanced column, therefore, scattered in a widely extended order, was confided the safety of the frontier. It was commanded by Colonel de Salaberry. It

---

* Letter to Secretary of War, 12th October, 1813.

became the duty of this officer to anticipate irruption or sortie, and to detect from the sound and flash of the distant gun the intended course of the projectile.

As early as September, the American General Hampton had transported across Lake Champlain the force collected at Burlington, and at the head of 5,000 men had attempted an invasion of the District of Montreal. On the 29th September he had despatched his *élite* under Majors Snelling and Hamilton to surprise an outlying picket at Odelltown. This was a hamlet buried in the dense forest, which for many leagues, in those days, covered the frontier. All the roads and pathways through the "bush" had been cut up, obstructed by *abattis*, and made impassable, during the preceding campaign by de Salaberry and his axe-men; still had Hampton pushed forward vigorously, his riflemen might have held the outskirts of the woodland, while his pioneers cleared away the obstacles in their rear. Three or four leagues of black-ash swamp once surmounted, and he would have emerged among the farms and populous parishes of an open and cultivated plain. But, both parties of the *élite* were misled or misdirected. The attack upon the picket was but partially successful—the alarm was given —the *abattis* were manned by a few frontier Light Infantry and by a handful of Indians under Captain Mailloux, who multiplied their number by an incessant fusilade, while yells of horrid augury reverberated through the gloom. These brave men held their own, until they were reinforced by the flank companies of the 4th Battalion of the embodied militia under Major Perrault * and by the Canadian Voltigeurs commanded by Colonel de Salaberry.

This indefatigable officer was Hampton's fate;—

> Ha! who comes here?
> Art thou some god, some angel, or some devil,
> That makes my blood cold, and my hair to stand?
> Speak to me. What art thou?

---

* *Vide* p. 85.

Ghost.	Thy evil spirit, Brutus!
Brutus.	Why com'st thou?
Ghost.	To tell thee thou shalt see me at Philippi.

and, on the pretext of want of water, in a very wet countrndy, a very wet season, Hampton withdrew from Odelltown—fell back on his own frontier, and moved his force westward, to find his Philippi on the banks of the Chateauguay.

Charles Michel d'Irumberry de Salaberry, Seigneur of Chambly and Beau Lac, was descended from a noble Basque family—of which a brave cadet had earned renown and rich feudal possessions under the French Crown, in Canada.* He was one of that chivalrous race of men, whose very names embellish Canadian story with picturesque illustrations. The younger branches of many noble French houses had sought service and settlement in a country peculiarly adapted to the genius and traditions of men to whom arms were the only career, and with whom the sword was the *guidon* to fortune. The process of French colonization in Canada had been unavoidably military. The cultivator of the soil was in ceaseless contest with the savagery of nature and of man. He could never abandon the sword for the plough-share. He was compelled to use both, with alternate hand. The feudal system of mediæval France was well calculated to encounter this condition of things. The same martial polity, which had, five centuries before, inspired the "Assizes de Jerusalem," engrafted its prototype the "Coutume de Paris" on the soil of Canada. The Saracen in the East, and the Savage in the West, would own no obedience but to the mailed hand. This military code provided at once for

---

* Of the family of the brave Colonel de Salaberry, C.B., the eldest son, **Alphonse**, is Adjutant General of Militia for Lower Canada. Louis, the second son, lives at Chambly. Charles, the third, is colonel of a regiment of Volunteers in the district of Quebec. Of the ladies of his family, one daughter is the widow of the late Augustus Hatt, Esquire, and now resides at Sorel.

colonization and defence, and harmonized with the antique associations of the colonists. "In 1598 Henry of Bearn authorized the granting of fiefs, châtellaines, and baronies in Canada to men of gentle blood for the tutelage and defence of the country."* And the Bearnoise or Basque family of de Salaberry profited, and not unworthily, by the wise liberality of their fellow countryman. Their father and the grandfather of Colonel de Salaberry had borne the "*panache blanche*" in full front of the fight against the standard of England, but from the hour when, by sacred treaty, their allegiance had been transferred to the sceptre of England, they bowed reverently to the last behest of their native Prince, and, at his command, gave "*foi et hommage*" to the British Crown.† And to that great obligation they, and the mass of their fellow countrymen, have ever been nobly faithful since. De Salaberry and three brothers took service in the British army. Two died under the blazing sun of Hindostan,—one fell in the deadly breach of Badajos. Our Canadian hero served in the West Indies. He had commanded the Grenadier Company of the 60th regiment, 4th battalion, in many fierce engagements. He distinguished himself in 1795 at the conquest of Martinique, and had survived the miasmata of Walcheren. On returning to Canada he turned

---

* Garneau, Vol. I, p. 182.

† In a note to Mr. J. M. Lemoyne's interesting collection, entitled "Maple Leaves," we find the following record of French Canadian services to the British Crown twenty-five years after the Conquest:—

"A party of distinguished Canadians on the 8th June, 1775, offered their services to Major Preston in Montreal to retake Fort St. John from the Americans, and did so on the 20th June, placing it in the hands of a detachment of the 7th Regiment, or Royal Fusiliers, under Captain Kineer. They were the Chevaliers de Belestre, de Longueuil, de Lotbinière, de Rouville, de Boucherville, de Lacorne, de La Bruière, de St. Ours, de Levy, Pertuis, Hervieux, Gamelin, de Montigny, d'Eschambault, and others. For this service, General Carleton publicly thanked them. In September of the same year, this party, with the

his military experience to good account, and raised the corps of Canadian Voltigeurs. At the head of this corps, as has been already related, with the advance of Colonel D'Échambault he had, in the campaign of the preceding year, repulsed the first attempt made by Dearborn on the debateable ground of La Cole.

On Hampton's retirement from Odelltown he was promptly followed up. Salaberry overtook him at the Four Corners, or cross roads of the Chateauguay—*via quâ se findit in ambas*—about five miles within the American frontier, and near the source of the river. Here an attempt was made to surprise the American camp, which failed through the accidental discharge of a musket, when Salaberry, finding himself to be discovered, collected about fifty of his Voltigeurs, and a handful of Indians, and made a vociferous onset on the advanced detachment of the enemy, consisting of about 800 men. The Americans fell back in confusion, and enabled him to withdraw without loss. These small affairs had infused mutual confidence into the commander, and his men, and contributed to the great success which was shortly to follow.

Under the smoke of this light skirmish, de Salaberry fell back on his supports, following the descending course of the Chateau-

---

assistance of a number of Volunteers, from Quebec and Three Rivers, Messieurs de Montisson, Duchesnay, de Rigouville, de Salaberry, de Tonancour, Beaubien, de Musseau, Moquin, Lamarque, Fauchier, and others, started for St. John's near Montreal, to relieve the 7th and 26th Regiments, then in charge of the fort; and who expected a siege; but after being beleaguered, the fort surrendered on the 2nd November to Gen. Montgomery. The Canadians and the two regiments were carried away prisoners of war—Congress refusing to exchange the Canadians ' they being too much attached to the English Government, and too influential in their own country.' Two—Messieurs de Montesson and de Rigouville—died prisoners of war. De Lacorne, Pertuis, and Beaubien had been killed during the siege. De Lotbinière had an arm shot off. De Salaberry was twice wounded."—Pp. 66, 67.

guay. He knew the ground thoroughly, having long before examined it, with the foresight of one charged with the safety of the outposts of the army.

He could now see the course of the projectile. He had indeed already anticipated its line of flight, and was already prepared to counteract the blow. For some days previous he had been occupied in choosing his positions and in fortifying them with the ready materials the Canadian forest offers. His dispositions for this purpose were made with great judgment.

It is impossible not to be struck by the meagreness of detail which characterizes both British and American narratives of this important action—but to the American the subject was not a pleasant one, and to the English writer not very intelligible. The scene of action was remote from the daily track of travel and of strife. It was neither seen nor sought. The battle was fought by French Canadian militia-men. These men dispersed to their homes—doubtless they " fought their battles o'er again " by their own fire-sides, but the English writer had not much opportunity to hear from their lips the changes of the fight. The Despatch of Sir George Prevost dwells more upon his own slight intervention at the close of the action than upon the incidents of the contest. The report of the American Adjutant General, King, is curt and conclusive : " 25th October. The plan of the attack adopted by the General was to detach Colonel Purdy with the *élite* and the 1st Brigade, forming the most efficient part of the army, across the river ; and by a night march gain the fording place on the left of the enemy's line, re-cross the river at that point, and at dawn of day attack the enemy's rear ; while Izzard's Brigade, under his own direction, should pursue the march, and at the same hour, attack it in front. The whole of this plan miscarried shamefully ;

Purdy's column, probably misled, fell into an ambuscade, and was quickly beaten and routed; and that of Izzard, after a few discharges, was ordered to retreat." And this report is a fair introduction to a more detailed story of the fight.

CHAP. XXIV.

Story of Chateauguay. The "Temoin oculaire." Hampton advances from Four Corners. De Salaberry faces right about, and returns to meet him. First rencontre—Halts—Throws up breastworks and abattis. Disposition of defenders—Ford in the rear. American attack on abattis—Impracticable. Attack on flank and rear, partially successful—Repulsed—Broken by flank fire. Retreating Americans fire on each other. Hampton, daunted, withdraws from front of abattis and retreats. Force engaged. Brilliant conduct of officers and men. Honour to De Salaberry.

It is always satisfactory that the party most interested should be enabled to tell his own story, and by a fortunate occurrence, this source of satisfaction has been supplied. The Redacteur of the "Courier d'Ottawa," Dr. L. E. Dorion, has re-produced most opportunely the narrative of a "Temoin oculaire," dated 3rd November, 1813. This narrative appears to have been published in some of the journals of the day. If a guess may be hazarded as to the authorship, it might be, perhaps not unjustly, ascribed to the late Commander Jacques Viger of Montreal. Ample in detail and minute in circumstance, it gives, with all the proverbial ease of the French *raconteur*, incidents which correspond in the main with the relations of more pretentious writers. The following account of the Battle of Chateauguay will be little more than the story told by the "Temoin oculaire" done into English. The original will be found in the Appendix.

The American army at the Four Corners, under Hampton, after having for some time attracted the attention of our troops, on the

21st October moved direct on our frontier. That same afternoon about 4 p.m. his advanced guard drove in our advanced videttes. They were thrown out to a place called "Piper Road," about ten miles from the church at Chateauguay. Major Henry, of the Beauharnois militia, in command at the English River, notified Major General de Watteville, who ordered up, at once, the two companies of the 5th Incorporated Militia, commanded by Captains Levesque and Debartzch, and about two hundred men of the Militia de Beauharnois. This force advanced about two leagues until, at nightfall, it halted at the extremity of a thick wood into which it would at that moment have been imprudent to penetrate. At daybreak they were joined by Colonel de Salaberry with his Voltigeurs and Captain Fergusson's Light Company of the Canadian Fencibles. Thus composed, de Salaberry pushed on, along the left bank of the river, about a league, and there encountered a patrol of the enemy. He instantly halted his force. He had some weeks before carefully reconnoitred this very ground, and knew that the whole course of the river presented no better position. The forest was intersected by ravines which drained a swamp on his right, and fell into the river which covered his left. Upon four of these ravines, which were like so many moats, *fossés*, in his front, he threw up breastworks. The three first lines were distant perhaps 200 yards from each other. The fourth was half a mile in the rear, and commanded a ford, by which an assailant coming from the right bank of the Chateauguay might have got into his rear. It was most important to guarantee this, the weak point of the position. Upon each of these lines of defence a parapet of logs was constructed, which extended into the tangled swamp on the right; but the front line of all, following the sinuosities of the ravine in front, formed almost an obtuse angle to the right of the road, and of the whole position. This whole day—the 22nd—was employed vigorously in strengthening these works, which in strength, natural and artificial, could not be surpassed. They had also the advantage of compelling the assailant to advance to the attack through a wilderness, remote from his supplies, while our troops had all they required, and were close upon their supports in the rear.

The right bank of the river was covered by a thick forest. In the rear, at the ford, care was taken to post about sixty men of the Beauharnois militia.

Nor did the Colonel limit his precautions to the works above spoken of. To secure himself to the utmost, he detached a party of thirty axe-men of the division of Beauharnois to destroy every bridge within a league and a half of his front. And about a mile ahead of the front line of defence above described, he threw down a formidable *abattis* of trees, with the branches extending outwards, and reaching from the bank of the river on his left, three or four arpents across the front to a *savanne* or swamp on the right, which was almost impassable. Thus the four inner lines were effectually covered, and the American artillery, known to number at least ten guns, was rendered useless. They could not be brought into action.

To these admirable arrangements, as much as to the heroism of his men, must be ascribed the brilliant results which ensued, and to the gallant de Salaberry, alone, must be ascribed the choice of the ground and the dispositions made.

On the 22nd, Major General de Watteville visited the outposts and approved entirely of the precautions taken, but the labour of strengthening the position continued without intermission up to the 25th September. When at about 10 a.m. the American skirmishers opened on the *abattis*, Lieutenant Guy of the Voltigeurs, who was in front with about twenty of his men, fell back, and was supported by Lieutenant Johnson of the same regiment, in charge of the picket, which protected the fatigue party. After a sharp exchange of musketry, the labourers retired within,—the covering party to the front of the *abattis*.

At this moment, de Salaberry, who had heard the first firing, rode up from the front line of defences. He brought with him three companies of the Canadian Fencibles under Fergusson, which deployed at once on the right rear of the *abattis*. The company of Captain J. B. Duchesnay was extended on the left, while the company of Captain Jucherau Duchesnay occupied, *en potence*, a position on the left rear among the trees on the bank of the river, so as to take the enemy in flank if they attempted to carry the ford in the rear, held by the Beauharnois militia.

It should be observed here, that in this part of its course, and between the *abattis* and the ford, the river made a curve or bow, so abrupt, that at the re-entering elbow of the curve, the fire of the defenders flanked the ford in support of the fire in front.

Then de Salaberry, who had already twice during this campaign, tested the American metal—who had longed for another trial—saw his opportunity, and profited by it. He was in the centre of the line—the companies of Fergusson, L'Ecuyer, and deBartzch on his right. In the swamp and wood lay Captain Lamothe and a corps of Indians; on the left and left rear the companies of the two Duchesnay's. The place of these troops taken from the first and second lines of defence was supplied from the third and fourth by the Canadian Fencible regiment, under Colonel Macdonell of Ogdensburg fame.

While these arrangements were being made with precision and rapidity, the enemy debouched from the wood into a large open space in front of the *abattis*. On the left bank of the river Hampton had the supreme command: under him served General Izzard, at the head of the 10th, the 31st, and other regiments, amounting to 3,000—or 3,500 men with three squadrons of cavalry and four guns—and yet the artillery was not brought into action. About 1,500 men were thrown on the right bank of the river under Colonel Purdy to force its way through the bush, and take the Canadian force, in reserve, at the ford below.

The enemy debouched on the plain in front of de Salaberry in column, and advanced in this formation close to the *abattis*, exposing the head of his narrow line to a fire in front, and his flank to the Indians and tirailleurs in the bush and swamp. This was his moment. An American officer had ridden forward, and had attempted to harangue the troops in French. Salaberry seized a rifle, fired, and the orator fell. At the same moment his bugler sounded the order to fire, and a blaze of musketry burst from the *abattis* and the swamp. The column halted, paused for a moment, made a turn to the left, formed line, and opened a vigorous fusilade—but the fire of the left was, by this movement, thrown into the wood, where it had but little effect. Not so with the fire of the right, which compelled our pickets to retire within the *abattis*. The enemy mistook this falling back for a flight, and raised a great shout, which we returned with interest, and it was all they got from us, for they never had possession of one inch of the *abattis*. While the cheers on the one side were re-echoed by cheers on the other, taken up by the troops in our rear, suddenly Salaberry ordered all our bugles to sound, to augment in imaginasion the strength of our force. The *ruse* had this effect. We learnt from prisoners afterwards that they had estimated our force at 6,000 or 7,000 men. But for all the shouting and bugling, the musketry fire never ceased. It was so hot and uninterrupted, that the enemy never attempted to carry the *abattis*. After a time their fire slackened, and they appeared to await other events —they looked to the other side of the river.

Here the bugles indicated an advance, and Colonel Macdonell, eager to add to the laurels he had won at Ogdensburg, moved rapidly in the direction of the fire with two companies from the first and second line of retrenchments under Captain Levesque. The Beauharnois militia, defending the ford, had been attacked by Purdy in superior force, and had been compelled to retire. Macdonell ordered Captain Daly with his company of the 5th Incorporated to cross the ford in their support.

At this moment de Salaberry, perceiving the fire in his front to relax, and the shouts of the combatants and the fire of musketry to increase on his left flank and rear, saw, at once, that a diversion was about to be operated at the ford, and betook himself to his left where the company of Juchereau du Chesnay was drawn up *en potence*, and came down to the river just as Daly crossed the stream. From a stump, he watched the advance of the enemy with a field glass, exposed the while to a heavy fire, and gave words of encouragement to Captain Daly as he waded through the water. This gallant officer got his men into order and most bravely thrust the enemy home. They fell back, rallied and reformed, and opened a well-sustained fire. Daly was over-matched. He and his brave Canadians slowly fell back. He had been wounded in the advance, and while retiring, while encouraging his men by word and example, he was wounded a second time and fell. Captain Bruyere of the Milice de Beauharnois was also wounded at the same time. Their men, unequal in numbers, were compelled to recede, slowly, and with face to the foe, under the command of the gallant Lieutenant Schiller, and once more was heard the joyful shouts and jeers of the advancing enemy—but their exultation was brief—for rushing forward, unobservant of the company formed *en potence* on the other side of the river, they became suddenly exposed to a crushing fire in flank, which at short distance arrested their march and threw them into utter confusion. Vain was the attempt to rally—they broke and scrambled back into the bush. There, it is believed, that advancing parties fired upon their retiring comrades, mistaking them for enemies. On the

R

other hand, Hampton, learning that his stratagem had failed, and that the attack on the ford, on which he had so much relied, had resulted so disastrously, drew off his left attack, which for an hour had been inactive, though incessantly persecuted by our skirmishers from the *abattis*. The Canadian troops remained in position, and slept that night on the ground on which they had fought.

In the morning, being reinforced by the company of Voltigeurs under Captain de Rouville and the grenadiers of Captain Levesque of the 5th Incorporated and sixty of the Beauharnois Division, de Salaberry confided to Colonel Macdonell the defence of the *abattis* against any renewed attack, and pushed forward his videttes cautiously—incredulous of Hampton's retreat. About twenty prisoners were taken, and the line of flight was indicated by muskets, knapsacks, drums, and provisions strewed in the way. Forty dead bodies were interred by our people, many graves were found, and notably, those of two officers of distinction, buried by their own men. The wounded were carried off, but we knew afterwards that the enemy estimated their own loss *hors de combat* at upwards of one hundred.

This brilliant achievement cost the Canadian force, two killed, sixteen wounded. Among the officers most prominent on this occasion—and all did their duty nobly—were Captains Fergusson, de Bartzch,* and Levesque of the 5th; Captain L'Ecuyer of the

---

* Captain de Bartzch, of the Voltigeurs, in after years the Hon.P.D. de Bartzch, of St. Charles on the river Richelieu, Seigneur of the Seigniory of that name, and as member of the Assembly and of the Legislative Council, an active able, and eloquent advocate of reform, so long as reform eschewed revolution—has bequeathed an honourable name to a family who, in the bloom of life, recall pleasant recollections of the promise of the bud. The eldest daughter of this gentleman married the Hon. Lewis T. Drummond, late Attorney General for Lower Canada. The second is the wife of the Hon. Cornwallis Monk, Judge of the Superior Court. The fourth married the Count de Rotter-

Voltigeurs; the two du Chesnays of the Voltigeurs,* who both distinguished themselves by their *sang froid* and precision in the execution of difficult manœuvres. To these must be added the

---

mund, a Polish exile and savant; and the third M. de Kierzkowski, son of the late Lieutenant-General Kierzkowski, an old and distinguished officer in the service of Russia. This gentleman has been returned, and held a seat, in both branches of the Canadian Legislature, as a member of the House of Assembly and member of the Legislative Council,

ad unguem
Factus homo,—non ut magis alter, amicus.

* The Brothers du Chesnay, whose names will ever stand in our Canadian story as the foremost in this conflict—the Ajaces of the fight,

αει σφών κλεος εσσεται κατ' αιαν,

were of an old family. Their first settlement in Canada dates from 1640. The family name is Juchereau de St. Denis,—du Chesnay (of the oak grove) being the designation of a fief which became the appanage of a younger branch bearing the patronymic of Juchereau. One of the two brothers, Juchereau du Chesnay, had served the British crown for some years in the 60th regiment —on foreign stations—and on the death of his father, retired from active service, in the interests of his estate and of his family. But the hereditary passion was inextinguishable. On the first sound of war he transferred to the militia the knowledge he had acquired in the line. He raised a company in the Canadian Voltigeurs, and during the war was constantly on the frontier. He was, as given in the text, actively engaged at Chateauguay. He was subsequently appointed Deputy Adjutant General of Militia and Superintendent of the Indian Department. His devotion to the Throne has descended as an heir-loom to those, whose friendship is a pleasure, and a pride to the contemporary annalist. His surviving children are the Hon. Juchereau du Chesnay, M.L.C., and Philippe, now Provincial Aide-de-Camp and Lieutenant-Colonel, Militia. Of his daughters, the eldest is the widow of the late Hon. Roch de St. Ours, M.L.C., formerly Sheriff of the District of Montreal, and the representative of one of the oldest and best families in French Canada. The second is the wife of T. C. Campbell, Esquire, C.B., late Major in the 7th Hussars, Seigneur of St. Hilaire de Rouville, and Colonel, Militia. And the third is married to Lieutenant-Colonel Ermatinger, who earned for himself, rank, and for Canada, distinction, in the service of Spain, and is now one of the Inspecting Field Officers of Militia of the Province.

The second brother, better known as the "Chevalier" du Chesnay, was also

gallant Captain Daly * of the Canadian Fencibles and Bruyere of the Chateauguay Chasseurs, both of whom were wounded. Captain Lamothe made the most of his handful of savages. Lieutenants Pinguet,† of the Light Infantry; Guy, Johnson, Powell, and Hebben of the Voltigeurs; Schiller, of Daly's company,—all

---

in the British service, previous to the war of 1812. On the outbreak of the contest he devoted his services to his country's cause, raised a company of Voltigeurs, and at Chateauguay, and on all other occasions, upheld, at the head of his French fellow countrymen, the honour of the British flag. A nephew, Narcisse, the son of an elder brother Antoine, a lad of 16 years of age, was also in the field at Chateauguay, actually engaged. " Those who were there behaved themselves so loyally that their heirs to this day are honoured for their sake." Froissart, Vol. II, p. 220.

* Joseph Daly, Esquire, of Montreal, H.M. agent for emigrants, is a nephew of this brave officer.

† Captain Pinguet.—This officer appears to have been a Quebecquois. Since writing the above, there has appeared in a Feuilleton, published in Quebec, and entitled "Soirées Canadiennes," two letters, indited by Captain Pinguet, one shortly before, and the other, immediately after the Battle of Chateauguay. In the second he says : " C'était le dimanche que l'aba:tis fut commencé, et le mardi, comme les bûcheurs finissaient quelque chose qui manquait, un parti de dix hommes de notre compagnie et de vingt des Voltigeurs, qui étaient en avant pour protéger les travaillants, aperçurent l'avant-garde de l'ennemi qui s'avançait. * * * Nous avions à combattre contre deux mille hommes de pied et deux-cents hommes de cavalerie; nous ne perdions pas de temps ; nos soldats ont tiré entre trente-cinq et quarante cartouches, et en si bonne direction que les prisonniers que nous fîmes le lendemain disaient que nos balles passaient toutes à l'égalité, soit de la tête, soit de la poitrine. Notre compagnie seule s'est battue là environ trois-quarts d'heure avant que de recevoir du renfort. * * * * * And to show that campaigning in Canada is not a mere *promenade militaire*, may be added : "Après la bataille, on nous a ramenés dans nos retranchements, où nous avons passé huit jours, à la pluie, au froid, sans feu et sans couvertures ; de là, nous sommes descendus aux maisons, où nous étions presque aussi mal que dans les bois ; nous y avons été huit jours, et avons reçu ordre de remonter. Je crois à présent qu'un homme est capable d'endurer sans crever, plus de misère qu'un bon chien."

displayed intelligence and vigour. Captains Longtin and Huneau of the Milice de Beauharnois gave to their men an honourable example. Of the former it is related, that on the commencement of the action, he knelt down at the head of his company and offered up a brief and earnest prayer. " And now, *mes enfans*," said he, rising, " having done our duty to God, we will do the same by our King." Here spoke out that olden spirit of chivalrous devotion which the history of a thousand years has made the heritage of the Canadian people.

Nor should we pass over in silence the names of the *simples soldats*,—Vincent, Pelletier, Vervais, Dubois, and Caron,—all of the Voltigeurs, who swam the river and cut off the retreat of the prisoners who were taken.*

It will be seen at once that the whole brunt of the action fell upon the advanced corps under the command of Colonel de Salaberry. This force barely numbered 300 combatants. The battle was fought in front of the first line of entrenchments, at the *abattis*, and at the ford in the rear. On this part of the field de Salaberry commanded alone, and to him alone is to be ascribed the glory of the victory.

---

* Among the officers in command of companies who had not the good fortune to be actually engaged—who were " well in hand," but not wanted—on the 26th October, may be noted the names of de Beaujeu, de Lery, de Rouville, de Tonnancour, Malhiot, Raymond, Bruère, the indefatigable McKay, and Berczy. The company, however, of this last officer was in the charge of Lieutènant Taché, now the Hon. Sir Etienne Taché, Colonel and Aide-de-Camp to the Queen— of whom more hereafter. A sister of Captain de Tonnancour married the Hon. Thomas Coffin, of Three Rivers, and his eldest son is Prothonotary of the Court of Queen's Bench, Montreal.

CHAPTER XXV.

Macdonell of Ogdensburg—The Canadian Fencibles—Descent of the St. Lawrence—Running the Rapids—Night March through the Bush—"Always on Hand"—French and English "Shoulder to Shoulder"—Natural Exultation of the French Canadians—Practical Reply to Dishonouring Imputations—Gratitude of the British Government—Queenston Heights—Chateauguay—Chevy Chace and the "Combat des Trentes"—Beaumanoir and Bembro—Croquart.

Had the gallant de Salaberry required the services of a fellow soldier, or had the fortune of war, even for a moment, deprived us of his own, there stood, happily, at his side the most efficient substitute Canada could supply. Macdonell of Ogdensburg had been lately appointed to the command of a battalion of French Canadian Fencibles, and was at Kingston drilling and organizing the force confided to him. On the 20th October, Sir George Prevost, then at Kingston, received intelligence of Hampton's irruption on the Beauharnois frontier. At the time, Wilkinson was known to be within a few miles in front, at the head of 10,000 men. Kingston was presumed to be his object. The distracting effect of this double menace, in front, and in flank and rear, demanded prompt and judicious counteraction. Here Sir George did well. He dared not weaken Kingston by withdrawing a single man of the line. As he mounted his horse for Lower Canada he sent for Macdonell, and inquired if his corps was in a fit state to meet the enemy; and was assured that they were ready to embark so soon as *they had done dinner*. Prevost gave his prompt subordinate *carte blanche*, enjoining, simply, a prompt rencounter with Hampton on the Beauharnois frontier. Left to himself and to his own resources,

Macdonell was not unequal to the emergency. He had offered men. He had now to find boats, and boatmen and pilots, to conduct those men in safety down the dangerous rapids of the St. Lawrence. In that named "of the Coteau du Lac" Lord Amherst lost in 1760 sixty-eight batteaux and eighty-eight men. Those who have descended the rapids of the St. Lawrence for a pastime, in a well-found steamer, manned and piloted and handled, to provide against all chance of accident, and can recall the combined sensation of awe and misgiving with which they sank and surged amid those boiling waters, whirled by rocks and shoals, where a touch would have been destruction, with the speed and rush and roar of a tempest, and who rejoice even now that the rapids are passed and the danger over, may be able to appreciate the resolution of men who dared the same danger at the call of duty, in huge unwieldy row-boats or batteaux, to which a disabled oar or a misdirection of the rudder must have brought instantaneous destruction. But no misgivings troubled the minds of these brave men or their resolute leader. His arrangements were rapidly made. Boats were soon procured—his own personal experience supplied pilotage—his soldiers volunteered to the oar. Every French Canadian is a boatman. The perilous waters to which they are accustomed demand the constant exercise of bravery and skill. The world does not produce better material for soldier or sailor. After a few hours' delay he embarked with his 600 men, encountered great dangers, but surmounted all; ran all the rapids successfully; crossed Lake St. Francis in a tempest; disembarked on the Beauharnois shore; and in the dead of the night threaded the forest in Indian file, reaching the bank of the Chateauguay, on the morning of the 25th September, in advance of Sir George Prevost, who had ridden down the opposite shore of the St. Lawrence aided by relays of horses. When the Commander-in-Chief asked him in a tone of some surprise " And where are your men ?"

"There, Sir," replied Macdonell, pointing to 600 exhausted soldiers sleeping on the ground, *not one man absent.** This willing young battalion of French militia, officers and men, had accomplished the distance from Kingston to the battle-field of Chateauguay—170 miles by water and 20·miles by land in 60 hours of actual travel—a fact which deserves to be ranked by the side of the marvellous march of the Light Division of the British army before the battle of Talavera, recorded with so much of just pride by the historian Napier.

Thus it was, that three companies occupied the rearmost lines of defence prepared by de Salaberry, and being thus in the rear, Daly's company had the proud satisfaction of repelling the American flank attack on the ford. Of the men, therefore, engaged, all were French. Of the officers, four names indicate their British lineage. Their gallantry proved it, and proved further, how thoroughly in such a cause, and on such a field—should occasion ever occur—the people of French Canada may rely on the staunch co-operation of their fellow citizens of British extraction.

The French population of Lower Canada are very proud of the victory of Chateauguay, and with just reason. The British population of the Upper Province had achieved a like success over the common enemy at Queenston Heights. It was gratifying to the natural pride of a great national origin, that the fortune of war should have thus equitably distributed her honourable distinctions. They had, moreover, a stronger motive, both for resentment and exultation. The American Government and democratic press, with unexampled effrontery, had cast upon a race " *sans peur et sans reproche,*" the dishonouring imputation of an easy political virtue. They had been charged with a readiness to violate plighted honour, and with disaffection to the British Crown. Truthful and

---

* *Vide* United Service Journal, June, 1848. Corresp.

generous in all relations, whether of peace or war, they resented this indignity, as a stain felt more keenly than a wound, and they gave the " *Bostonais* " their answer on the field of Chateauguay.

This noble and opportune service had the effect of twenty victories. Twenty days had hardly elapsed since the defeat of Proctor on the Thames. Muttered rumours of disaster had scarcely reached remote districts, ere the cloud of anxiety and doubt was dispelled by the exploit of Chateauguay, and the Red Cross Banner of England gleamed forth unsullied, in the light of that valour which it had so often encountered, proved, and respected, under the Lilies of France.

Great Britain honoured this worthy feat of arms in a becoming manner. Standards were conferred upon the regiments engaged. A Battle Medal was given to every soldier. De Salaberry was made a Commander of the Bath. Sir George Prevost, who had ridden up from his quarters in the rear at the close of the action, extolled in a Despatch dated from Montreal on the 30th October, the conduct of the men engaged, and dwelt with superfluous complacency " on the determination of all classes of His Majesty's subjects to persevere in an honourable and loyal line of conduct," which upon that occasion, at least, might have been allowed to speak for itself.

Queenston Heights and Chateauguay are to the people of Canada what Chevy Chace and the "Combat des Trentes" were, in the olden time, to their martial ancestry—the fountain and the nursery of traditions, which create character and foreshadow a national career not unworthy of the sources from whence they spring. As " the child is father to the man," so to nations, honourable traditions are the best guarantee of future greatness, and the descendants of those who fought on the battle fields of Canada, accepting the obligations noble memories impose, are as proud of their antecedents, as those who glory in the iron legend of Beaumanoir and Bembro—of Knollys, Calverty, and Croquart —or of those who,

> With stout Erle Percy there were slain,
> Sir John of Adgerton,
> Sir Robert Ratcliff and Sir John,
> Sir James the bold Heron.

The " Combat des Trentes " is, probably, not so familiar to English ears, as the fierce Border foray immortalized in the Ballad of Chevy Chace. The story has been well told, is full of national interest, and is not an inappropriate pendant to scenes upon which the Canadian loves to linger. Both the " Combat des Trentes " and the " woeful hunting " of Chevy Chace, befell in the same century, but the encounter of the " Thirties " preceded that " on Cheviot side " by many years. Chevy Chace dates probably from the year 1388. The " Combat des Trentes " took place 27th March, 1301.*

About twenty miles from the town of St. Malo, " *St. Malo, beau port de Mer*," on the river Rance, stands the romantic town of Dinan, and, in a dell hard by, where ripen the best figs in Brittany, *experto crede*, may still be seen the ruins of the Chateau and Monastery of Beaumanoir. Thirty-five years ago, the mailed effigies of the warriors of a half-forgotten race lay recumbent on their tombs in the chancel of the roofless abbey, spared by the ravages of revolution, but crumbling rapidly beneath those of time. The name of Beaumanoir was one of high renown in the days of du Guesclin and of Olivier de Clisson, when the English contested, on the soil of France itself, the *suzeraineté* of the French crown. The Lord of Beaumanoir was one of the leaders in this remarkable " Combat des Trentes," of which the following account is given in

---

* Battle of Otterbourne (historically the same as
   the foray of Chevy Chace), ... August 15, 1388
  Combat des Trentes .... March 27, 1351

the Histoire de Bretagne, quoted in a note to Johnes' edition of Froissart, Vol. II, p. 191 :—

"After the death of Sir Thomas Daggeworth, the King appointed Sir Walter Bentley, Commander in Brittany. The English, being much irritated at the death of Daggeworth, and not being able to revenge themselves on those who slew him, did so on the whole country, by burning and destroying it. The Marshal de Beaumanoir, desirous of putting a stop to this, sent to Bembro, who commanded in Ploërmel, for a passport to hold a conference with him. The Marshal reprobated the conduct of the English, and high words passed between them; for Bembro had been the companion in arms to Daggeworth. At last, one of them proposed a combat of thirty on each side. The place appointed for it was at the half-way oak tree between Josselin and Ploërmel, and the day was fixed for the 27th March, 1351, being the fourth Sunday in Lent. Beaumanoir chose nine knights and twenty-one esquires. Bembro could not find a sufficient number of English in his garrison —there were but twenty—the remainder were Germans and Bretons. Bembro first entered the field of battle, and drew up his troop. Beaumanoir did the same. Each made a short harangue to his men, exhorting them to support their own honour and that of their nation. Bembro added, that there was an old prophecy of Merlin, which promised victory to the English. The signal was given for the attack. Their arms were not similar, for each was to choose such as he liked. Billefort fought with a mallet 25 lbs. weight, and others with what arms they chose. The advantage at first was with the English, as the Bretons had lost five of their men. Beaumanoir exhorted them not to mind this, as they stopped to take breath; when each party having had some refreshment, the combat was renewed. Bembro was killed. On seeing this, Croquart cried out, ' Compagnons, don't let us think of the prophecies of Merlin, but depend on our courage and arms; keep yourselves close together, be firm, and fight as I do.' Beaumanoir, being wounded, was quitting the field to quench his thirst, when Geoffry du Bois called out, 'Beaumanoir, drink thy blood, and thy hurt will go off.' This made him ashamed and return to the battle. The Bretons at last gained the day, by one of their party breaking, on horseback, the ranks of the English—the greater part of whom were killed. Knollys, Calverty, and Croquart were made prisoners, and carried to the Castle of Josselin. Tintimiac on the side of the Bretons, and Croquart on the English, obtained the prize of valour. Such was the issue of this famous Combat of Thirty, so glorious to the Bretons, but which decided nothing as to the possession of the Duchy of Brittany." *

---

* The Chronicler adds in the text, with respect to Croquart, "He was originally but a poor boy, and had been page to the Lord d'Ercle in Holland. He had the reputation of being the most expert man-at-arms of the country. He was said to be worth 40,000 crowns, not including his horses, of which he had twenty or thirty, very handsome and strong, and of a deep roan colour. King John offered to knight him, and to marry him very richly if he would quit the English party, and promised to give him 2,000 livres a year; but Croquart would not listen to him. It chanced one day as he was riding a young horse, which he had just purchased for 300 crowns, and was putting him to his full speed, that the horse ran away with him, and in leaping a ditch, stumbled into it, and broke his master's neck." Such was the end of Croquart.

END OF VOL. I.

NOTE.

The anonymous correspondent through whose valuable agency the interesting narrative of a "Témoin oculaire" has been revived, after an oblivion of fifty years, expatiates on the apparent apathy of his fellow countrymen, and points to the monument on Queenston Heights as an example and a reproach. He asks why nothing has been done to commemorate the scene of this great national exploit, and to point out to posterity the battle field of Chateauguay. This writer will be pleased to hear that the subject has not been altogether neglected, and that although much remains to be done, a step has been taken in the right direction, which, it is hoped, may lead to more practical results. There is, in the immediate vicinity of the battle field, a piece of Ordnance property, in superficies about five acres, occupied by an old block house. On the suggestion of the officer in charge, this piece of land has been set apart as the site of a future national monument. Through the active instrumentality of the Hon. Sir Etienne Taché, the Hon. George E. Cartier, Attorney General, and the Hon. P. Vankoughnet, then Commissioner of Crown Lands, an Order in Council was passed, dated 7th December, 1859, " reserving this piece of land from sale, and appropriating it for the purpose of erecting a monument commemorative of that distinguished feat of Canadian arms—the Battle of Chateauguay."

APPENDIX.

APPENDIX.

―――o―――

No. 1.

(*Extracted from the Report of the Loyal and Patriotic Society of Upper Canada. Published, Montreal, Lower Canada, 1817. Printed by William Gray.*)

To THOMAS JEFFERSON, *Esquire, of Monticello, Ex-president of the United States of America.*

Sir,

In your letter to a member of Congress, recently published, respecting the sale of your library,* I perceive that you are angry with the British for the destruction of the public buildings at Washington, and attempt, with your accustomed candour, to compare that transaction to the devastations committed by the Barbarians in the middle ages. As you are not ignorant of the mode of carrying on the war adopted by your friends, you must have known that it was a small

---

* MONTICELLO, 21st Sept., 1814.

"DEAR SIR,— .... I learn from the newspapers that the vandalism of our enemy has triumphed at Washington over science as well as the arts, by the destruction of the public library, with the noble edifice in which it was deposited. Of this transaction, as that of Copenhagen, the world will entertain but one sentiment. They will see a nation suddenly withdrawn from a great war, full armed and full handed, taking advantage of another, whom they had recently forced into it—unarmed and unprepared—to indulge themselves in acts of barbarism which do not belong to a civilized age."

retaliation after redress had been refused for burnings and depredations, not only of public but private property, committed by them in Canada; but we are too well acquainted with your hatred to Great Britain to look for truth or candour in any statement of yours where *she* is concerned. It is not for your information, therefore, that I relate in this letter those acts of the army of the United States in the Canadas, which provoked the conflagration of the public buildings at Washington, because you are well acquainted with them already; but to shew the world that to the United States and not to Great Britain must be charged all the miseries attending a mode of warfare originating with them, and unprecedented in modern times.

A stranger to the history of the last three years, on reading this part of your letter, would naturally suppose that Great Britain, in the pride of power, had taken advantage of the weak and defenceless situation of the United States to wreak her vengeance upon them. But what would be his astonishment when told that the nation, said to be unarmed and unprepared, had provoked and first declared the war, and carried it on offensively for two years, with a ferocity unexampled, before the British had the means of making effectual resistance. War was declared against Great Britain by the United States of America in June, 1812,—Washington was taken in August, 1814. Let us see in what spirit your countrymen carried on the war during this interval.

In July, 1812, General Hull invaded the British province of Upper Canada, and took possession of the town of Sandwich. He threatened (by a proclamation) to exterminate the inhabitants if they made any resistance; he plundered those with whom he had been in habits of intimacy for years before the war—their plate and linen were found in his possession after his *surrender to General Brock;* he marked out the loyal subjects of the King as objects of peculiar resentment, and consigned their property to pillage and conflagration. In autumn, 1812, some houses and barns were burnt by the American forces near Fort Erie, in Upper Canada.

In April, 1813, the public buildings at York, the capital of Upper Canada, were burnt by the troops of the United States, contrary to the articles of capitulation. They consisted of two elegant halls, with convenient offices, for the accommodation of the legislature and of the courts of justice. The library and all the papers and records belonging to these institutions were consumed at the same time. The church was robbed, and the town library totally pillaged. Commodore Chauncey, who has generally behaved honourably, was so ashamed of this last transaction, that he endeavoured to collect the books belonging to the public library, and actually sent back two boxes filled with them, but hardly any were complete. Much private property was plundered, and several houses left in a state of ruin. Can you tell me, Sir, the reason why the public buildings and library at Washington should be held more sacred than those at York? A false and ridiculous story is told of a scalp having been found above the Speaker's chair, intended as an ornament.

In June, 1813, Newark came into the possession of your army (after the capture of Fort George), and its inhabitants were repeatedly promised protection to themselves and property, both by General Dearborn and General Boyd. In the midst of these professions, the most respectable of them, although non-combatants, were made prisoners and sent into the United States; the two churches were burnt to the ground; detachments were sent, under the direction of British traitors, to pillage the loyal inhabitants in the neighbourhood, and to carry them away captive; many farm houses were burnt during the summer; and at length, to fill up the measure of iniquity, the whole of the beautiful village of Newark, with so short a previous intimation as to amount to none, was consigned to the flames. The wretched inhabitants had scarcely time to save themselves, much less any of their property. More than four hundred women and children were exposed without shelter on the night of the 10th of December, to the intense cold of a Canadian winter, and great numbers must have perished, had not the flight of your troops, after perpetrating this ferocious act, enabled the inhabitants of the country to come in to their relief.

Your friend Mr. Madison has attempted to justify this cruel deed on the plea that it was necessary for the defence of Fort George. Nothing can be more false. The village was some distance from the fort; and

APPENDIX.

instead of thinking to defend it, General McClure was actually retreating to his own shore when he caused Newark to be burnt. This officer says that he acted in conformity with the orders of his government; the government, finding their justification useless, disavow his conduct. McClure appears to be the fit agent of such a government. He not only complies with his instructions, but refines upon them by choosing a day of intense frost, giving the inhabitants almost no warning till the fire began, and commencing the conflagration in the night.

In Nov., 1813, the army of your friend General Wilkinson committed great depredations in its progress through the eastern district of Upper Canada, and was proceeding to systematic pillage, when the commander got frightened, and fled to his own shore, on finding the population in that district inveterately hostile.

The history of the two first campaigns proves, beyond dispute, that you had reduced fire and pillage to a regular system. It was hoped that the severe retaliation taken for the burning of Newark, would have put a stop to a practice so repugnant to the manners and habits of a civilized age; but so far was this from being the case, that the third campaign exhibits equal enormities. General Brown laid waste the country between Chippewa and Fort Erie, burning mills and private houses, and rendering those not consumed by fire, uninhabitable. The pleasant village of St. David was burnt by his army when about to retreat.

On the 15th of May a detachment of the American army, under Colonel Campbell, landed at Long Point, district of London, Upper Canada, and on that and the following day, pillaged and laid waste as much of the adjacent country as they could reach. They burnt the village of Dover, with the mills, and all the mills, stores, distillery, and dwelling houses in the vicinity, carrying away such property as was portable, and killing the cattle. The property taken and destroyed on this occasion, was estimated at fifty thousand dollars.

On the 16th of August some American troops and Indians from Detroit, surprised the settlement of Port Talbot, where they committed the most atrocious acts of violence, leaving upwards of 234 men, women, and children in a state of nakedness and want.

On the 20th of September, a second excursion was made by the garrison of Detroit, spreading fire and pillage through the settlements in the western district of Upper Canada. Twenty-seven families, on this occasion, were reduced to the greatest distress. . . . . . . Early in November, General McArthur, with a large body of mounted Kentuckians and Indians, made a rapid march through the western and part of the London districts, burning all the mills, destroying provisions, and living upon the inhabitants. If there was less private plunder than usual, it was because the invaders had no means of carrying it away.

On our part, Sir, the war has been carried on in the most forbearing manner. During the two first campaigns, we abstained from any acts of retaliation, notwithstanding the great enormities which we have mentioned. It was not till the horrible destruction of Newark, attended with so many acts of atrocity, that we burnt the villages of Lewiston, Buffalo, and Black Rock. At this our commander paused. He pledged himself to proceed no farther, on the condition of your returning to the rules of legitimate warfare. Finding you pursuing the same system this last campaign, instead of destroying the towns and villages within his reach, to which he had conditionally extended his protection, he applied to Admiral Cochrane to make retaliation upon the coast. The Admiral informed Mr. Monroe of the nature of this application, and his determination to comply, unless compensation was made for the private property wantonly destroyed in Upper Canada. No answer was returned for several weeks, during which time Washington was taken. At length a letter, purporting to be answered, arrived, in which the Secretary dwells with much lamentation on the destruction of the public buildings at Washington; which, notwithstanding the destruction of the same kind of buildings in the capital of Upper Canada, he affects to consider without a parallel in modern times. So little regard has he for truth, that, at the very moment of his speaking of the honour and generosity practised by his government in conducting the war, General McArthur was directed by the President to proceed upon his burning excursion.

Perhaps you will bring forward the report of the Committee appointed by Congress to inquire into British cruelties, and to class them under the heads furnished by Mr. Madison, as an offset for the facts that have been mentioned. The Committee must have found the subject extremely barren, as only one report has seen the light; but since the articles of accusation are before the public, and have been quoted by the enemies of England as capable of ample proof, let us give them a brief examination:

1st. Ill-treatment of American prisoners.

2nd. Detention of American prisoners as British subjects, under the pretext of their being born on British territory, or of naturalization.

3rd. Detention of sailors as prisoners, because they were in England when war was declared.

4th. Forced service of American sailors, pressed on board English men-of-war.

5th. Violence of flags of truce.

6th. Ransom of American prisoners taken by the savages in the service of England.

7th. Pillage and destruction of private property in the bay of Chesapeake, and the neighbouring country.

8. Massacre of American prisoners surrendered to the officers of Great Britain by the savages engaged in its service. Abandoning to the savages the corpses of American prisoners killed by the English, into whose hands they had been surrendered. Pillage and murder of American citizens, who had repaired to the English under the assurance of their protection; the burning of their houses.

9th. Cruelties exercised at Hampton, in Virginia.

1st. Ill-treatment of American prisoners.

General Brock sent all the militia taken at Detroit home on their parole, accompanied by a guard to protect them from the Indians, detaining only the regulars, whom he sent to Quebec, where they met with the most liberal treatment, as the honest among them have frequently confessed. General Sheaffe acted in the same manner after the battle of Queenston, keeping the regulars, and dismissing the militia on their parole. Nor was this liberal course departed from, till the gross misconduct of the American government, in liberating, without exchange, those so sent home, and in carrying away non-combatants, and seizing the whole inhabitants of the districts which they invaded, rendered it absolutely necessary.

When they were not able to take all the armed inhabitants away, they made those they left sign a parole—a conduct never known in the annals of war—the conditions of which not only precluded them from afterwards bearing arms, but from giving, in any manner, their services to government. The farmers were dragged out of their houses, and carried into the States. Clergymen were forced to give their parole; in fine, it appeared to make no difference whether a man was in arms or not,—he was sure to experience the same treatment.

Many people, when prisoners, have been treated in the most infamous manner. Officers, though sick and wounded, have been forced to march on foot through the country; while American officers taken by us, were conveyed in boats or carriages to the place of destination.

Our captured troops have been marched, as spectacles, through the towns, although you affect to complain of Hull's and other prisoners being marched publicly into Montreal. The officers of the 41st Regiment were confined in the penitentiary, at Kentucky, among felons of the most infamous description. They were treated with harshness, often with cruelty; and persons who wished to be kind to them were insulted by the populace.

Even the stipulations respecting prisoners, agreed to by the American government, have been most shamefully broken. Sir George Prevost and Mr. Madison agreed that all prisoners taken before the 15th day of April, 1814, should be exchanged on or before the 15th day of May last, to be conveyed into their respective countries by the nearest routes. On that day the Governor-in-Chief, faithful to his engagements, sent home every American prisoner; but the government of the United States seemed for a long time to have totally forgotten the stipulation. A few prisoners were sent back in June, but many of the officers and all the soldiers of the 41st Regiment were detained till towards the end of October. To the soldiers of this regiment (as indeed to all others) every temptation had been presented, to induce them to desert and enlist in their service, by money, land, &c. After it was found impossible to persuade any number of them to do so, the American government encamped them, for nearly two months, in a pestilential marsh near Sandusky, without any covering. There, having neither shelter nor the necessary quantity of provisions, they all got sick, many died; and, in October, the remainder were sent to Long Point, sick, naked and miserable. From this place they could not be conveyed, till clothes had been sent to cover their nakedness. Great numbers sunk under their calamities, and the utmost care and attention were required to save any of them alive. Such an accumulation of cruelty was never exhibited before.

The government of the United States assumed the prerogative of relieving officers from parole, without exchanging them; and even Commodore Rodgers took twelve seamen out of a cartel, as it was proceeding to Boston Bay, and was justified for this outrage by his government.

2nd. Detention of American prisoners as British subjects.

It is notorious that a great many of the American army have been British subjects since the commencement of the war; and, had we determined to punish these traitors with death, if found invading our territories, and, after giving them warning, acted up to such a determination, it would have been strictly right; and in such case very few would have entered Canada. While these persons act merely as militia, defending their adopted country against invasion, some lenity might be shown them; but when they march into the British Provinces for the sake of conquest, they ought to be considered traitors to their king and country, and treated accordingly.

3rd. Detention of sailors as prisoners, because they were in England when war was declared.

This accusation is ridiculous, as sailors are always considered in the first class of combatants; but it comes with an ill grace from those who have detained peaceable British subjects, engaged in civil life, and banished, fifteen miles from the coast, those of them who happened to be in America at the declaration of war, and treated them, almost in every respect, like prisoners of war, according to Bonaparte's example.

4th. Forced service of American sailors, pressed on board of English men-of-war.

This accusation has been often made, but never coupled with the offer of Mr. Forster, to discharge every American so detained, on being furnished with the list. The list was never furnished.

5th. Violence of flags of truce.

This accusation of Mr. Madison contains about as much truth as those that have been already examined. We shall give two examples of the treatment experienced by the bearers of flags of truce from the British army.

Major Fulton, aide-de-camp to General Sir George Prevost, was stopped by Major Forsyth, of the United States army, at the outposts, who insulted him most grossly, endeavoured to seize his despatches, and threatened to put him to death. So much ashamed were Forsyth's superiors at this outrage, that he was sent for a short time to the rear.

General Proctor sent Lieut. Le Breton to General Harrison, after the battle of Moravian Town, to ascertain our loss of officers and men; but, instead of sending him back, General Harrison detained him many weeks, took him round the lake, and, after all, did not furnish him with the required information, which had been otherwise procured in the meantime.

6th. Ransom of American prisoners, taken by the savages in the service of England.

Some nations of the natives were at war with the Americans, long before hostilities commenced against England; many others not. When attempts were made to conquer the Canadas, the Indians beyond our territories, part by choice and part by solicitation, came and joined us as allies; while those within the Provinces had as great an interest in defending them, as the other proprietors of the soil. To mitigate as much as possible the horrors of war, it was expressly and repeatedly told the Indians that scalping the dead, and killing prisoners or unresisting enemies, were practices extremely repugnant to our feelings, and no presents would be given them but for prisoners. This, therefore, instead of becoming an article of accusation, ought to have excited their gratitude; for the presence and authority of a British force uniformly tended to secure the lives of all who were defenceless, and all who surrendered. It almost without exception saved the lives of our enemies; yet the American government brands us as worse than savages, for fighting by the side of Indians, and at first threatened our extermination if we did so, although they employed all the Indians they could. Many individuals have acknowledged their obligation to us for having been saved by the benevolent and humane exertions of our officers and troops; but no officer of rank ever had the justice to make a public acknowledgment. The eighth accusation is much the same as this, and must have been separated in order to multiply the number of articles. It is notorious that some British soldiers have been killed by the Indians, protecting their prisoners. This was the case at General Winchester's defeat, and at General Clay's. The grossest exaggerations have been published. General Winchester was declared in all the American papers to have been scalped, and mangled in the most horrid manner, when he was in his quarters at Quebec. In a General Order, dated Kingston, 26th July, 1813, among other things respecting Indians, it is said, that the head-money for the prisoners of war brought in by the Indian warriors, is to be immediately paid by the Commissariat, upon the certificate of the general officer commanding the division with which they are acting at the time. Let us now see how the poor Indians are treated by the Americans, after promising that they have done their utmost to employ as many Indians as possible against us. It is a fact that the first scalp taken this war was by the Americans, at the river Canard, between Sandwich and Amherstburgh. At this place an Indian was killed, by the advance of General Hull's army, and immediately scalped.*

At the skirmish of Brownston, several Indians fell, and were scalped by the American troops.

The Kentuckians were commonly armed with a tomahawk and long scalping-knife; and burned Indians as a pastime.

At the river Au Raisin, Captain Caldwell, of the Indian department, saved an American officer from the Indians, and, as he was leading him

---

* An Indian never scalps his enemy until after he is dead, and does so to preserve a proof or token of his victory.

off, the ungrateful monster stabbed him in the neck, on which he was killed by Capt. Caldwell's friends.

The American troops, under General Winchester, killed an Indian in a skirmish near the river Au Raisin, on the 18th January, 1813, and tore him literally to pieces, which so exasperated the Indians, that they refused burial to the Americans killed on the 22nd. The Indian hero, Tecumseh, after being killed, was literally flayed in part by the Americans, and his skin carried off as a trophy.

Twenty Indian women and children, of the Kickapoo nation, were inhumanly put to death by the Americans a short time ago, near Prairie, on the Illinois River, after driving their husbands into a morass, where they perished with cold and hunger. Indian towns were burnt as an amusement, or common-place practice. All this, however, is nothing, compared to the recent massacre of the Creeks. General Coffee, in his letter to General Jackson, dated 4th November, 1813, informs him that he surrounded the Indian towns at Tullushatches, in the night, with nine hundred men; that, about an hour after sunrise, he was discovered by the enemy, who endeavoured, though taken by surprise, to make some resistance. In a few minutes the last warrior of them was killed. He mentioned the number of warriors seen dead to be 186, and supposes as many among the weeds as would make them up two hundred. He confesses that some of the women and children were killed, owing to the warriors mixing with their families. He mentions taking only eighty-four prisoners of women and children. Now, it is evident that, in a village containing two hundred warriors, there must have been nearly as many women and men, perhaps more; and, unquestionably, the number of children exceeded the men and women together. What, then, became of all these? Neither does General Coffee mention the old men. Such things speak for themselves. The poor Indians fought, it appears, with bows and arrows, and were able only to kill five Americans. Their situation was too remote, for them to receive assistance from the British. Their lands were wanted, and they must be exterminated. Since this period, the greater part of the nation has been massacred by General Jackson, who destroyed them wantonly, in cold blood. There was no resistance, if we except individual ebullition of despair, when it was found that there was no mercy. Jackson mentions, exultingly, that the morning after he had destroyed a whole village, sixteen Indians were discovered hid under the bank of the river, who were dragged out and murdered. Upon these inhuman exploits, President Madison only remarks to Congress, that the Creeks had received a salutary chastisement, which would make a lasting impression upon their fears. The cruelties exercised against these wretched nations are without a parallel, except the coldness and apathy with which they are glossed over by the President. Such is the conduct of the humane government of the United States, which is incessantly employed, as they pretend, in civilizing the Indians. But it is time to finish this horrid detail. We shall, therefore, conclude with a short extract from a letter of the Spanish Governor of East Florida, Benigno Garzia, to Mr. Mitchell, Governor of the State of Georgia, to show that the policy of the government of the United States, in regard to the Indians, is now generally known:

"The Province of East Florida may be invaded in time of profound peace, the planters ruined, and the population of the capital starved, and, according to your doctrine, all is fair; they are a set of outlaws if they resist. The Indians are to be insulted, threatened, and driven from their lands; if they resist, nothing less than extermination is to be their fate."

7th and 9th.—Pillage and destruction of private property, in the Bay of Chesapeake and the neighbouring country, and cruelties exercised at Hampton, in Virginia.

It requires astonishing effrontery to make these articles of accusation, after the depredations and cruelties committed by the army of the United States in the Canadas.

In the attack upon Craney Islands, some boats in the service of Great Britain ran aground. In this situation they made signals of surrender; but the Americans continued to fire upon them from the shore. Many of them jumped into the water, and swam towards land; but they were shot as they approached, without mercy. A few days after, Hampton was taken, and some depredations were committed by the foreign troops who had seen some of their comrades so cruelly massacred: but before any material damage was done, they were remanded on board. Several letters from Hampton mention the behaviour of the British, while there, as highly meritorious, and contradict the vile calumnies of the Democratic print, which Mr. Madison copies in his message to Congress.

This brief account of the conduct of your government and army, since the commencement of hostilities (which might have been greatly extended), will fill the world with astonishment at the forbearance of Great Britain, in suffering so many enormities, and such a determined departure from the laws of civilized warfare, to pass so long without signal punishment.

Before finishing this letter, permit me, Sir, to remark, that the destruction of the public buildings at Washington entitled the British to your gratitude and praise, by affording you a noble opportunity of proving your devotion to your country. In former times, when you spoke of the magnitude of your services, and the fervour of your patriotism, your political enemies were apt to mention your elevated situation, and the greatness of your salary. But, by presenting your library a free-will offering to the nation, at this moment of uncommon pressure, when the Treasury is empty, and every help to the acquisition of knowledge is so very necessary to keep the government from sinking, you would have astonished the world with one solitary action in your political life worthy of commendation.

Nor are your obligations to the British army unimportant, though you have not aspired to generous praise. An opportunity has been given you of disposing of a library at your own price, which, if sold volume by volume, would have fetched nothing. You have, no doubt, seen that old libraries do not sell well after the death of the proprietors; and, with a lively attention to your own interests, you take advantage of the times.

    I am, Sir,
      With due consideration, &c.,

        (Signed,) JOHN STRACHAN, D.D.,
           Treasurer of the Loyal and Patriotic
            Society of Upper Canada.

YORK, 30th January, 1815.

No. 2.

BATAILLE DE CHATEAUGUAY.

M. L'ÉDITEUR,—Il y a cinquante ans que 300 braves donnaient à l'univers entier le spectacle d'un des plus beaux faits d'armes dont peut se glorifier notre jeune pays. Sur la frôntière de leur patrie, animés du courage chevaleresque que leur avait légué leurs ancêtres et marchant sur les pas de leur valeureux chef, De Salaberry, ils repoussent et mettent en fuite une armée infiniment supérieure quant au nombre et pleine de l'orgueil que lui inspirait ses prouesses passées. Sans doute, Monsieur l'éditeur, vous avez déjà compris, et le victorieux nom de "Châteauguay" est venu involontairement se placer sur vos lèvres, ce nom rempli d'émotions et tout palpitant d'intérêt, mais hélas! tombé dans l'oubli. Quoi! un demi-siècle est à peine encore écoulé, nous possédons encore au milieu de nous quelques uns de ces anciens vétérans qui virent le drapeau étoilé s'enfuir devant la bravoure toute française de nos "Voltigeurs," et néanmoins la plus belle page de notre histoire est ignorée par une grande partie de la jeunesse canadienne. Cette mémorable journée, qui fait pâlir l'assertion mensongère qui met en doute la bravoure et le courage du Canadien-français, devrait être gravée dans le cœur de tout bon citoyen, et sa mémoire consacrée par quelque marque publique qui la transmettrait à la postérité la plus reculée. Il y a quelques années, avec grande pompe, on posait la première pierre d'un monument élevé au général Brock et à son aide-de-camp, le colonel McDonald. Pourquoi le Bas-Canada ne ferait-il pas ce qu'a fait le Haut ? Pourquoi un monument, témoignage irrécusable de notre vénération, ne s'éléverait-il pas sur la tombe du héros Canadien comme sur celle du Breton ? Est-ce qu'aux plaines de Châteauguay ne se rattachent pas d'aussi glorieux souvenirs qu'aux " Queenston's Heights?" Oh! oui, et cependant, sur le champ qui renferme les ossements de nos pères, l'œil ne rencontre pas même la simple petite croix de bois à laquelle le fils religieux peut aller suspendre une couronne de laurier. Qu'on élève donc un marbre à ceux qui défendirent si vaillamment notre sol contre l'invasion étrangère, comme à ceux tombés pour la défense de nos droits civils et politiques ; ou bien, mieux encore, qu'un seul couvre leurs cendres à tous, et qu'il dise aux étrangers qui visitent le pays qu'arrosent le St. Laurent, l'Ottawa et le Saguenay, que les Canadiens-français, eux aussi, ont eu dans le passé leurs braves et leurs martyres.

CASTOR.

Montréal, 15 janvier 1863.

P.S. Ci-inclus, vous trouverez, M. l'éditeur, le récit de l'événement mémorable auquel je fais allusion dans la correspondance ci-dessus ; j'espère que vous le publierez, persuadé qu'il sera lu avec le plus grand plaisir par vos lecteurs. Je fais l'extrait suivant d'un ancien journal.

3 novembre 1813.

Comme un détail circonstancié de l'affaire récente sur la rivière de Châteauguay pourrait ne pas déplaire à vos lecteurs, je vous prie d'insérer dans votre gazette l'ébauche suivante. Quelque diffuse et quelque défectueuse qu'elle soit, comme description, elle a au moins le mérite de l'exactitude, ayant été écrite par un

TÉMOIN OCULAIRE.

L'armée américaine stationnée à *Four Corners*, sous le général Hampton, après avoir si longtemps fixé l'attention de nos troupes, commença enfin à s'approcher de nos frontières, le 21 du mois dernier. Le même jour, vers 4 heures de l'après-midi, son avant-garde poussa notre piquet stationné à *Piper's Road*, à environ dix lieues de l'église de Châteauguay. Aussitôt que le major Henry, de la milice de Beauharnais, commandant à la rivière des Anglais, eût reçu avis de l'approche de l'ennemi, il en informa le major De Watteville et fit avancer immédiatement les capitaines Lévesque et Debartzch avec les compagnies du flanc du 5ème bataillon de la milice incorporée, et environ deux cents hommes de la division de Beauharnais. Cette force s'avança d'environ deux lieues cette nuit-là, et s'arrêta à l'entrée d'un bois au travers duquel il n'aurait pas été prudent de passer. Le lendemain au matin, de bonne heure, ils

APPENDIX.

furent joints par le lieut.-col. De Salaberry, avec ses Voltigeurs, et la compagnie légère du capitaine Ferguson, du régiment canadien. Le lieut.-colonel De Salaberry remonta à près d'une lieue sur la rive gauche de la rivière, à l'autre extrémité, et une patrouille de l'ennemi s'étant montrée à quelque distance, il fit faire halte à sa petite force. Le lieutenant-colonel, qui avait eu l'avantage de reconnaître tout le pays au-dessus de Châteauguay dans une expédition sur la frontière américaine, quelques semaines auparavant, savait que le bord de la rivière ne pouvait fournir une meilleure position. Le bois était rempli de ravines profondes, sur quatre desquelles il établit quatre lignes de défense, l'une après l'autre. Les premières lignes étaient distantes l'une de l'autre d'environ deux cents pas; la quatrième était à peu près un demi-mille en arrière, et commandait sur la rive droite de la rivière un gué qu'il était très-important de défendre, afin de protéger la rive gauche. Il fit faire sur chacune des ces lignes une espèce de parapet qui s'étendait à quelque distance dans le bois, pour garantir sa droite. Le parapet sur la première ligne formait un angle obtus à la droite du chemin, et s'étendait le long des détours du fossé. Toute cette première journée fut employée à fortifier cette position, qui, quant à la force, ne le cède à pas une de celles qu'on aurait pu choisir. Elle avait aussi l'avantage de forcer l'ennemi, s'il était disposé à attaquer, de traverser une grande étendue de terrain inhabité et de s'éloigner de ses ressources, tandis qu'au contraire nos troupes avaient tout à souhait et étaient bien soutenues à l'arrière.

La rive droite de la rivière était couverte d'un bois épais, et l'on eut aussi soin de se mettre en garde auprès du gué, et l'on posta en avant de l'autre un piquet de soixante hommes de la milice de Beauharnais.

Le lieutenant-colonel ne borna pas son attention aux ouvrages ci-dessus. Pour assurer sa protection davantage, il ordonna à un parti de trente bûcherons, de la division de Beauharnais, d'aller en avant de la première ligne, afin de détruire les ponts, et de faire des abatis. En conséquence, tous les ponts furent détruits dans l'espace d'une lieue et demie, et il fut fait un abatis formidable à environ un mille en avant de la première ligne, s'étendant du bord de la rivière à trois ou quatre arpents dans le bois, où il joignait, sur la droite, une terre marécageuse, ou *savanne*, par laquelle il était presque impossible de passer. Les quatre lignes étaient ainsi complètement à couvert. On savait bien que l'ennemi avait une dixaine de canons, et il lui devenait impossible de les amener.

C'est à la force de la position choisie et fortifiée de la sorte, ainsi qu'à l'héroïsme de notre petite armée, que nous devons la victoire brillante qui a été obtenue. Les talents et l'habileté d'un officier commandant ne se distinguent pas moins sans doute dans le choix de son terrain avant la bataille, que dans la disposition de ses troupes au fort de la mêlée, et l'on ne fera que rendre justice au lieutenant-colonel De Salaberry en disant que lui seul doit être loué de *l'arrangement admirable établi pour la défense de son poste.*

Après que le colonel De Salaberry eut fait ces dispositions judicieuses, le major-général De Watteville vint voir son camp, et lui fit l'honneur d'approuver tout ce qu'il avait fait.

Quoique les abatis eussent été achevés le second, on tint continuellement en cet endroit des partis de travailleurs, afin de le rendre encore plus formidable ; on envoya des troupes en avant pour les protéger, et il y avait toujours en outre à l'arrière un piquet nombreux. Le 29 du mois passé, vers dix heures du matin, une avant-garde de l'ennemi vint à portée de mousquet de l'abatis. Le lieutenant Guy, des Voltigeurs, qui était en front avec une vingtaine de ses hommes, fut contraint de reculer après avoir échangé quelques coups de fusils, et fut soutenu par le lieutenant Johnson, du même corps, qui commandait le piquet à l'arrière des travailleurs, qui se virent dans la nécessité de retraiter et ne se remirent pas à l'ouvrage de tout le jour.

Dès que le lieutenant-colonel De Salaberry eut entendu le feu, il partit du front de la première ligne. Il prit avec lui trois compagnies du capitaine Ferguson, du régiment canadien, qu'il déploya à la droite et à l'avant de l'abatis ; celle du capitaine J. B. Duchesnay, à qui il ordonna d'occuper la gauche, en s'étendant en même temps du côté de la rivière, et celle du capitaine Juchereau Duchesnay qui, avec environ 50 ou 60 miliciens de Beauharnais, fut placée derrière, en potence, à la gauche de l'abatis, de manière à pouvoir prendre l'ennemi en flanc, s'il avançait contre la milice de Beauharnais, sur la rive droite de la rivière. J'oubliais de dire qu'il y avait environ une vingtaine de sauvages avec les hommes de la compagnie du capitaine Ferguson sur la droite. Le lieutenant-colonel se plaça au centre de la ligne du front. Il voyait alors devant lui un ennemi avec lequel il s'était deux fois efforcé d'en venir aux prises depuis le commencement de cette campagne ; l'occasion tant désirée se présentait, et l'évènement a montré comment il a su en profiter. Entre l'abatis et al première ligne étaient placées la companie de Voltigeurs du capitaine Ecuyer et la compagnie légère du capitaine Debartzch, du 5me bataillon de la milice incorporée, ayant leurs piquets de flanc sur la droite. Un gros corps de sauvages, sous le capitaine Lamothe, était répandu dans le bois, à la droite du capitaine Debartzch. Le lieutenant-colonel McDonell, de l'infanterie légère de Glengarry, se transporta, avec une partie de sa brigade légère, de la 3me et 4me lignes à la 1re et la 2me. Tous ces mouvements se firent avec une grande rapidité.

Sur ces entrefaites, l'ennemi commença à se former dans une grande plaine qui aboutissait presque à une pointe en front de l'abatis. Le général Hampton commandait en personne sur la rive gauche de la rivière ; il avait avec lui le 10me, le 31me et autres régiments, faisant enviren trois mille ou trois mille cinq cents hommes, avec trois escadrons de cavalarie et quatre pièces d'artillerie. Néanmoins, l'artillerie ne fut pas employée dans l'action. Un gros parti de l'ennemi, se montant à environ quinze cents hommes, pénétra à travers les bois sur la rive droite de la rivière ; il était composé du 4me, 33me, 35me, et des bataillons de Chasseurs volontaires. Le reste de l'armée américaine se formait derrière la force qui était sur la rive gauche.

Peu après que le colonel De Salaberry eut fait les dispositions, comme on a déjà dit, une forte colonne d'infanterie s'avança par la plaine au devant de là, et le colonel, voyant que cette colonne s'était exposée à être prise en front et en flanc, avantage qu'il avait attendu quelque temps, il tira le premier, et l'on s'aperçut que son feu avait jeté bas un officier à cheval ; c'était un bon augure. Alors il ordonna au trompette de sonner la charge, et aussitôt les compagnies du front firent un feu vif et bien dirigé qui arrêta quelques minutes la marche de l'ennemi. Il demeura quelque temps en repos, puis, faisant un tour à gauche, il se forma en ligne, et dans cette position, lâcha plusieurs volées. Néanmoins, par ce mouvement, le feu de la gauche de sa ligne porta entièrement sur la partie du bois qui n'était pas occupée par nos troupes ; mais le feu de sa droite fut assez fort pour obliger nos piquets à venir chercher un abri derrière l'abatis. L'ennemi prit ce mouvement pour le commencement d'une retraite, et fut bien trompé, car il ne put s'emparer d'un pouce de l'abatis. Les *huzzas* retentissaient d'un bout à l'autre de son armée : mais nous ne lui cédâmes pas même dans le combat de cris ; nos compagnies du front crièrent à leur tour, et les *huzzas* furent répétés par celles de la queue, et ensuite par les troupes de la première ligne, qui fit jouer les trompettes dans toutes les directions pour porter l'ennemi à croire que nous étions en plus grand nombre. Cette ruse de guerre eut l'effet désiré, car nous avons ensuite appris des prisonniers qu'ils estimaient notre force à 6 ou 7000 hommes. Après ces clameurs mutuelles, on tira pendant quelques volées de part et d'autre. L'ennemi n'essaya pas une fois de pénétrer dans l'abatis. Il continua cependant son feu, qui fut rendu à propos, particulièrement par ceux de la gauche. Peu après, il commença à se ralentir, comme si l'attention de l'ennemi eût été dirigée de l'autre côté de la rivière. Là les trompettes, qui étaient au front, donnèrent le signal d'avancer, en conséquence de quelques manœuvres, et le lieutenant-colonel McDonell, curieux d'ajouter de nouveaux lauriers à ceux qu'il avait déjà cueillis à Ogdensburgh, vint de la première et seconde ligne avec la compagnie du capitaine Lévesque, comme je crois, et une autre.

Vers la fin de l'engagement sur la rive gauche, l'ennemi qui, sur la droite, avait fait reculer les miliciens de Beauharnais, commença sur notre gauche un feu vif, qui lui fut rendu par la gauche de la compagnie du capt. J. B. Duchesnay et la droite de celle du capitaine Juchereau Duchesnay. Alors le lieutenant-colonel De Salaberry ordonna au lieutenant-colonel McDonell, qui avait repris sa position, d'empêcher l'ennemi d'avancer. Le capitaine Daly, qui fut choisi pour ce service, traversa au gué, emmena avec lui les restes de la milice sédentaire de l'autre côté, et s'avança avec rapidité le long de la rivière.

Le feu de l'ennemi ayant presque cessé à l'abatis, et le lieutenant-colonel De Salaberry voyant que l'action allait devenir sérieuse sur la droite, laissa sa situation au centre du front et se plaça sur la gauche avec les troupes jetées derrière en potence. Là, il monta sur un gros tronc d'arbre, et quoique très-exposé au feu de l'ennemi, l'examina de sang-froid avec la longue-vue. Alors, il donna ses ordres en français au capitaine Daly, et lui enjoignit de répondre dans la même langue, afin de n'être pas entendu de l'ennemi. Le capitaine Daly poussa vaillamment les ennemis devant lui pendant quelque temps ; mais, se ralliant sur leurs troupes de derrière, qui étaient presque en ligne avec la force sur la rive gauche, ils attendirent son approche et le reçurent avec un feu bien entretenu. Il fut blessé dès l'abord ; nonobstant sa blessure, il continua de pousser en avant avec sa compagnie, et dans le temps qu'il encourageait ses hommes, et par ses paroles et par son exemple, il fut blessé pour la seconde fois et tomba. Le capitaine Bruyère, de la milice de Beauharnais, fut aussi blessé dans le même temps, mais légèrement. Leurs hommes, n'étant plus en état de résister à une force si supérieure, furent contraints de reculer, ce qui se fit dans une fort bon ordre, sous le commandement du lieutenant Schiller ; et l'on entendit, encore une fois, les cris joyeux des ennemis, mais leur joie fut celle d'un moment ; car ils ne furent pas plutôt arrivés vis-à-vis de la potence, que, par l'ordre du lieutenant-colonel De Salaberry, les troupes qui se trouvaient là firent sur eux un feu vif et bien dirigé, qui les arrêta tout-à-coup dans leur marche hardie et les mit dans la plus grande confusion. Vainement tâchèrent-ils de résister ; ils se dispersèrent et retraitèrent avec précipitation. Il était alors environ deux heures et demie de l'après-midi ; et le général Hampton, voyant que ses troupes sur la rive droite ne réussissaient pas mieux que celles de la rive gauche, ordonna à ces dernières de retraiter, après être demeurées inactives pendant près d'une heure, bien qu'elles fussent assaillies de temps à autre par nos escarmoucheurs, qui étaient parfaitement à couvert dans l'abatis. Nos troupes restèrent dans leur position et couchèrent, cette nuit-là, sur le terrain qu'elles avaient occupé durant la journée. Le lendemain, au point du jour, elles furent renforcées par la compagnie de Voltigeurs du capitaine Rouville et la compagnie de grenadiers du capitaine Lévesque, du 5me bataillon de la milice incorporée, et de soixante hommes de la division de Beauharnais, le tout sous le commandement du lieutenant-colonel McDonell. Ce fut à cet officier distingué que le lieutenant-colonel De Salaberry confia le soin de la défense de l'abatis. On poussa des piquets à deux milles plus avant qu'on avait encore fait; la journée se passa dans l'attente d'une seconde attaque, mais nul ennemi ne se montra. Ses piquets étaient postés de telle sorte qu'une vingtaine d'hommes tombèrent entre nos mains sur la rive droite de la rivière. On trouva aussi, sur cette même rive, une grande quantité de fusils, de tambours, de havresacs, de provisions, etc. Tout indiquait fortement dans quel désordre l'ennemi avait été jeté et avait effectué sa retraite. Nos troupes enterrèrent plus de 40 de leurs gens, outre ceux qu'ils enterrèrent eux-mêmes, et parmi lesquels se trouvaient deux ou trois officiers de distinction. On trouva deux chevaux morts sur la rive gauche, et l'ennemi emmena dans des charriots plusieurs de ses blessés de ce côté de la rivière.

Le 28 au matin, le capitaine Lamothe, avec environ 150 sauvages, alla reconnaître l'ennemi, qui, suivant le rapport du colonel Hughes, des ingénieurs, avait abandonné son camp le jour précédent. Un parti des miliciens de Beauharnais, soutenu par le capitaine Debartzch, brûla et détruisit les ponts nouvellement érigés à un mille de l'ennemi, qui avait transporté son camp à environ une demi-lieue de *Piper's Road*, c'est-à-dire à environ deux lieues de sa première position. Le capitaine Lamothe pénétra dans le bois avec ses sauvages, et malgré l'infériorité de sa force, cet officier actif et zélé engagea un combat partiel avec l'ennemi, qui eut un homme tué et sept blessés.

Le 30, un parti de chasseurs sauvages, sous le capitaine Ducharme, donna avis que l'ennemi avait, le 29, abandonné son camp à *Piper's Road* dans le plus grand désordre, et était sur le chemin des Quatre-Fourches.

Ici finit l'expédition du général Hampton contre le Bas-Canada. Je me suis étendu dans la description de la scène du combat, de la position et des mouvements des troupes engagées, sans craindre de lasser la patience du lecteur. Sur un tel sujet, l'attente empressée d'un public canadien recherchera naturellement avec anxiété toute espèce d'information, et dans un démêlé aussi difficile et aussi mémorable, il n'est pas de circonstance, quelque petite qu'elle soit, qui n'ait son intérêt particulier.

D'après toutes les informations qu'on a pu tirer des prisonniers, il paraît que l'intention de l'ennemi était de s'avancer par la rivière de Chateauguay jusqu'aux bords du St. Laurent, pour y attendre la co-opération du général Wilkinson, qui devait prendre Kingston dans sa route en descendant;

"*Rusticus expectat dum defluat amnis.*"

On a aussi appris des prisonniers que la force de l'ennemi se montait à 7,000 hommes d'infanterie, 400 de cavalerie et 10 ou 12 pièces de canon. Le lecteur éloigné ou imbu de préjugés ne croira peut-être pas que toute la force engagée de notre côté n'excédait pas 300 hommes; mais c'est le fait; nous l'affirmons sans crainte d'être contredit. Le reste de notre armée *était en réserve par derrière.*

Il est tout-à-fait flatteur de pouvoir ajouter que ces trois cents hommes et leur brave commandant étaient tous Canadiens, à l'exception du brave capitaine Ferguson, de trois hommes de sa compagnie et de trois officiers appartenant à d'autres corps. Qu'on le dise toutes les fois qu'on fera mention de la bataille de Chateauguay, et il faudra que le préjugé cache sa tête hideuse et que les murmures de la malveillance soient étouffés par la honte et la confusion.

Les officiers et soldats engagés dans cette journée mémorable se sont tous couverts de gloire. Le capitaine Ferguson, de l'infanterie légère du régiment canadien, et les deux capitaines Duchesnay se sont grandement distingués dans le commandement de leurs compagnies respectives et en exécutant plusieurs mouvements difficiles avec autant de sang-froid et de précision qu'en un jour de parade. La bravoure du capitaine Daly, de la brigade de flanc de la milice, qui conduisit, *à la lettre,* sa compagnie au milieu des ennemis, ne pouvait être surpassée. On n'a pas moins remarqué, dans ce combat sévère, le courage et la bravoure du capitaine Lamothe, du département des sauvages, du lieutenant Pinguet, de l'infanterie légère canadienne, du lieutenant et adjudant Hebben, des Voltigeurs, du lieutenant Schiller, de la compagnie du capitaine Daly.

Les lieutenants Guy et Johnson, des Voltigeurs, formèrent leurs piquets sur la ligne de défense, après qu'ils se furent retirés, et se conduisirent avec une grande bravoure durant tout l'engagement. Le capitaine Ecuyer, des Voltigeurs, et le lieut. Powell, de la compagnie du capitaine Lévesque, se sont fait beaucoup d'honneur par leurs efforts pour s'assurer des prisonniers dans les bois, en s'exposant à un péril imminent. Les capitaines Longtin et Huneau, de la milice de Beauharnais, se sont fait remarquer par leur bonne conduite ; le premier se mit à genoux au commencement de l'action, fit une courte prière avec ses hommes, et leur dit, en se relevant, *qu'à présent qu'ils avaient rempli leur devoir envers leur Dieu, ils faisaient leur devoir pour leur Roi.* Louis Langlade, Noël Annance et Barlet Lyons, du département des sauvages, étaient dans l'action du 26 et l'affaire du 28. Leur conduite a été remarquable durant tout ce temps.

Je ne passerai pas sous silence les noms des soldats Vincent, Pelletier, Vervais, Dubois et Caron, des Voltigeurs, dont quelques-uns traversèrent la rivière à la nage, et firent prisonniers ceux qui refusaient de se rendre.

A l'égard du lieutenant-colonel De Salaberry, le plus égoïste doit avouer que ses services importants le rendent digne des remercîments et de la reconnaissance de sa patrie.

On ne sait ce qu'on doit admirer d'avantage, ou son courage personnel comme individu, ou son habileté et ses talents comme commandant. Nous le voyons, longtemps avant le combat, montrer le plus profond jugement dans le choix de sa position et la fortifier ensuite par tous les moyens que lui suggèrent sa sagacité. Nous le voyons, au fort de l'action, embrasser tout par des vues grandes et étendues, défendant chaque point, et pourvoyant à tout accident. Mais son mérite et celui de sa petite armée devient encore plus éclatant quand nous réfléchissons à l'état critique des temps, immédiatement avant cette brillante victoire. Les affaires paraissaient désespérées dans le Haut-Canada ; le découragement commençait à faire sentir ses tristes effets ; on nous avait même dit, sous haute autorité, "que très-probablement, le moment approchait où il " serait *finalement* déterminé si l'attente présomptueuse de l'ennemi " devait être réalisée par l'invasion et la conquête de cette province, ou

" s'il ne devait trouver que la défaite dans son entreprise." Ce moment est passé : les amis de leur pays se le rappelleront avec reconnaissance ; l'aspect des affaires est changé. L'ennemi, pour nous servir d'une phrase à la mode, a bien " pollué notre sol," mais il a été repoussé par un commandant Canadien, à la tête d'une troupe de Canadiens qui ne se montait pas à la vingtième partie de la force qui leur était opposée.

* * *

www.ingramcontent.com/pod-product-compliance
Lightning Source LLC
Chambersburg PA
CBHW031331230426
43670CB00006B/307